Christ In Our Midst

Incarnation, Church and Discipleship in the theology of Pilgram Marpeck

ANABAPTIST AND MENNONITE STUDIES

Anabaptist and Mennonite Studies is a publication series sponsored by the Institute of Anabaptist Mennonite Studies, Conrad Grebel University College, University of Waterloo, published in cooperation with Pandora Press. The aim of the series is to make available significant academic works relating to Anabaptist and Mennonite history and theology.

1. A. James Reimer, *Mennonites and Classical Theology: Dogmatic Foundations for Christian Ethics* (Kitchener, ON: Pandora Press, 2001) ISBN 0-9685543-7-7

2. Helen Martens, *Hutterite Songs* (Kitchener, ON: Pandora Press, 2002) ISBN 1-894710-24-X

3. Karl Koop, *Anabaptist-Mennonite Confessions of Faith: The Development of a Tradition* (Kitchener, ON: Pandora Press, 2004) ISBN 1-894710-32-0

4. John Howard Yoder, *Anabaptism and Reformation in Switzerland* (Kitchener, ON: Pandora Press, 2004) ISBN 1-894710-44-4

5. Rodney James Sawatsky, *History and Ideology: American Mennonite Identity Definition through History* (Kitchener, ON: Pandora Press, 2004) ISBN 1-894710-53-3

6. Harry Huebner, *Echoes of the Word* (Kitchener, ON: Pandora Press, 2005) ISBN 1-894710-56-8

7. Werner O. Packull, *Peter Riedemann: Shaper of the Hutterite Tradition* (Kitchener, ON: Pandora Press, 2007) ISBN 978-1-894710-76-3

8. Neal Blough, *Christ In Our Midst: Incarnation, Church and Discipleship in the Theology of Pilgram Marpeck* (Kitchener, ON: Pandora Press, 2007) ISBN 978-1-894710-77-0

Christ In Our Midst

Incarnation, Church and Discipleship in the theology of Pilgram Marpeck

by
Neal Blough

Published by
Pandora Press

Library and Archives Canada Cataloguing in Publication

Blough, Neal
    Christ in our midst : incarnation, church and discipleship in the theology of Pilgram Marpeck / Neal Blough.

(Anabaptist and Mennonite studies, ISSN 1494-4081 ; 8)
Originally published in French under title: Christologie anabaptiste.
Includes bibliographical references.
ISBN 978-1-894710-77-0

    1. Marbeck, Pilgram, ca. 1495-1556. 2. Jesus Christ--History of doctrines--sixteenth-century. 3. Jesus Christ--Person and offices. 4. Anabaptists--Doctrines--Early works to 1800. I. Title. II. Series.

BX4946.M3B57 2007   232.092   C2007-901055-5

The publishers wish to acknowledge the generous support of William Klassen, Robert Kruse, and the Jubilee Charitable Trust in the publication of this book.

CHRIST IN OUR MIDST: INCARNATION, CHURCH AND DISCIPLESHIP IN THE THEOLOGY OF PILGRAM MARPECK
Copyright © 2007 Pandora Press
        Published by Pandora Press
        33 Kent Avenue
        Kitchener, Ontario N2G 3R2
All rights reserved.
        ISBN: 978-1-894710-77-0
        ISSN: 1494-4081

Chapters I, II, IV, V of the original French publication have been substantially revised; the Introduction, chapters III, VI and VII are new.

Cover Illustration: Caravaggio, "Supper at Emmaus," Pinocateca di Brera, Milan, Italy. Reproduced under license from the Italian Ministry for Cultural Goods and Activities.

Book cover designed by Christian Snyder
Book contents designed by Beth MacIntosh
All Pandora Press books are printed on Eco-Logo certified paper.

Table of Contents

Preface   7

Introduction   11

Chapter 1 Pilgram Marpeck's Anti-Spiritualist Writings in Strasbourg   25

Chapter 2 Anabaptism and the Reformation: Pilgram Marpeck's Strasbourg Confession of Faith (1532)   47

Chapter 3 Widening the Debate Again: Exposé of the Babylonian Whore   81

Chapter 4 The Christological Synthesis of 1542   101

Chapter 5 Marpeck's Christology and the Controversy with Schwenckfeld   133

Chapter 6 Salvation and ethics: Marpeck, the Reformation and Medieval Theology   187

Chapter 7 Christ In Our Midst: Incarnation, Church and Discipleship Then and Now   225

Index   255
Bibliography   263

Preface

More than twenty years have elapsed since the French publication of my doctoral dissertation on Pilgram Marpeck's Christology.[1] Since that time, various people have suggested that an English translation would be welcome. However, time constraints mired any progress on my part and years slipped by as they have a way of doing. A heartening step in this direction occurred when Reuben Glick Shank, under the auspices of the Institute of Mennonite Studies, undertook the translation of several chapters of the dissertation as well as a more recent article (chapter VI of this book). This proved to be the stimulus necessary to move things forward. But as the title reflects, the project is no longer a mere translation but stands on its own as a different book.[2] This modification can be attributed to several reasons.

---

[1] *Christologie anabaptiste. Pilgram Marpeck et l'humanité du Christ*, (Geneva : Labor et Fides, 1984).
[2] Approximately 40% of the original is not in this book, there are three new chapters, and those chapters which do come from the dissertation have been reworked and modified in light of more recent research.

First of all, the last twenty years have given rise to important developments in the realm of scholarship pertaining to Marpeck. My original research was completed before the availability of subsequent work and findings by historians and theologians such as Stephen Boyd, Walter Klaassen, Werner Packull, John Rempel, C. Arnold Snyder, J. Denny Weaver and Thomas Finger, among others whose publications will be cited throughout this book.[3]

Careful historical scholarship has uncovered new traces of the extent of Marpeck's influence in the sixteenth-century and beyond. Stephen Boyd has unearthed previously unknown aspects of Marpeck's biography that help to understand both his life and his theology. Walter Klaassen has convincingly argued that the *Exposé* (written around 1532) could be added to the Marpeck corpus of writings. This implies not only that Marpeck was dialoguing with Bucer during his last months at Strasbourg in the early 1530's, but that he was also attempting to address Luther and the larger context of the Reformation. At the time of my initial research it was thought that Marpeck and his "circle"[4] left no real influence in the Anabaptist communities that survived the mid sixteenth-century. Arnold Snyder and Hanspeter Jecker have since demonstrated that the Marpeck tradition had influence in Swiss Brethren circles into the 17th century. Werner Packull and Martin Rothkegel also have discovered that Marpeck's writings were part of larger ongoing debates than was initially known. This all implies that the scope of Marpeck's interests and influence were greater than imagined only twenty years ago.

From a theological point of view but with differing approaches, C. Arnold Snyder, John Rempel, Denny Weaver and Thomas Finger have all emphasized the importance of Marpeck in elaborating a contemporary

---

[3] The works of those mentioned in the introduction will be cited throughout the book. The most recent summary of historical scholarship on Marpeck is William Klassen's "The Legacy of the Marpeck Community in Anabaptist Scholarship," *Mennonite Quarterly Review* (January 2004), 7-28.

[4] Historians use the term "Marpeck-circle" or "Marpeck community" to refer both to the network of scattered Anabaptist congregations that considered him as a leader as well as to the fact that several of the writings attributed to Marpeck were probably authored together with his colleague Leupold Scharnschlager and others.

Anabaptist theology. Pilgram Marpeck is considered as having been less sectarian and legalistic, more socially involved and sacramental, and thus more helpful in elaborating a contemporary theology than those sixteenth-century Anabaptists who had been forced by circumstances to view Christian presence in the world as one of "separation."

My own continued research on Marpeck has also led to insights and conclusions that were not part of the original project. Articles or extracts of articles subsequently published elsewhere are included in this volume, albeit in a reworked fashion. Those chapters that issue from the dissertation (I, II, IV, V) have been revised in light of more recent scholarship which has resulted in some passages having been nuanced, changed or simply left out.[5] Two additional chapters (VI & VII) plus the introduction are new and appear here for the first time.

Other experiences have also contributed to expanding my understanding of Marpeck. Teaching church history for fifteen years has served to underscore how much I did not know when undertaking the original project. Introducing and teaching Marpeck over the years to Mennonites, Protestants, Evangelicals, Pentecostals and Catholics, both in Europe and in Africa, in addition to participation in various forms of ecumenical dialogue, has convinced me of the merit and utility of his theology in discussions of Anabaptism with those of other confessional origins. All of this combined, as well as the continuing and growing interest of historians and theologians in Marpeck's writings has encouraged me to offer this work as part of the ongoing attempt to understand his thought. While this book is strictly an historical study for the most part, the final chapter does enter into current debates on the ongoing relevance of Marpeck's theology.

The original study contained a chapter on the life and writings of Marpeck. Given the considerable evolution in what is now known about Marpeck and the number of recent publications on Marpeck in English,

---

[5] Reuben Glick Shank did the original translation of chapters 2, 4, 5 and 6, and is to be thanked for his very good and careful work. Nevertheless, I subsequently introduced modifications (mostly of content and very rarely of style) into his translations.

such a chapter will not be part of this work.[6] Nevertheless, one of my basic operating premises maintains the significance and requisite detailed study of the historical context in which any theology is elaborated. It is my hope that each chapter contains sufficient reference to the context at hand, but for those readers not familiar with the life of Pilgram Marpeck (c. 1495-1556), a short "historical prologue" containing helpful data has been included at the beginning of chapters 1 and 4. It is important to know that Marpeck was not trained as a formal theologian, but as an engineer. He also had extensive experience in the political and social realms of cities in which he lived (Rattenberg in Austria, Strasbourg in Alsace, and Augsburg in southern Germany). It is perhaps his life as an "urban professional" that renders his theology so attractive to present day inheritors of sixteenth-century Anabaptism.

Special thanks are due to John Rempel and C. Arnold Snyder for their encouragement to move forward with this project, to Reuben Glick Shank and the Institute of Mennonite Studies for their precious aid with translation, to William Klassen for his "behind the scenes" facilitation and for helping to find the funds necessary for the publication, and to my wife Janie for her editorial ability in improving the English readability of this preface and of chapter VII.

---

[6] Summaries of Marpeck's life and writings can be found in Johann Loserth, "Pilgram Marpeck," *The Mennonite Encyclopedia* III, 491-500; Harold S. Bender, "Pilgram Marpeck, Anabaptist Theologian and Civil Engineer," *MQR* (July 1964), 231-265 ; Walter Klaassen & William Klassen, trans. & eds., *The Writings of Pilgram Marpeck* Scottdale, PA: Herald Press, 1978), 15-41 (hereafter cited as *WPM*); William Klassen, "Pilgram Marpeck. Liberty without Coercion," in Hans-Jürgen Goertz, *Profiles of Radical Reformers* (Scottdale, PA: Herald Press, 1982), 168-177. The most extensive historical work to this point has been done by Stephen Boyd, *Pilgram Marpeck. His Life and Social Theology* (Mainz: Verlag Philipp Von Zabern, 1992). Cf. as well Boyd, "Marpeck, Pilgram," in *The Mennonite Encyclopedia*, volume V, 538-539. Walter Klaassen and William Klassen are currently preparing a new biography of Marpeck which is close to publication.

Introduction

The aim of this book is to analyze and present the theology of the Anabaptist reformer, Pilgram Marpeck (1495?-1556). Before entering into this specific task, this introduction will first seek to locate Marpeck in his time and place, for theology is never done in a vacuum, but always responds to specific questions and contexts. As an educated lay person deeply interested in church reform, Pilgram Marpeck became committed to the Anabaptist reforming path by 1528 and reflected theologically on the issues of his day from an Anabaptist perspective. But he was a unique Anabaptist reformer. His awareness of a wide variety of contemporary and historical theological positions, his unique life experiences and his intellectual gifts placed Marpeck in a special position to engage and articulate his Anabaptist convictions, something he did in conversation with the rich theological currents of his time, as will become evident in the study that follows.

The Reformation Context

The broadest context for this study is the ecclesiastical and theological upheaval of sixteenth century Western and Central Europe commonly known as the Reformation.[1] Looking to the Reformation could mean taking a specific person or movement, i.e. Martin Luther, Ulrich Zwingli or the origins of Anabaptism, as a starting point. But that would be starting too soon. Presupposing a clear and neat divide between the medieval and Reformation periods runs the risk of not seeing how deeply the Reformers and the Anabaptists drank from the well of medieval assumptions, practices and theology. Reform was not a new theological or ecclesiastical concept at the beginning of the sixteenth century. When Martin Luther (supposedly) posted 95 Theses on indulgences on the door of one of Wittenberg's churches in 1517 he was responding to issues that had been gestating for centuries.

Long before Luther and Marpeck, movements such as the Waldensians and Franciscans (12th and 13th centuries) had formulated stinging critiques of a wealthy, powerful and crusading medieval church. The papal schism of 1378 was seen as a major scandal by most European Christians and inspired a reform movement which culminated in the Councils of Constance and Basel in the early 15th century. At this point, many were convinced that ecumenical councils (and not the papacy) should have the final word in defining church dogma and settling conflicts in order to bring about "reform within both the head and the members" of the Church.

During this same "conciliar period," dissident movements formed around John Wyclif (England) and John Huss (Prague), demonstrating both a new consciousness of "national"[2] identities as well as a continuing dissatisfaction with what was perceived as an overly centralized and theologically deficient Roman Church. Urban spiritual movements such as Third Order Franciscans and the Devotio Moderna reflected a growing

---

[1] For an excellent synthetic treatment of this period (although somewhat weak on Anabaptism) see Diarmaid MacCulloch, *The Reformation, A History*, (New York: Viking Press, 2004).

[2] MacCulloch warns that "nationalism" is an anachronism when applied to the sixteenth century. He prefers the term "commonwealth." Ibid., 42.

interest among lay people who wanted to seriously live out their Christian faith in the context of their families and professional life, i.e. without being clergy or members of a religious community. This same period saw the rise of the Renaissance and of Christian humanism. Benefiting from the Greek manuscripts and skills of intellectual refugees fleeing a now Muslim Constantinople, Christian scholars such as Erasmus were calling the church back to Scripture and the early church fathers – who were more open to Platonic influences – and away from much more recent scholastic developments in theology, which relied more on Aristotle.

All of these issues fed directly into the sixteenth-century Reformation. In several contexts, "Protestant" ideas became the ideal means for taking distance from Rome and affirming new local, regional or "national" identities. New urban and lay spiritualities paved the way for the idea of a "priesthood of all believers." Because of humanism, the classical past (i.e. Scripture and the early Patristic period) could now be used to critique the more recent (i.e. scholastic) past. Numerous ideas and important forces were already in motion when Martin Luther came upon the scene.

Even such a brief look at the period preceding 1500 helps us to have a more nuanced understanding of what subsequently happened in the sixteenth century. Traditional Catholic and Protestant historiography has depicted the Western Church of 1500 as being decadent and in total decline. More recent studies point instead to strong religious vitality and aspirations, something which helps to explain why so many people were dissatisfied and wanted to see the church reformed.[3] Cultures wallowing in complacency and decadence do not consciously seek change. Ecclesiastical change became possible in 1500 not only because of widespread dissatisfaction, but also because the faith of large numbers of people led them to envision something else. New looks at the past were giving birth to new visions of the future.

It was thus the case that around 1500, most people agreed that the "patient," i.e. the Church, was "ill" and in need of "healing." Nevertheless,

---

[3] Cf. Bernd Moeller: "Piety in Germany around 1500" in Steven E. Ozment, *The Reformation in Medieval Perspective* (Chicago, Quadrangle Books, 1971), 50-75.

diagnoses and proposed treatments differed radically. During a first and relatively short period, many who aspired to change – humanists, theologians, princes, city officials, and the "common people" – collaborated and saw themselves as allies. But as is often the case, shared opposition to a perceived common enemy can hide important differences. As time went on, important divergences became apparent not only between Catholic and Protestant reformers (i.e. Erasmus and Luther) but also between those who were no longer within the Catholic fold (i.e., Luther, Müntzer, Zwingli, Sattler, Hubmaier, et al.). Instead of healing the church, "Reform" began tearing her apart.

Of course, the religious and theological debates of the sixteenth century took place in larger political, economic and cultural settings. The early sixteenth century was an explosive period full of contradictory expectations, a fact which helps explain divergent diagnoses and conflicting remedies in regards to the Church. Humanism and the "Renaissance" sensibilities argued of an end of the "Dark Ages" and the beginning of new intellectual horizons. A New World was being discovered by Spanish and Portuguese explorers as a result of which the Hapsburg emperor Charles V quickly became ruler of vast territories outside of Europe, an immense empire that aroused intellectual curiosity and economic expectations. On the other hand, theologians such as Luther built their reforming theology on a radically pessimistic Augustinian anthropology. According to this perspective, the entire human race is stuck in a quagmire of evil. The threat of Turkish invasion on the eastern edge of Charles' empire, accompanied by widespread poverty, famine, economic exploitation and ecclesiastical corruption fed eschatological currents that proclaimed the imminence of Christ's return and the end of history. While some were imagining a new world, others foresaw the end of the world.

In the midst of this coexisting optimism and pessimism, there were also contradictory political and economic tendencies at work. In the early 1520s, the "common people" in the Empire were longing to recover lost privileges of self-government and access to rivers and forests for fishing, hunting and firewood. On the other hand, in an increasingly urban Europe, princes, territorial rulers, emperors and kings aspired to more centralized power and rationalized governmental structures and techniques. These same leaders also aspired to more control over ecclesiastical properties, revenues and pastoral care in their respective territories. Urban merchants and artisans were shaping new economical practices and theories. A Catholic king (Francis I) and a Catholic emperor (Charles V), who was also king of Spain reigned in constant rivalry with each other but were forced to collaborate against a common Turkish enemy. All of these factors had direct bearing on how the Reformation played out.

Pilgram Marpeck and his Context

It was in such a multi-faceted Reformation context that Pilgram Marpeck attempted to pastor, comfort and solidify scattered Anabaptist communities in various parts of German-speaking Europe. Marpeck himself was very much aware of a good many of these elements. Probably more so than any other sixteenth century Anabaptist leader, Pilgram Marpeck was personally close to key events and influential people that shaped the larger Reformation.

In his native Rattenberg, situated within the eastern Austrian part of the Empire, Pilgram was born into a wealthy and politically active family. Just as his father had been, Marpeck was also involved in the municipal affairs of Rattenberg, serving as councillor and even as mayor for one year. It was in these early years of the 1520s that Luther's ideas began to fuse and inspire dissent. Marpeck himself was serving in official capacities as Rattenberg began to deal with issues between Catholics and "Lutherans." As mining magistrate, Marpeck was directly responsible to King Ferdinand of Austria, the emperor's brother. Since the mines for which he was responsible were an important source of revenue for the empire, Marpeck was very much aware of the large-scale economic issues and tensions at work. When the Peasants' War swept through the area in 1526, Marpeck saw first-hand how Reformation ideas could fire the imagination of peasants and miners who aspired to a better life. He also witnessed the birth of Anabaptism in his native area of the Tyrol and was asked to identify those of his employees who had sympathy with the new movement's ideas and practices. Because of his refusal to do so, he lost his job and he and his wife Anna were obliged to leave Rattenberg.

On his way to Strasbourg in 1528, Marpeck stopped first in Moravia where he was baptized and ordained as an Anabaptist elder. Once in Strasbourg, the free Alsatian imperial city that was a haven to many religious dissidents of his time, Marpeck quickly became a citizen and was hired by the city to engineer and build waterways for floating wood from the mountains into Strasbourg. He also functioned as an Anabaptist leader. Personally acquainted with Martin Bucer, the leading reformer of the city, Marpeck was an eye-witness to efforts to put into place a Reformed church in collaboration with the city council. When the emperor Charles threatened war against the Protestants princes in the early 1530s, Marpeck observed the beginnings of the Schmalkaldic League of which Strasbourg became a member. All of these events contributed to the end of Anabaptism as an ecclesial and theological possibility in Strasbourg and necessitated once again that Marpeck give up an important professional position. After a dozen years of exile and wandering, Marpeck spent the last years of his life in Augsburg, where in 1547 he observed Charles' troops entering victoriously into the city after having defeated the German Protestant armies.

Pilgram Marpeck had important first-hand knowledge of central Reformation events and ideas, and also was well acquainted with the varieties of Anabaptism. His original encounter had been with the nascent Austrian and Moravian strains of the Anabaptist movement. He certainly would have been aware of the fact that his employer, the Hapsburg ruler Ferdinand I of Austria, put the noted Anabaptist theologian Balthasar Hubmaier to death at the stake in Vienna in March of 1528. In Strasbourg he knew Wilhelm Reublin, who had participated in Anabaptist beginnings both in Zurich and Waldshut as well as having been present with Michael Sattler at Schleitheim in 1527. Strasbourg also provided the opportunity to become acquainted with Melchior Hoffman, Caspar Schwenckfeld, and perhaps even Michael Servetus. Marpeck had the nerve to help translate and edit an important writing of Bernhard Rothmann, a pastor and leader in Anabaptist Münster, and to see to its republication. Travels and correspondence brought first-hand experience with the Swiss Brethren and the Hutterites. As his writings reveal, he was well aware of the weak points and dangers of Anabaptism, i.e. the catastrophe of Münster, the legalism of some of the Swiss Brethren, and the authoritarianism of the Hutterites.

All of this means that as he pondered the theological issues of the day, Pilgram Marpeck was able to draw on a wider range of experience and intellectual currents than could most other sixteenth century Anabaptist writers and leaders. In fact, the theology that came to expression in his writings needs to be read as a kind of conversation with a wide variety of theological and reforming currents both within the Anabaptist movement and the wider Christian world of his time. His broad political and professional experience in various urban settings along with his first hand knowledge of several varieties of Anabaptism allowed Marpeck to work at the theological issues of the day in a fascinatingly original way.

In the midst of a very complex situation, specific questions and issues were being raised. Because of the Reformation, because there were now rival claims to being the "true Church," new questions were being asked without those involved always knowing what the answers would look like or what the consequences would be to the solutions they proposed – sometimes very different consequences resulted than they had imagined. Most of the theological and ecclesiological issues extended well beyond the borders of Anabaptist reform in and of it itself, but Anabaptists such as Marpeck needed to deal with them. New questions required new answers. But new answers were often forged with categories and concepts inherited from previous centuries of theological discourse and ecclesiastical structures and practices. As the ensuing chapters will show in greater detail, the majority of Marpeck's writings were responses to very specific issues and evolved in conversation with inherited and contemporary positions.

Authority within the Church

Erasmus' call to return to the Bible, echoed even more strongly by Luther and his followers, made Scripture a fundamental source for theologizing in a new way. Up until the sixteenth century, it had been presupposed that the theology of the Church Fathers and medieval doctors upheld and explicated Scripture. As a corollary, this also meant that there was considerable theological pluralism in the late Middle Ages and that Reformers of various stripes had many different schools of thought that could inspire their critiques as well as their new answers.

In the generations preceding 1500, debates turned around the question of who had the final say concerning which church Fathers and theologians had the correct reading of Scripture. The conciliar movement of the fifteenth century insisted that the ecumenical councils had the final word. The Renaissance popes shied away from that conclusion and preferred papal authority as the answer. Luther began his career as a reformer by calling for a council in 1520, but after being excommunicated, the appeal of Scripture as the final authority over against both pope and council seemed to be a new way out of an inextricable dilemma. The Reformation principle of *sola scriptura* proclaimed loudly something that many people felt instinctively: the church as an institution (including councils and Popes) could err and had erred, and needed to be held accountable to scriptural authority.

Generations, if not centuries of theological reflection were jettisoned and Scripture began to function as the one and final explicit source of theological reflection. Erasmus had contributed to this by his claim that the meaning of biblical texts was clear and simple to anyone who approached them in faith. Luther and Zwingli, as well as the early Swiss Anabaptists enthusiastically embraced this new method of theologizing. Nevertheless, by the time Marpeck began his theological career, it was becoming clear that the insistence on the final authority of *sola scriptura* had not anticipated the fundamental question of hermeneutics. Luther and Zwingli both claimed the ultimate authority of the Bible, but their total disagreement over how to conceive of Christ's presence in the Eucharist was evidence that the Catholic insistence on the necessity of determining an ecclesiastically authorized reading of Scripture was not totally unjustified. Anabaptist critiques of infant baptism merely amplified Protestant disagreement on how to interpret authoritative Scripture.

Such debates led to more theologically and historically aware methods of approaching Scripture. The magisterial reformers would insist on "was Christum treibt" or the "analogy of faith," i.e. the principal of justification by faith as the hermeneutical key to Scripture. The need to refer to church fathers, especially Augustine, was also increasingly recognized by some as a necessary hermeneutical tool. Among the Anabaptists, the same kind of hermeneutical shift was also evident. For example, Balthasar Hubmaier's first treatise on baptism (1525) was based almost totally on Scripture.[4] Only a year later, he published a new justification for believers' baptism that strongly relied on the authority of the patristic and medieval sources as well as contemporary theologians.[5]

As we shall see, Pilgram Marpeck's theology clearly recognized the need for theological and historical criteria for reading Scripture. His writings are full of references to biblical texts, but he was also consciously aware of patristic and medieval theological concepts (Incarnation, Trinity) that had been used as theological guideposts along the way for reading and interpreting Scripture. While accepting and building on the fundamental intuitions of Anabaptism, Marpeck's developing theology went beyond the simple biblicism of the Swiss Brethren and attempted to situate "Anabaptist" theology in the larger history of Christian thought. As will become quite clear, Marpeck came to the conviction that the key to thinking and speaking about God (theology) was to understand Christ (Christology). The notion of the Incarnation – consciously formulated in trinitarian categories – thus became the hermeneutical key to Scripture for Marpeck, his principal means of navigating through both the Old and New Testaments. As did the Reformers (and all of Christian theology for that matter), Marpeck posited a Christological reading of Scripture. But as will become quite clear, his was a different Christology from that of Luther, Zwingli or Schwenckfeld.

---

[4] Balthasar Hubmaier, "On the the Christian Baptism of Believers," in H. Wayne Pipkin and John H. Yoder, *Balthasar Hubmaier Theologian of Anabaptism*, (Scottdale, PA: Herald Press, 1989), 95-149.
[5] Balthasar Hubmaier, "Old and New Teachers on Believers' Baptism," in ibid., 245-274.

Anthropology and Justification by Faith

One important source of the hermeneutical impasses between reformers was that they brought differing theological and philosophical presuppositions to their reading of Scripture. Several debates over differing presuppositions are reflected in Marpeck's Christology.

One of the main reasons that Luther and Erasmus parted ways had to do with their differing assumptions about human nature, especially in relation to sin and free will. As will be seen in chapter 6, Luther shared the anthropological assumptions of a radical Augustinianism that had been revived in the several generations prior to the Reformation. According to this perspective, human nature is totally corrupt and incapable of accomplishing any good in the eyes of God. In contrast, Erasmus – and much of medieval theology – held to a more optimistic view of human nature, claiming that human beings could respond to God's grace and were capable of accomplishing acts pleasing to God with the help of grace. The difference between these two perspectives became a main point of separation also between "Reformation" and "Radical Reformation," with radical reformers siding with Erasmus against Luther.

Medieval Catholic theology spoke of infused grace via the sacraments as the means for human actions to become pleasing to God. Anabaptists, having refused such an understanding of sacramental mediation, needed a different way to express anthropological insights. A totally new theology of baptism was necessary, both against Catholicism as well as over against the reformers. In much the same way, medieval Eucharistic theology was no longer seen as an acceptable explanation of the Lord's Supper as a "means of grace." As will become evident in several debates that will be analysed in the following chapters, Marpeck's developing Trinitarian Christology allowed him to articulate an understanding of the Christian life in which the direct presence of the Holy Spirit replaced sacramentally infused grace as the fundamental category for explaining how faithful Christian discipleship was possible.

Closely related to the question of anthropology was the central Reformation concept of justification by faith. Luther's understanding of justification was formulated in the context of his radically pessimistic anthropology. According to Luther, God's gracious initiative in Christ excluded any possibility of human effort in the process of coming to salvation, downplayed the role of Christ as teacher and example, and led to a strong doctrine of predestination. As will become clear, Marpeck's Christology attempted to safeguard the Reformation critique of works' righteousness while at the same time critiquing Luther's theology of justification.

Inner and outer

As had previously been the case with medieval mysticism, Erasmus' theology had a strong underpinning of neoplatonism which gave priority to the inner and spiritual realms of the Christian faith. This reflected a shift in European mentality that was starting to move toward the Enlightenment and at the same time a critique of that strand of medieval piety that relied heavily on the sacred power of objective ritual objects. This interiorizing tendency was a given for those who had been influenced by Erasmus, including Reformers such as Zwingli and Bucer as well as the early Swiss and South German-Austrian Anabaptists (although in different ways). At work here was a new interiority that placed a strong emphasis on the individual appropriation of faith and devalued outward expressions of faith and penitential "good works" (pilgrimages, shrines, rituals). Zwingli and others radicalized this inward tendency, sometimes denying any intrinsic relationship between inner and outer, between spiritual and material.

By the time Marpeck arrived on the scene, the official reformers had placed "outward" affairs of church observance in the hands of civil government. Luther and Zwingli were totally speaking past each other, coming to very different conclusions about how God uses "outer means." In reaction to the bitter and violent disputes over "outer" questions such as ecclesiology, baptism and Eucharist, more radical Spiritualists proposed jettisoning most outward expressions of the faith in favour of a purely interior "spiritual" faith and "spiritual" (i.e. invisible) community of believers. The Spiritualists, sharing as they did some fundamental beliefs with Anabaptists, began making significant inroads into Anabaptist communities.

Spiritualism was perhaps the major issue that Marpeck's theology had to face. Once again, he dealt with it via his Christology. In a surprising way, we will see how much he owed to Luther quite early on in his writing career. Over the years, Marpeck developed a theology based on a Lutheran sacramental logic combined with an almost Calvinist understanding of "real" (though spiritual) presence. His eclectic and sometimes awkward borrowing of theological themes all pointed in one direction: the visibility of the church and a communal Spirit-filled presence that reflected the humanity of Christ in the world.

Church and State

After having been excommunicated in 1520, Martin Luther was sorely pressed to find an alternative structure for church authority. Bishops would no longer do – at least not Catholic bishops. In 1523, in order to bypass episcopal straight jacketing of pastoral offices, Luther suggested that local congregations should be free to choose their own pastors. During the same period, Zwingli suggested that ecclesiastical tithes could be better used to pay local pastors. These ideas contributed to the popular uprising known as the Peasants' war which extended all the way to Marpeck's Tyrol. After the blood bath and constant accusations that "Reformation" meant "anarchy," it was no longer feasible to imagine congregationalism, and Luther placed the Reformation in the hands of the princes; Zwingli, Bucer and later on Calvin, collaborated very closely with the municipal structures of imperial free cities. This solution was not all that new, since for several generations there already had been a tendency for lay civic leaders to take responsibility for local religious affairs.[6] Nevertheless, the Reformation put into place new structures of collaboration between church and state. Princes and city councils in effect replaced bishops in the structure of church polity.

Once Hubmaier's efforts to establish a civic or communal Anabaptism were no longer a viable option, the major Anabaptist response to this

---

[6] MacCulloch, *Reformation*, 49.

question was given at Schleitheim (1527) and recommended separatism and the absolute refusal to participate in governmental affairs. Having been a civil servant and accustomed to exercising authority, and finding himself in an imperial free city where Anabaptism had not yet been totally excluded (Strasbourg), Marpeck was more open to Christian participation in the public realm. At the same time, he kept alive the Anabaptist critique of violence used to protect Christian faith over against Bucer and Luther, while at the same time refusing any theological justification of political power that could be used in direct exchange for official status for the Church.

Once again, it was Marpeck's Christology that allowed him to move forward in a new direction. Learning from Caspar Schwenckfeld and medieval descriptions of the meaning of Christ's descent into hell, Marpeck was able to distinguish between the Old and New Covenants in a new and creative way. His Anabaptist intuitions led him to describe a visible church which reflected Christ's non-violent presence in the world via the Holy Spirit, sent at Pentecost.

The following chapters will demonstrate the extent to which Pilgram Marpeck's Christology was at the heart of how he dealt theologically with a whole series of important Reformation questions. His was a Christology that took up and amplified important Anabaptist intuitions that had not yet been developed in a serious or consistent manner by Anabaptists before him. His was a Christology that took seriously Reformation critiques of the medieval church, attempting to argue from Scripture and to move away from an *ex opere operato* understanding of sacraments. His was a Christology that entered without hesitation into the important theological debates of the day. His was a Christology that recognized the importance of anchoring itself within the larger Christian tradition, of using shared "catholic" categories such as the Incarnation, the Trinity and the doctrine of the two natures of Christ.

Perhaps most importantly, Pilgram Marpeck articulated a practical and Anabaptist Christology, an understanding of Christ that could not be separated from the church's mission and presence in the world nor from discipleship. Marpeck's use of traditional Christological categories was neither a sell-out to "constantinianism" nor an "ivory tower" overly intellectualized theology cut off from everyday life and from issues of the church in the real world. As we hope to demonstrate in the following chapters, Pilgram Marpeck's Christology sought nothing else than to point to the "Christ in our midst."

Chapter 1

Pilgram Marpeck's Anti-Spiritualist Writings in Strasbourg

Historical Prologue

Having moved from the Bavarian town of Rosenheim, Marpeck's father, Heinrich, served Rattenberg, Austria, as a councilman, mayor and district magistrate. Pilgram likewise became engaged in city affairs. After the death of Pilgram's first wife, Sophia, with whom he had one daughter, Margareth, Pilgram Marpeck married Anna and they adopted three foster children. Professionally he worked in the city hospital, organized the city's crossbow competition, and acted as a purchasing agent for the mining guild's infirmary before entering office as mining magistrate in 1525. Politically, he served on the outer and inner city councils and as mayor (1522), taking an active role in regulating the city's craftsmen negotiating the release of the reform-minded preacher, Stephan Castenbaur (Agricola), and hiring a priest to fill the pastoral office in the city's parish church. As mining magistrate, Marpeck was required by Archduke Ferdinand to hand over miners who, like he, were sympathetic to Anabaptist preachers Leonhard Schiemer and Hans Schlaffer.

After initial consent, Marpeck resigned his office a few days after Schiemer's execution. From Rattenberg, he travelled to Bohemia and Moravia where he most likely received baptism and a commission as an Anabaptist elder.

After joining the Strasbourg gardener-wagoner guild and buying citizenship in 1528, Marpeck led a communal group of Anabaptists and social radicals, for which he was arrested and release sometime before 1530. From 1530 to his expulsion in 1532, he served the city as lumbering supervisor, overseeing the cutting and delivery of wood from the city forest near Hausach on the Kinzig river. During this time he led a group of Anabaptists, most closely associated with the Swiss Brethren, and contributed to the differentiation among the city's Anabaptist groups by criticizing the spiritualistic tendencies of Hans Bünderlin and Christian Entfelder and the apocalyptic speculations of Melchior Hoffman.[1]

The first major theological and chronological building-block of Marpeck's Christology is found in his polemical engagement with the spiritualist wing of the Radical Reformation in Strasbourg. It is here for the first time that we see the importance of the Incarnation and of the humanity of Christ (*menscheit Christi*) as a theme that will constantly be rehearsed and replayed in the ensemble of Marpeck's writings.

As will become evident, Pilgram Marpeck's understanding of the Incarnation has two main functions within his theology – the one "material" and the other "historical." The material function of the humanity of Christ is found in his anti-Spiritualist writings to emphasize the importance of outer/material reality and the "ceremonies" (baptism, the Lord's Supper, discipline, etc.). It is to this aspect of the Incarnation to which this chapter will attend. Neither treatise examined here is explicitly Christological, except for a small section of the *Clear Instruction*. Nevertheless, it is in these two writings that Marpeck deals with the Spirit and the Letter, the inner and the outer, in ways that anticipate his later writings.

---

[1] Taken directly from Stephen Boyd, "Marpeck, Pilgram," in *ME* volume V, 538.

A Clear Refutation

A copy of this first treatise was not found until 1958 and identified as having been written by Marpeck in 1959.[2] It was written mainly against Hans Bünderlin of Linz (1499-1533), a former priest, influenced by Luther and Anabaptism before adopting a more spiritualist theology. Having come to Strasbourg during the period of Marpeck's stay in Alsace, Bünderlin published two booklets in 1529 and a third in 1530. Bünderlin was apparently well-known in Anabaptist circles in Strasbourg, to the point that his books were being read during their meetings.[3] We must remember that in 1530, fierce debates were raging among European Christians as to the meaning and practice of the sacraments. Luther's teaching on justification by faith led to a major shift in Eucharistic theology and practice, thus establishing a breach between Catholics, Lutherans and Zwinglians. Within the Reformation camp, Luther and Zwingli had been unable to come to an agreement on the Eucharist. The birth of the Anabaptist movement and ensuing debates on baptism had already been the source of people being put to death. The spiritualist wing of the Reformation expressed strong disappointment over the fracturing of the body of Christ on the basis of these "outward" manifestations of the faith hence the radical critique of "ceremonies" by the Spiritualists.

It was the growing influence of spiritualist thinking and its attractiveness in Anabaptist circles that led Marpeck to refute Bünderlin's *Erklerung durch vergleichung der Biblischen geschrifft...* (1530). As did other Spiritualists, Bünderlin called into question the usefulness of "outer ceremonies" in the life of the Church. He claimed that the ceremonies were no longer valid 1) because of having been falsified by the Antichrist, 2) because of having no explicit command to use them since the death of the apostles, and 3) because the apostles had no authority to transmit them beyond their own generation.

Marpeck's response to Bünderlin's Spiritualism begins by claiming that the ceremonies were founded in the words and commands of Christ

---

[2] *WPM*, 569, note 2.
[3] M. Krebs and H.G. Rott (eds). *Quellen zur Geschichte der Täufer*, VII Band, Elsass I Teil, Stadt Strassburg, (Gütersloh: Gerd Mohn, 1959), 225 (hereafter cited as QGT VII).

himself. Christ's coming marked the beginning of a new period in history called the New Testament.[4] Christ's ordinances are valid during this entire period, until his return. Even if people had abused and falsified these ordinances, it was not a valid reason to no longer use them. Their validity was to be found in the words of Christ and of the apostles. For example, Christians are to celebrate the Supper because Paul had written that it was necessary to "proclaim the Lord's death until He comes."[5]

Even though the ceremonies are founded literally and outwardly in the words of Christ and Scripture, Marpeck knew that he could not stay only at the "outward," literal level in his argumentation. Christ's words are valid in the present because of the Spirit. "Where, however, the Spirit of Christ is present ... there Christ's pure ordinance is joined to it."[6] An outward or literal basis for the ceremonies would not suffice. Christ, through his Spirit, acts in the life of believers to convince them of the necessity of the ceremonies. The same Spirit also purifies the ceremonies of all abuse. There is no need of miracles or special signs in order to participate in the ceremonies as the Spiritualists claimed. The inner experience of the Spirit verifies the outward testimony of Scripture. Comparing the Reformation to the return of the Israelites from exile, Marpeck writes that

> Just as the Israelites, rescued out of Babylonian captivity... restored the ancient ceremonies, so too does Christ today, through His servants rescued out of the prison of the Antichrist, restore and renew His instituted ceremonies ... by means of His inner command and His bestowal of the certainty of His Spirit.[7]

While arguing that Christ's commands justify the ceremonies, Marpeck also insists that such practices have no use if they do not come out of an inner calling: "If the inner mandate of Christ is not present, all is in vain."[8]

---

[4] *WPM*, 45. Marpeck elaborated on this point much more fully in his Strasbourg Confession of 1532, which will be studied in the following chapter.
[5] *WPM*, 48.
[6] *WPM*, 45-46.
[7] *WPM*, 46.
[8] *WPM*, 54.

Even though the above remarks are not strictly "Christological," they lay the groundwork for two major categories of Marpeck's thought in general: Christ's *outer* and *visible* word, and the *inner* and *invisible* Spirit. Understanding how Marpeck ties together the inner and outer, the spiritual and the material will be one of the main tasks of our work.

A Clear Refutation presents at least two different ways of describing the relationship between inner and outer. The first way is used to respond to claims that there are no commands that render necessary the celebration of the ceremonies. According to the Strasbourg Spiritualists, the apostles received commands from Jesus which were confirmed by signs and wonders. Since Jesus is no longer present and there are no more signs and wonders, the written words of the New Testament are not enough. For Marpeck, the traditional outward ceremonies of the Church are justified through the inward urging of the Spirit. Even without miracles, "through the Spirit of Christ, there is sufficient inner command."[9] Inward call was also sufficient to justify the passing on of the ceremonies to others.

> Apollos and other renowned apostles ... moved about, preaching and baptizing, without external command or commission, but ... were sent inwardly by Christ's Spirit.[10]

Rather than being transmitted institutionally, the ministry of the first generation apostles was passed on through the inner power of the Spirit. In the same way, anyone baptized inwardly through the Spirit should not despise water baptism or other ceremonies commanded by the words of Christ. In this first way of describing the relationship between inner and outer, it is the former which moves the latter to action. "For as one can see, the heart moves our external members."[11] Christ's Spirit works first of all inwardly. But this inward action always leads to the outward and visible.

> Where Christ has come in the flesh by faith ... that same man, with his flesh and all external members, indeed, the whole man

---

[9] *WPM*, 49.
[10] *WPM*, 51.
[11] *WPM*, 65.

obedient in external ceremonies, will confess the instruction and the life of Christ.¹²

This first way of describing the relationship between inner and outer leads to a second. The Incarnation, i.e., Christ's coming in the flesh becomes the central element in Marpeck's argumentation against the Spiritualists. We will come back to this line of reasoning later. It is more fully developed in *A Clear and Useful Instruction*.

Because of its stronger emphasis on the inner calling of the Spirit as the justification for the ceremonies, it is tempting to think that *A Clear Refutation* was indeed Marpeck's first effort at a theological response to Spiritualism. His attempted response is based more upon the Spirit than on the Incarnation, a fact which most probably reflects the fact that his first Anabaptist roots were indeed in the South-German tradition, which was more influenced by Spiritualism and Mysticism than was Swiss Anabaptism.¹³

The Gospel of All Creatures and Suffering for Christ

Several other elements found in *A Clear Refutation* are evidence of Marpeck's roots in the South German-Austrian stream of Anabaptism. The first of these is his usage of the "Gospel of all creatures." Unfortunately, the very notion of the "Gospel of all creatures" is based on a faulty understanding of Mark 16:16 made possible by the German translation of the New Testament. By confusing the genitive and dative cases in German, the phrase "proclaim the Gospel *to* all creatures" could also be read as "proclaim the Gospel *of* all creatures" (*Evangelium aller Kreatur*). The term was first used in this sense in a treatise usually attributed to Hans Hut, *Von dem Geheimnis der Taufe* (On the Secret of Baptism).¹⁴

---

[12] *WPM*, 52. This fundamental premise will remain to the very end in Marpeck's thought. Spirit-renewed intentions always produce corresponding outward actions.
[13] Werner O. Packull, *Mysticism and the Early South German-Austrian Anabaptist Movement* 1525-1531, (Scottdale, PA: Herald Press, 1977).
[14] The text can be found in Heinold Fast, *Der linke Flügel der Reformation*, (Bremen: C. Schünemann Verlag, 1962), 79-99.

The notion itself points to a kind of natural theology which affirms the possibility of knowing the Gospel by observing the creatures and the natural order of the world. In Hans Hut's thought, the notion is a protest against the "scribes" of the Reformation who attributed too much importance to the outer word and held the monopoly of its interpretation. With the "Gospel of all creatures," the simple peasant could also have direct access to the Gospel by observing the world about.[15]

By referring to Job 12:7-8, Marpeck states in *A Clear Refutation*, that "all visible creatures are placed in the world as apostles and teachers."[16] In other words, the "creatures" are part of the visible world that is used also for the ceremonies. Apparently, the Spiritualists (called "*Geister*" by Marpeck) wanted to do away with the "Gospel of creatures" on the basis of John 6:45: "They will all be taught (i.e. inwardly) of God."[17] In other words, they wanted to do away with all outward manifestations of the faith on the basis of the inner and spiritual.

This question cannot be dealt with in detail, but it is clear that the use of the "Gospel of all creatures" demonstrates Marpeck's original roots in a more spiritualist and mystical form of Anabaptism via Thomas Müntzer, Hans Hut, Hans Denck, Leonhart Schiemer and Hans Schlaffer.[18] Following Werner Packull, Stephen Boyd had shown the Gospel of all creatures was familiar to Marpeck most directly because of the influence of Schiemer and Schlaffer's missionary activities in the Tyrol before the Anabaptist engineer left Rattenberg for Strasbourg. Boyd also suggests that the *Theologia Deutsch*, edited and published by Luther in 1516 and 1518, had a major impact on Austrian Anabaptism.

---

[15] "The Gospel of or in all creatures could be illustrated with examples from the daily routines of peasants and artisans, namely the divine purpose of cleansing through suffering. Accordingly, true faith, born though the inner experience of the ' bitter ' Christ, stood at the center of the salvation process." Werner O. Packull, *Hutterite Beginnings: Communitarian Experiments During the Reformation* (John Hopkins University Press, 1995), 56.

[16] *WPM*, 48.

[17] Cf. *WPM*, 56. The English translation does not make this clear and I am basing my remarks on the original German text.

[18] Packull, *Mysticism*, 106-107; Stephen Boyd, *Pilgram Marpeck*, 21-41; Thomas N. Finger, *A Contemporary Anabaptist Theology* (Downers Grove: InterVarsity Press, 2004), 117.

In the writings of both Schiemer and Schlaffer, the Gospel of all creatures is involved with the personal suffering entailed in self-renunciation for Christ. Schiemer had written:

> (Paul) says further that the Gospel I preached to you is preached in all creatures... And indeed the means by which all creatures come to be useful to the human is suffering... And just as an animal is not useful to the human for food unless the body dies, so no human becomes blessed, who does not die for Christ's sake.[19]

By linking the suffering of the creatures to the suffering of Christ and the believer, Marpeck was making a soteriological statement. From the very beginning of his writings, we see elements that reflect a critique of Luther's understanding of justification by faith. As did Luther, Marpeck affirmed that salvation comes from faith. But as Müntzer and Hut had done in previous writings, Marpeck closely tied the notions of suffering and repentance to faith.

> Whoever does not suffer (meaning through a genuine act of repentance) will not rule with Him (Rom. 8). Since not all men repent, not all will share in the sufferings of Christ.[20]

According to such a perspective, the believer plays a more active role in the process of justification than in Luther's theology. Once the message of salvation has been heard, whoever believes must repent and live a new life. Christ has died for all and all can theoretically benefit from this death, but each one must make a conscious choice, which involves inner suffering, to do so.

There is an obvious anti-predestination strain here: "...Where man is not willing, God cannot and will not....Therefore the unwilling, disobedient man will no more receive the Spirit of God than he will participate in the expiation of Christ."[21] Or said in a more positive vein:

> The man who, through genuine works of repentance (that is, through faith in Jesus Christ), submits to the fellowship of

---

[19] Schiemer, quoted by Boyd, *Pilgram Marpeck,* 32. For Schlaffer, see ibid., 37-38.
[20] WPM, 61
[21] *Ibid.*

suffering under God's hand and discipline will also participate in the suffering and expiation of Christ, and upon him God's spirit will be poured ... by faith.[22]

Such willingness to suffer with Christ allows the believer to know Christ and to become more and more like him. Knowledge of God is associated with such knowledge of Christ and the believer thus participates in the divine nature.[23] We note here for the first time in Marpeck's writings an uneasiness with Luther's understanding of justification by faith, an element we will continue to track throughout the entire study. It will also be shown that Marpeck's interest in the "creatures" will be integrated to a larger theology where the Incarnation and the order of God's creation play fundamental roles.

That Marpeck had his roots in the more mystical anti-Lutheran strain of Anabaptism is not a surprise. But the move he makes in his next treatise is. One can only speculate that Marpeck quickly became aware of the weaknesses of an anti-Spiritualist argumentation based principally on the inner work of the Holy Spirit. Other theological tools were readily available, and as he did throughout his entire life, he borrowed what seemed most useful to the task at hand.

A CLEAR AND USEFUL INSTRUCTION [24]

As will become clear, there are good reasons to think that Marpeck's next Christological building block was borrowed from Martin Luther's anti-Spiritualist writings. This will be demonstrated by comparing Marpeck's *Klarer Unterricht* (*Clear Instruction*) of 1531 (in which the concept of the "humanity of Christ" was developed for the first time) and Luther's use of the same concept in some of his anti-*Schwärmer* writings of the 1520's. The similarities are various and striking. Both were writing against Spiritualists who denied the usefulness of "outer means"; both contended that because of the Incarnation inner reality is known through the outer; and both

---

[22] *Ibid.*
[23] *WPM*, 63.
[24] This section reworks and updates my earlier article "Pilgram Marpeck, Martin Luther and the Humanity of Christ," *MQR* (April 1987), 203-212.

saw Christ's humanity in the outward ceremonies and life of the church. When Marpeck wrote *A Clear Instruction* in 1531, Luther's anti-Spiritualist writings were both available and read in Strasbourg;[25] hence there is no reason to assume that Marpeck could afford to ignore such a useful tool in his polemic against Hans Bünderlin and Christian Entfelder.

The concept of the humanity of Christ

William Klassen's research has made it possible to use *A Clear Instruction* as a source of Marpeck's theology.[26] While there is no reason at present to doubt Marpeck's authorship of this book, it is not as clear that it was written primarily against Schwenckfeld as Klassen claims, but rather against Christian Entfelder.[27] This 1531 treatise was part of the same debate between Strasbourg Anabaptists and Spiritualists that was evident in *A Clear Refutation*. As before, one of the basic points of disagreement had to do with the usefulness and necessity of the outward means, or ceremonies, of the church and the visibility of the Christian community.

In such a context, where the necessity of the outer and material manifestations of the Christian faith were being radically questioned, it became clear to Marpeck that neither his previous argument based on primacy of the inner working of the Spirit nor the typical Anabaptist insistence on (outer) scriptural commands were theologically adequate to counter Spiritualist charges of legalism and literalism. For Entfelder, Bünderlin *et al.,* knowledge of God and the ensuing Christian life were seen as inner and spiritual. This basic neo-platonic starting point was formulated in such a way as to preclude the importance of the outer material realm of reality in Christian faith and practice.

In response to this point of view Marpeck affirmed, as he had previously in *A Clear Refutation*, that the true essence of knowledge of

---

[25] Cf. *Christologie Anabaptiste*, 70, note 77.
[26] Cf. William Klassen's work on this question: "Pilgram Marpeck's Two Books of 1531," *MQR* (January 1959), 18-30; and *Covenant and Community. The Life, Writings and Hermeneutics of Pilgram Marpeck* (Grand Rapids: Eerdmans, 1968), 36-45.
[27] The reasons for my doubts will become clear in the next chapter.

God is indeed inner and spiritual.[28] *A Clear Instruction* attempted to go beyond a merely literal foundation for the "ceremonies" (a word that became a technical term in this debate, referring to all outer means). The true foundation is inner, "out of the deepest conviction of the heart, out of belief, and out of the inward living Word."[29] Everything that the believer knows and does originates in the Spirit; good works proceed "from the working of the Holy Spirit."[30]

As he had done previously, Marpeck took seriously the Spiritualist starting point: true knowledge of God is inner and spiritual. But the next building block in this theology would develop a closer link between inner and outer than could the "Gospel of all creatures." The Spiritualists posited a dualistic framework in which inner and outer reality must be kept apart. Marpeck challenged this assumption, arguing now that one may not separate these two realms, that they are two different but intimately related components of a larger, unified reality. The link between the two would from now on be found directly in Marpeck's apparently new-founded understanding of the Incarnation or the "humanity of Christ."

The major thrust of *A Clear Instruction* is clear and simple. Since God became flesh in Jesus Christ, he has necessarily bound himself to the outer and material realms of this world to make himself known. One "knows" God (a knowledge which was "inner" in Spiritualist vocabulary) only through the outward means (*eusserliche mittel*). Spiritual reality is known only by means of the material, and therefore the humanity of Christ has first of all a primary epistemological function: through this humanity, knowledge of God can be attained.

From this basic assumption of the epistemological significance of the humanity of Christ, the ceremonies are then conceived of as a kind

---

[28] C. Arnold Snyder has formulated this quite well: "It is important to note that in the debate between Marpeck and the spiritualists the primary role of the Spirit of God was not at issue. Marpeck, no less than Denck and Bünderlin, maintained that a personal experience of the renewing Spirit of God was necessary in order for one to become a Christian believer." Cf. *Anabaptist History and Theology: An Introduction*, (Kitchener, ON: Pandora Press, 1995), 313.
[29] *WPM*, 76.
[30] *WPM*, 77.

of prolongation in time and space of the Incarnation. For this reason, Marpeck's doctrine of the humanity of Christ has important ecclesiological and ethical implications. What follows immediately in *A Clear Instruction* is a description of the various functions which Marpeck attributed to the humanity of Christ.

The Humanity of Christ and Knowledge of God

According to *A Clear Instruction*, inner knowledge can be attained only through outer means. "The secrets of God lie hidden under the outward speech, words, deeds and ceremonies of the humanity of Christ."[31] In order to know the inner Spirit of God, one needs an outer key. This key, the humanity of Christ, opens the door behind which the knowledge of God is hidden. "This breath or Spirit of God would have remained an eternal secret without the humanity and the physical voice of Christ."[32] In other words, without this manifestation of the humanity of Christ spiritual knowledge is impossible: "Through Christ's humanity, the inward must be revealed and recognized."[33]

This is not an epistemology whereby human reason can deduce inner reality from outward appearances, nor is it a natural theology whereby the order of nature leads to an "unmoved mover." According to *A Clear Instruction*, human reason is subject to Christ's humanity, which can be linked to the suffering to which the "Gospel of all creatures" pointed. In other words, the outer key is not just any outward manifestation of material reality; it is exclusively related to the revelation of God's self-giving and suffering love in the Incarnation and its prolongation in the life of the church.

The Humanity of Christ and the Ceremonies

Once the primary epistemological function of the humanity of Christ is understood, it is easy to follow Marpeck's extension of the concept to

---

[31] *WPM*, 81-82.
[32] *WPM*, 76.
[33] *Ibid.*

other realms. Throughout his treatise, Marpeck consistently identified the humanity of Christ with the ceremonies. These ceremonies are the outward manifestations of Christian faith, which the Spiritualists either rejected or saw as unimportant. What, more exactly, are these ceremonies and how do they function as the "humanity of Christ?"

First of all, Marpeck did not limit the ceremonies to baptism and the Lord's Supper, the two "Protestant" sacraments. The first page of *A Clear Instruction* lists the ceremonies as it describes the position of Marpeck's adversaries.

> Moreover, they say that, at present, no longer does anyone have the power to employ the ceremonies of Christ, such as baptism, the Lord's supper, teaching, the ban, and the laying on of hands, and that those who do employ these ceremonies do so apart from God's command.[34]

All that Christ and the apostles asked of disciples becomes a part of the humanity of Christ and is thus a "ceremony." The roles of the ceremonies vary. Some play the epistemological role already mentioned, leading people to a knowledge of God. Others have a nurturing or teaching function, assisting the believer in the walk of discipleship. Marpeck did not assign a specific role to each of the ceremonies. Nonetheless, it is clear that they are the means used by God to act concretely and materially within history. For example, reading the Scriptures and preaching communicate the message of salvation; water baptism commits the believer to God and the church; teaching and discipline help Christians progress in their discipleship; the Lord's Supper maintains the unity of the Christian community.

The ceremonies prolong God's presence in time and space, thus serving humanity in the same way as did Jesus of Nazareth. It is important to underline the idea of service, since the Spiritualist critique of the sacraments was that they had become idols that enslaved Christians. For Marpeck, using the ceremonies does not make one a slave of the letter or turn ceremonies into idols. The ceremonies are not ends in themselves, but means which God uses in the process of self-revelation.

---

[34] *WPM*, 71.

> For this reason, the true believers are lords over all outward ceremonies of Christ, and employ them for their service (Col. 2:16-23); the ceremonies are to serve them and not they the ceremonies. Thus, through Christ, their Master, they may by His Spirit the more energetically serve the one eternal God, and live according to His will and pleasure. In doing so, they do not deify the ceremonies, as they did in the past, and they avoid esteeming the ceremonies so highly that believers do not employ them. They also avoid the opposite extreme of those who completely cast the ceremonies aside and regard them as unnecessary. For Satan cannot tolerate Christ's maintaining the correct and true means. And, therefore, even today the physical Christ serves us in His members, and He will serve us until the end of the world...[35]

For Marpeck, rejecting these ceremonies and the knowledge of God which they bring is tantamount to rejecting the salvation accomplished by God in the Incarnation.

> Therefore, whoever presumes to discover the secrets of God, or presumes to be taught by God, without the outward, that is, the exterior or visible, casts away ... the very means by which he could be taught, could learn, or discover the divine secrets, for it is precisely the humanity of Christ which is our mediator before the Godhead (I Tim. 2:5), and not the Godhead before the humanity.[36]

The Humanity of Christ, the Church and Ethics

When applied to ecclesiology, such an understanding of the humanity of Christ has interesting implications. As we have seen, the ceremonies are the *Menschheit Christi*, i.e., a prolongation of the Incarnation and the service which Christ rendered to humanity. The humanity of Christ refers first to the Incarnation, the person, words, teaching and work of Christ; second to the teachings and deeds of Jesus and the apostles, and finally to the words and acts of those who make up the church throughout history.

---

[35] *WPM*, 83-84.
[36] *WPM*, 82.

Marpeck identified the humanity of Christ with the Pauline concept of the body of Christ when speaking of the church. This "outward" definition of the church and its assimilation into the humanity of Christ was extremely troublesome for the Spiritualists.

> Oh, it annoys the fleshly to the highest degree that the Son of Man, in a physical way, should act and walk upon the earth by means of His members (I Cor. 6: 9-20; Acts 13: 2-47; I Cor. 12: 4-31; Eph. 4: 3-16), His body (Eph. 5: 30), His flesh and bone. It annoys them that those who are regarded by the world as humble, insignificant, simple and foolish (I Cor. 1: 18-25), who preach the crucified Christ and follow Him in the cross should have the keys to the kingdom of Heaven, to bind and to loose, to forgive and to retain sin upon earth...[37]

To our knowledge, no Anabaptist writing at this early point in history established such a close theological and sacramental linkage between the Incarnation and the "body" of Christ.

It is important to note that Marpeck extends the notion of "ceremony" beyond the two rituals of baptism and the Lord's Supper. *A Clear Instruction* also includes as a ceremony the putting into practice of Jesus' teachings. In the same way that one is baptized or partakes of communion, one follows in the footsteps of Jesus. As will be shown in much greater detail in other chapters, this typical Anabaptist *Nachfolge Christi* ethic was incorporated into Marpeck's understanding of justification by faith. Faith justifies and sanctifies at the same time. Through faith, the Holy Spirit dwells in believers and gives the power to keep the commandments of Jesus. Faith in Christ frees believers from the slavery of disobedience. Thus, the notions of the humanity of Christ, faith, the church, the Holy Spirit and ethics are all closely related in Marpeck's theology.

> Where this physical voice of Christ – which Christ even today channels through men and the Scriptures, which are preserved for us and are still a witness to Him – is believed sincerely, our spirit is free and the drawing of the Father revealed. The Spirit of Christ, our assurance (Rom. 8: 31-39) in all works,

---

[37] *WPM*, 81

deeds and gifts, possesses all power and authority, even until the end of the world.³⁸

In this perspective, baptism and love of neighbour (or of enemy) are both ceremonies which actualize the words of Christ and then continue the dynamic put into place by the Incarnation. Both have their origin in Christ's teaching and believers, through the power of the indwelling Spirit, live out these words and thus they themselves become part of the "humanity of Christ."

We have thus seen how Marpeck used the concept of Christ's humanity against the Spiritualists, first as an epistemological tool for tying together inner and outer reality, and second as a way to undergird theologically an Anabaptist concern for the visibility of the church and a discipleship ethic. As we will see, the later writings develop and systematize this understanding of the humanity of Christ. When compared to *A Clear Refutation*, *A Clear and Useful Instruction* provides an important step forward in Marpeck's theology. The more spiritualistic orientation of Marpeck's South German-Austrian origins takes on a more clearly Lutheran flavour as becomes evident when we compare Marpeck's thinking with several of Luther's writings of the 1520s against the *Schwärmer* ("enthusiasts" or "spiritualists").

The Humanity of Christ in Luther's Anti-Spiritualist Writings

Any reference to Luther's concept of the humanity of Christ will notice the similarity of context and concern in the two different settings. Whether in the anti-Karlstadt and anti-Müntzer writings of 1524-1525 or in the Eucharistic controversy with Zwingli several years later, a major question was the usefulness and necessity of the "outer means." In Luther's view those who question either the outer Word or the real presence of Christ in the Supper deny the reality of the Incarnation.³⁹

---

³⁸ *WPM*, 76-77.
³⁹ Marc Lienhard, *Luther témoin de Jésus-Christ*, (Paris: Le Cerf, 1973), 198. "D'après Luther, c'est le Christ même qui est en cause lorsque Calrstadt et d'autres que Luther qualifie d'enthousiastes, vont mettre en question soit la nécessité des 'moyens exérieurs' que sont la Parole et les sacrements, soit la présence réelle du Christ dans la Cène."

Luther fought against a theology which affirmed that the "flesh" is of no value and that God must be found in his true spiritual essence. In his treatise *Dass diese Worte "Das ist mein Leib" noch fest stehen wider die Schwarmgeister* (1527) Luther described the position of his adversaries, revealing therein a theology similar to that of Marpeck's Spiritualist opponents in Strasbourg.

> They think that the divine Word has to do only with spiritual things and not with outer or corporal things. That is still the sowing of Müntzer's and Karlstadt's spirit, who could bear nothing outward.[40]

For Luther, as for Marpeck, the outer means represented a continuation of the Incarnation. Obviously, the real question in this debate was Christological; even several years later when the discussions focused almost exclusively on the Eucharist, the controversy was still essentially one of Christology.[41] Thus, the starting point for both Luther and Marpeck was the desire to defend the usefulness and the necessity of the outward means, against the Spiritualist denial of their importance.

The Humanity of Christ and Knowledge of God in Luther's Theology

As was the case for Marpeck in *A Clear Instruction*, Luther conceived of the *eusserliche ding* (outer things) as leading to knowledge of God. Once again, the doctrine of the Incarnation was the starting point. In Christ, God became an *"eusserlich ding"* to give humanity the possibility of knowing him.[42] Since the Word became flesh and is the way to the Father, human knowledge of God is bound to outer and physical signs of revelation.[43] Along this way leading to God we find the *eusserlich ding*, which in Luther's theology are called the humanity of Christ.[44] For Luther, as for Marpeck,

---

[40] *Luthers Werke,* Kritische Gesamtausgabe (Weimar: Böhlaus, 1883ff), XXIII, 261 (hereafter *WA*). (Our translation).
[41] Cf. Lienhard, *Luther Témoin,* 198.
[42] K.O. Nilsson, *Simul: Das Miteinander von Göttlichem und Menschlichem in Luthers Theologie* (Göttingen: Vandenhoeck und Ruprecht, 1966), 155.
[43] Regin Prenter, *Spiritus Creator* (Munich, 1954), 270.
[44] *Ibid.,* 283.

the Spirit could not function other than through the outer things or means.⁴⁵ In a sermon on the book of Exodus published in 1526, Luther put the following words into the mouth of Jesus:

> ...keep your eyes steadfastly on me. Through my humanity one comes to the Father. The Father has enclosed himself in my humanity and has revealed himself to the whole world through my humanity.⁴⁶

As we saw for Marpeck, Luther was dealing with the question of how one arrives at or attains spiritual and inner knowledge. In Luther's perspective, in order to arrive at the "top" it is necessary to start at the "bottom." In 1525 he wrote:

> ...the outer things must come first. The inner things come after and through the outer, because God has decided to give the inner to no one without the outer.⁴⁷

Luther's theology conceives of God as hidden (*verborgen*) in Christ's humanity, the consequence being that one can know God only through faith. Marpeck used *verborgen* similarly.⁴⁸

As was Marpeck, Luther was far from expressing a simple "natural theology" when speaking of outer things. Rather, he saw a veiled (*verborgen*) revelation in the Incarnation and the prolongation of the latter in the outer means, which was at the heart of his doctrine of justification by faith. To know God by other means or through human reason would be a form of works-righteousness. One could claim for Marpeck what Marc Lienhard

---

⁴⁵ *WA*, XXIII, 193. "...der geist bei uns nicht sein kan anders denn in leiblichen dingen."

⁴⁶ *Ibid.*, XVI, 145. "...halt deine augen feste auff mich, durch meine menscheit komet man auff den vater. Der Vater schleusset sich in meine Menscheit, und hat sich der Vater durch meine menscheit der gantzen Welt furgelegt."

⁴⁷ *Ibid.*, XVIII, 136. "...die eusserlichen Stücke sollen und müssen vorgehen. Und die innerlichen hernach und durch die eusserlichen komen, also das ers beschlossen hat, keinem menschen die innerlichen Stücke zu geben on durch die eusserlichen Stücke."

⁴⁸ Cf. H.Band, *Luthers Lehre von verborgenen Gott* (Berlin, 1957), 31. In a very similar vein, Marpeck wrote: "Die gehaimnussen Gottes liegen *verborgen* under den eusserlichen reden/thaten/und ceremonien der menscheit Christi" (*Klarer Unterricht*, Biii).

has written of Luther: "Spiritual is that dimension of faith whose object is hidden by its opposite."[49]

The Ceremonies and the Church in Luther's Concept of the Humanity of Christ

Marpeck's rather broad conception of the ceremonies went beyond what was to become the classical Protestant understanding of the sacraments as baptism and the Lord's Supper. For this reason it is tempting to think that he "stretched" the humanity of Christ more so than did Luther, especially if one considers Luther's doctrine of the real presence, which would appear to limit the physical presence of Christ to the Eucharist. Nevertheless, there are more similarities between Marpeck and Luther in this regard than first meet the eye. In Luther's theology, God is bound to the Incarnation and to the doctrine of the two natures of Christ. This means simply that there is no revelation of God outside of the humanity of Christ. "There where you place God, you must also place his humanity. These two can be neither separated or divided."[50]

Therefore, any place or way in which God is revealed becomes the "humanity of Christ." For Luther, this humanity can be found in baptism, in preaching, in the Scriptures, etc.;[51] so the list gets longer. The notion of ceremonies in Marpeck's theology is obviously similar. That which at first glance appears a bit strange – i.e., to speak of ceremonies as the humanity of Christ – could be explained by supposing that Marpeck was familiar with Luther's anti-Spiritualist writings and was able to adapt his reading to his own debate in Strasbourg. Even the development of an ecclesiology from the doctrine of the humanity of Christ (which would appear to have been a specific Anabaptist concern) in which Jesus is present in his members is hinted at in Luther's writings. One text speaks of Christ who can be found "in the manger, on the cross, in baptism, in the Lord's Supper, in

---

[49] M. Lienhard, "La doctrine du Saint-Esprit chez Luther," *Verbum Caro*, I, XXVI, (1965), 22.
[50] *WA*, XXVI 333: "Wo du mir Gott hinsetzest, da mustu mir die menscheit mit ihm setzen. Sie lassen sich nicht sondern und von einander trennen."
[51] See Prenter, 284-285, and Lienhard, *Luther témoin*, 227-43.

preaching or in my neighbour or brother."[52] The following citation goes even farther:

> The Spirit can only be in us through physical (corporal) things, such as the Word, water, the body of Christ and his saints on earth.[53]

Conclusion

What kind of conclusions can be drawn from such a comparison? In regard to the concept of the humanity of Christ, this comparative study points to the very probable influence of Luther in this one area of Marpeck's theology. Both used the doctrine of the Incarnation as a way of arguing against the Spiritualists. If one grants that *A Clear Refutation* was Marpeck's first writing, it appears that he found his South German-Austrian Anabaptist roots not to be sufficient for the task at hand, and turned to Luther to help better formulate his anti-Spiritualist argumentation in *A Clear Instruction*. This "Lutheran" influence was to have important ramifications for Marpeck's theology and would lead him away from the mostly Zwinglian position which characterized many of the Swiss Anabaptists in relation to the sacraments.[54]

Pilgram Marpeck was not saying something entirely new in the short history of Anabaptist theology to which he was contributing in 1531, but he was arguing the point in a new and more "theological" way. Because of the need to respond to the Spiritualists in a more sophisticated manner, Marpeck reaffirmed a fundamental premise, i.e., obedience to Jesus' and the apostles' commands, and undergirded it with the doctrine of the Incarnation. It was at this point where Luther's anti-Spiritualist writings appear to have been helpful for arguing against Bünderlin and Entfelder.

It must of course also be kept in mind that the logic of Luther's insistence on the outer and material manifestations of Christian faith

---

[52] *WA*, XXXIII, 81-82.
[53] *WA*, XXIII, 193.
[54] How Marpeck differed from both Luther and Zwingli would only become clear as the years went by.

was not a radical departure from medieval thinking. In fact, from the Catholic point of view, Luther was a Spiritualist because of his critique of transubstantiation. If Luther's anti-*Schwärmer* writings helped Marpeck formulate his concept of the humanity of Christ, he was not picking up something unique to Luther, but rather a major tenet of Christian sacramental thinking throughout the entire medieval period.

It must also be noted that Marpeck's concept of the humanity of Christ differed from Luther's (but was similar to the medieval point of view) because it included ethics. For Marpeck, following Christ is a ceremony (sacrament), which means that the question of a more general influence of Luther on Marpeck needs to be addressed. It is most important to measure "Lutheran" influence on Marpeck at points that are crucial in understanding the difference between the Anabaptists and the Reformers. If, as Werner Packull and Alistair McGrath suggest,[55] Luther's formulation of the doctrine of justification by faith was a major break with medieval anthropology and soteriology, it will be necessary to see where Marpeck stood on these issues.

A more careful examination throughout this book of several key points will show that Marpeck was clearly "Anabaptist" and not very "Lutheran" in relation to justification by faith and ethics. From his earliest to his latest writings, he consciously included sanctification within his doctrine of justification rather than separating the two concepts as did Luther. Therefore Marpeck also rejected the notion of *simul justus et peccator* (simultaneously justified and sinner) so close to the heart of Luther's theology,[56] and his usage of the theme of Christian liberty in his exchange with the Swiss Brethren in the 1542s shows a "Lutheran vocabulary" with an "Anabaptist content."[57]

---

[55] Packull, *Mysticism*, 25 speaks of the difference between Marpeck and medieval mysticism. Alistair McGrath argues convincingly that Luther's understanding of justification was different not just from mysticism but from medieval Western theology in general. See *Iustitia Dei. A History of the Christian Doctrine of Justification*, 3rd ed., (Cambridge: Cambridge University Press, 2005), 215. This will be dealt with in greater detail in chapter 7.
[56] *Christologie anabaptiste*, 214-218.
[57] *Ibid.*, 203-13.

Any claim of Luther's influence on Marpeck therefore needs to be made carefully. As has been argued in the preceding pages, there is a strong probability that Luther's anti-Spiritualist writings contributed to Marpeck's formulation of the humanity of Christ, but beyond that point, comparison will have to be done on a case-by-case basis.

If, as we suspect, Marpeck was reading Luther, it meant that he was a conscious and willing participant in the theological debates of the Reformation. Werner Packull has shown how the Anabaptist-Spiritualist debates of Strasbourg were actually taking place on a much wider geographical level, spreading east to Moravia where Marpeck had been baptized and Entfelder and Bünderlin had been active.[58] What I originally understood as a debate more or less limited to Strasbourg has been widened because of Packull's careful scholarship. Anabaptists and Spiritualists were debating from Alsace to Moravia, fully participating in the theological controversies of the 1530s. But the lines we now draw with hindsight between magisterial and radical reformations, between Reformers and dissidents, between Anabaptists and spiritualists were not yet totally visible in 1530, and were perhaps especially hard to see in Strasbourg.

During the same period when Marpeck was seriously engaging the spiritualist option, apparently so attractive to many Anabaptists, he was simultaneously involved in an even more significant debate with the "official" Reformation in Strasbourg via Martin Bucer and with the wider Reformation context – including Luther – on the role of civil government in relation to ecclesiastical reform. It is to these debates – and how they impacted Marpeck's theological development – that the next two chapters are devoted.

---

[58] Packull, *Hutterite Beginnings*, 154-158.

Chapter 2

Anabaptism and the Reformation:
Pilgram Marpeck's Strasbourg Confession of Faith (1532)

Preliminary Comments

This chapter examines the next step in the construction of Marpeck's theology by taking a detailed look at the Christological elements of Pilgram Marpeck's Confession of Faith presented to the Strasbourg City Council in January 1532. Anabaptism was becoming less and less welcome in Strasbourg and Marpeck composed this document before being asked to leave the city.[1] It is not a confession of faith in the classic sense of the term, but rather a defense of adult baptism developed within a discussion of the relationship between the old and new covenants. In this case the discussion took place primarily between Marpeck and Martin Bucer. Since

---

[1] For the larger context of Marpeck in Strasbourg, see D. E. Ziegler, "Marpeck versus Butzer: A Sixteenth Century Debate over the Uses and Limits of Political Authority," in C.S. Smith, *Sixteenth Century Essays and Studies*, Volume II (Saint Louis: The Foundation for Reformation Research, 1971), 95-107; chapter 3 in Boyd, *Pilgram Marpeck*; chapters 2 and 3 in John D. Derksen, *From Radicals to Survivors* ('t Goy-Houton: Hes & De Graaf Publishers, 2002). The broader "theo-political" context of the Reformation, the city of Strasbourg and Marpeck's role is developed in greater detail in chapter 3, below.

Bucer wrote a detailed refutation of Marpeck's 1532 confession of faith,[2] it is possible to follow the debate from both sides.

As will be seen, the debate is quite distinct from that found in the two previous anti-Spiritualist writings. Nevertheless, the "humanity of Christ" remains an essential category in Marpeck's argumentation and takes on new meaning in light of new questions.

The fifteenth article of the confession is a good summary of Marpeck's position over against Bucer's.

> To him who believes and is baptized, the gospel of Christ, of Christ himself as the Savior for whom the ancients hoped and waited with great patience, conveys salvation, and the remission and forgiveness of sin. It utterly takes away all fear and bondage, sin, death, and hell, comforts and strengthens bruised hearts and gives them strength and power to do the will of God.[3]

The historical function of the humanity of Christ

Theological background

Marpeck's further development of the meaning of the "humanity of Christ" took place in a debate about adult baptism and the relationship between the Old and New Testament. Contra Marpeck, Bucer used the analogy of circumcision to justify infant baptism. Since all male infants were circumcised in the old covenant, infants should be baptized in the new. According to Bucer, baptism, like circumcision, is a sign of the covenant (*bundt zeychen*).[4] Such theological continuity between circumcision and baptism of children was possible because Bucer saw no essential difference between the old and new covenants.

> If we examine all Scripture before God, we find that the only difference between the old people and the new people is that

---

[2] QGT VII, 416-527 (n° 303). For Bucer's theology and further background on the Reformation in Strasbourg, see Martin Greschat, *Martin Bucer, A Reformer and his Times*, (Louisville: Westminster John Knox Press, 2004).
[3] *WPM*, 110.
[4] "Bucers Apologie der Kindertaufe gegen Pilgram Marpeck," QGT VII, 402.

these first ones had a more childish faith than ours. For Christ was preached to them from behind a veil, whereas for us he was unveiled.[5]

This close identification of the two covenants and testaments is at the heart of the debate between Marpeck and Bucer. Closely related to the issue of baptism, the questions of the oath, violence, and Church/State relationships were also a part of the debate.[6]

In response to Bucer, Marpeck wanted very much to demonstrate the existence of an important difference between the two testaments. This differentiation between the two covenants was to become a key foundation of Marpeck's thought, and the means by which he explains this difference is unique among the various Anabaptist groups.[7] His argument uses the Incarnation (humanity of Christ) to emphasize the historicity of the covenants. Simply stated, the new covenant follows the old and, along with it, a different reality enters history. It is the nature of the faith of the "ancients" (the patriarchs and prophets of the Old Testament) which becomes the object of debate between Bucer and Marpeck. By what measure and means were these "ancients" saved by Christ?

For Marpeck, the faith of the ancients was founded in the promise of God. Their faith was oriented toward a future reality, i.e. an unfulfilled reality. The promise was made to Adam and Eve after the fall and renewed throughout the Old Testament, particularly in the prophecies concerning the coming of the Messiah and of a new covenant. Contra Bucer, who proposed that the two covenants are essentially identical, Marpeck affirmed that the Old Testament itself necessarily implies a future accomplishment within time and history. Referring to Genesis 12: 1-3, he writes:

> For He says: "In or through your seed all people shall be blessed"; He does not say: "In your seed *are* all people blessed";

---

[5] Ibid., 400.

[6] The question of the relation between the two testaments is one of the most significant theological differences between the Anabaptists and the Reformers. For a detailed analysis of how the issue played out in Zurich, see J. H. Yoder, *Anabaptism and Reformation in Switzerland* (Kitchener, ON: Pandora Press, 2004), 165-175.

[7] R. S. Armour, *Anabaptist Baptism: A Representative Study* (Scottdale, PA: Herald Press, 1966), 144; Klassen, *Covenant and Community*, 107.

but rather, "they *shall* all be blessed," not as something already done, but as something that will be done.[8]

In this perspective, the history of the Old Testament is a period of waiting: waiting for deliverance and for forgiveness, waiting for the possibility to keep the commandments and to have the law written in the heart.

Defining the Historical Function

The fulfillment of God's promise takes place in the Incarnation, that is, in the life, death, and resurrection of Jesus Christ. Marpeck describes this Incarnation as "the humanity of Christ," the same terms encountered in *A Clear Instruction*. As seen in the previous chapter, over against the Spiritualists, the humanity of Christ illumines the relationship between the "inner" and the "outer" and grounds the necessity for the "outer means" or ceremonies. In the *Confession of 1532*, Marpeck applies the concept of the humanity of Christ to time and history. Just as God uses external means to accomplish and announce salvation, so also God works within the bounds of history. Thus Marpeck conceives of the redemption achieved in Christ as inextricably historical. The Incarnation offered Marpeck the means to distinguish between the two covenants and to claim that with Christ certain realities appeared in history that previously were absent.

According to Marpeck's reasoning, before the suffering and death of Christ, the "ancients" were living a faith of hope.[9] They were all prisoners of sin "until the humanity of Christ released them"[10] and they remained under God's curse until the coming of the Son "in His humanity."[11] Prior to this event, the way to heaven was blocked for everyone.[12] Marpeck's emphasis on the humanity of Christ leads him to highlight the importance of the physical and bodily suffering of Jesus. The redemption and atonement that was awaited by the ancients was linked to the historical events of Jesus' suffering, death, descent into hell, resurrection and ascension. Marpeck

---

[8] *WPM*, 117. (My italics)
[9] *WPM*, 109.
[10] *WPM*, 117.
[11] Ibid., 124.
[12] Ibid., 109.

referred to the hour at which Christ was crucified, and to the fact that righteousness flows from the humanity of Christ.[13]

Where were all the ancients who died before the coming of Christ? The doctrine of Christ's descent into hell responds to this question. Between the time of his death and resurrection, Jesus descended into hell to announce the Gospel to those who had hoped and believed in him.

> All went down into the pit; the faithful were comforted in the hope of the promised covenant and Abraham's seed (which Christ calls Abraham's bosom), but all were shackled, bound, and imprisoned until the time of the Son of God, who himself preached the gospel to them in the lowest places of the earth. He has led the captive into the heights…[14]

Marpeck also affirms that the Holy Spirit was given to humanity in a new way after the ascension of Jesus,[15] which, at the same time, implies that the law was not written on the hearts of the people before Christ's coming.[16] Christ has always existed as the second person of the Trinity, but only with the humanity of Christ was the promised redemption of the Old Testament accomplished.

Marpeck's position is truly quite simple: no "complete" redemption was possible before the humanity of Christ. The Incarnation brought a new reality into history, and created a new historical situation and a new people. The second part of this chapter on "the work of Christ" will examine in greater detail this "new reality" but we want beforehand to explore the origins of Marpeck's distinction between the covenants. Was this building-block in his theology original with him, or did he borrow it from elsewhere? Just as Marpeck probably made use of Luther's anti-Spiritualist writings to introduce the category of the "humanity of Christ," a good case can be made for the influence of Caspar Schwenckfeld on Marpeck's Confession.

---

[13] Ibid, 117..
[14] *WPM*, 125. Marpeck doesn't deal directly with the question of whether or not the "ancients" were in a state of physical suffering and whether or not "hell" and the "bosom of Abraham" are one and the same reality.
[15] *WPM*, 119.
[16] *WPM*, 109

The Humanity of Christ: Marpeck and Schwenckfeld

What Marpeck was trying to do was nothing new. Many Anabaptists made a radical distinction between the two testaments. Historians have claimed that Marpeck's way of differentiating the testaments in terms of the "humanity of Christ" was unique among Anabaptists. William Klassen believes Marpeck may have learned of this concept from Melchior Hoffman, who was in Strasbourg at the time.[17] Klassen also notes that the Anabaptist movement in general owes this radical Old/New Testament differentiation to Karlstadt, but doubts that Marpeck was much indebted to him on this question.[18]

Marpeck himself left clues concerning the source of this concept. One of his later writings suggests that he learned the understanding of the Incarnation from Schwenckfeld. As we will see in more detail in chapter 6, in the 1540s, Marpeck and Schwenckfeld were adversaries in a controversy concerning several issues, including the difference between the testaments. On this very point, Marpeck and his colleagues believed that they had been in agreement with Schwenckfeld, but that the latter had radically changed his mind. In the second part of the *Verantwurtung uber Casparn Schwenckfeld Judicium*[19] (*Response*), Marpeck and his colleagues gathered citations from Schwenckfeld's writings to demonstrate how previously they had been in agreement and that now, fifteen years later, Schwenckfeld had changed his mind. One of Schwenckfeld's texts cited by the *Response* was directed specifically against Bucer, and thus dates from the period of his sojourn in Strasbourg (1529-1533). The *Response* tells us that Marpeck and his fellow Anabaptists in Augsburg were familiar with this treatise of Schwenckfeld against Bucer; in fact, they had even copied it. The author(s) of the *Verantwurtung* wrote:

---

[17] Klassen, *Covenant and Community*, 177.
[18] Ibid., 178.
[19] J. Loserth (ed.) *Quellen und Forschungen zur Geschicht der oberdeutschen Taufgesinnten im 16. Jahrhundert, Pilgram Marbecks Antwort auf Kaspar Schwenckfelds Beurteilung des Buches des Bundesbezeugung von 1542* (Wien & Leipzig, 1929). (Cited henceforth as "Loserth").

> We are told that in that time someone gave to one of us a booklet written against Bucer and made it known that Caspar Schwenckfeld was the author. The same person would have copied this booklet...[20]

This "same person" was most likely Marpeck or Scharnschlager and "in that time" probably refers to the period during which Marpeck and Schwenckfeld were together in Strasbourg.

T. Bergsten and D. Husser have affirmed that Marpeck and Schwenckfeld were on friendly terms in Strasbourg and that they often were to be found in the same social settings.[21] While direct proof is lacking that while in Strasbourg, Marpeck copied Schwenckfeld's treatise against Bucer a comparison of the document's contents with that of other texts from Schwenckfeld's time in Strasbourg shows a striking resemblance between Schwenckfeld's position and Marpeck's as taken in his *Confession of 1532*.

Evidence for the similarity between Schwenckfeld's argumentation and Marpeck's confession of faith is found in the *Response* amongst the many citations from Schwenckfeld's treatise against Bucer. The following arguments are similar:

(1) Abraham and the other patriarchs neither received nor experienced the fulfillment of the promise but were awaiting it;

(2) the heavens "were not open" before the coming of Christ in history;

(3) Christ had to come in the flesh to fulfill the promise by his suffering;

(4) the Holy Spirit was not given to men and women before the Incarnation and the ascension.[22]

Loserth, the editor of the *Response*, identifies the treatise against Bucer with a letter Schwenckfeld wrote to the "brethren in Strasbourg." This

---

[20] Loserth, 409.
[21] Torsten Bergsten, "Pilgram Marbeck und seine Auseinandersetzung mit Caspar Schwenckfeld," *Kyrkohistorik Arsskrift*, 1957-1958, 45; D. Husser, "Caspar Schwenckfeld et ses adeptes entre l'Eglise et les sects à Strasbourg," in G. Livet and F. Rapp eds, *Strasbourg au coeurs religieux du XVIe siècle* (Strasbourg: Istra, 1977), 514.
[22] Loserth, 410-415.

letter, found in the *Corpus Schwenckfeldianorum*,[23] is dated February 13, 1532, thus a month after Marpeck's departure from Strasbourg. This dating might have facilitated the comparison process but Loserth was mistaken in identifying the citations in the *Response* with the letter to the "brethren in Strasbourg." Even if Marpeck was taking great liberties in regards to Schwenckfeld's document, a comparative reading of the texts shows that the source of the citations in the *Response* could hardly have been taken from the letter of February 1532.[24] More likely there were two documents addressing this subject with similar arguments. The treatise against Bucer cited in the *Response* is not the same document as the letter to the brethren in Strasbourg. The editors of the *Corpus Schwenckfeldianorum* affirm that the treatise against Bucer is a lost document.[25]

Thus it remains unclear whether the treatise against Bucer cited and copied by the Marpeck circle was written before or after the *Confession of 1532*. Nevertheless the fact that this treatise cannot be dated and that the letter from Schwenckfeld to the brethren in Strasbourg dates from the month following Marpeck's departure does not mean that Marpeck did not know Schwenckfeld's position regarding the distinction between the testaments before he wrote his confession. Several of Schwenckfeld's other writings dating from Marpeck's time in Strasbourg deal explicitly with this same subject. For example, Schwenckfeld's *Underschaid des Alten und Newen Testaments, der Figur und Waarheit*,[26] which dates probably from 1531, expresses more or less the same position. Also a letter from Schwenckfeld to Leonard von Liechtenstein of Nikolsburg lists eighteen differences between the Old and the New Testaments.[27]

---

[23] Chester David Hartranft (editor), *Corpus Schwencfeldianorum*, volume 4 (Leipzig: Breitkopf & Härtel, 1914), 520-556 (Cited henceforth as CS).

[24] For example, in the case of a citation on page 414 (Loserth), where Schwenckfeld speaks of Zacharias in Luke 1, Loserth compares it to a passage in the letter to the brethren in Strasbourg where Schwenckfeld cites the prophet Zacharias in the Old Testament. See also CS 8, 425-426.

[25] CS 8, CCXCV, "Lost Treatise against Martin Butzer," 425-426.

[26] CS 4, 414-443.

[27] See QGT VII, 363, 412. Schwenckfeld wrote this letter at the request of Bucer's colleague Wolfgang Capito (CS 4, 451). It is surprising that Capito asks someone who distinguishes between the testaments in the same way Marpeck did to write this letter, only weeks before

The greatest similarities are indeed observed in comparing Marpeck's confession and Schwenckfeld's letter to the brethren in Strasbourg. These two documents, written less than a month apart, present strikingly similar phrases and vocabulary, and the same logic and argumentation concerning the Incarnation as the means to distinguish between the Old and the New Testaments. In addition both documents are addressed to the same adversary, Martin Bucer. A summary of the common arguments may proceed as follows:

(1) The "ancients" lived a faith of hope; they had to wait for "the humanity of Christ."[28]

(2) Thus none went to heaven before the coming of Christ.[29]

(3) Redemption is accomplished in the Incarnation, by the suffering of the Son of God at a specific moment in history.[30]

(4) By his descent into hell, Christ liberated those who waited for him.[31]

(5) Only after that event was the Holy Spirit offered to the hearts of men and women.[32]

Marpeck was forced to leave Strasbourg. It is true that Schwenckfeld did not draw the same conclusions from this distinction as Marpeck, but he was also made to leave Strasbourg a few years later.

[28] *Marpeck* (QGT VII, 445): "...sonnder alles unnder der vermaledeyung bliben und wartten muessen, ... bis Crisstus der sun gottes selbs kommen ist, in seiner mennschait." *Schwenckfeld* (CS 4, 542): "In solchem glauben der verheissung nemlich dass Christus solt ins fleisch komen und uns im fleisch durch Creutz und Leiden erlosen sind di Veter all erhalten worden."

[29] *Marpeck* (QGT VII, 417): "Und ist niemant vor Cristo gein himel gefaren." *Schwenckfeld* (CS 4, 522): "... vor Christo kein mensch in Himmel ist eingangen."

[30] *Marpeck* (QGT VII, 434): "...di gerechtigkait so vor dem vatter gillt, durch sein mennschait erst worden ist." *Schwenckfeld* (CS 4, 536): "Die gantze Rechtfertigung... erst durch das sterben unnd blutwergiessen Christi dem menschen sind erworben."

[31] *Marpeck* (QGT VII, 440-441): "Darumb ist er abgestigen zu der hell, und hat erst allen altfattern das euangelium, den trost und die verzeihung und vergebung der sundt gepredigt..." *Schwenckfeld* (CS 4, 545): "... die Vater all hinunter in die Helle gefaren un da der erlosung... erwarten."

[32] *Marpeck* (QGT Vii, 439-440): "Es ist der geist Crissti kainen menschen... geben worden vor dem sterben und leiden Crissti, der solher geist und trost der gwissen erst erkauft, erlanngt unnd erworben hat..." *Schwenckfeld* (CS 4, 536): "..der heilig geist ... erst durch das sterbern unnd blutvergiessen Christi dem menschen erworben (ist)."

Did Marpeck perhaps influence Schwenckfeld? This appears doubtful for several reasons. First of all, Marpeck and his colleagues valued the writings of Schwenckfeld sufficiently to copy them and use them for many years. Secondly, Schwenckfeld's arguments concerning the humanity of Christ are developed in greater theological depth, which seems to indicate that Marpeck only used the parts that served his debate against Bucer. A third reason to believe that the Anabaptist theologian was borrowing from Schwenckfeld (and not the reverse) is that Marpeck often borrowed from others. For example, the previous chapter illustrated the parallel between Marpeck and Luther regarding the humanity of Christ. Or yet again Marpeck's *Vermanung (Admonition)* of 1542 is in large part an adaptation of a text written by Bernard Rothmann.

The case can thus be made that Marpeck's understanding of the "humanity of Christ," as a means to distinguish between the old and new covenants, was dependent on Schwenckfeld. (1) Schwenckfeld had written against Bucer on the differences between the Testaments. There exist a number of writings by Schwenckfeld conveying a position very similar to Marpeck's in his *Confession of 1532*. These documents by Schwenckfeld date from the period when Marpeck resided in Strasbourg. (2) A striking parallel exists between Marpeck and Schwenckfeld's positions in the *Confession of 1532* and the letter to the brethren in Strasbourg. These documents were written less than a month apart. (3) Marpeck's circle admits to having copied a document written by Schwenckfeld against Bucer (although this document's date is unknown). (4) Marpeck's writings demonstrate a tendency to borrow from others.

Of course none of this proves directly that Marpeck is indebted to Schwenckfeld on this point. But, when seen together, the cumulative effect of these different reasons render it highly plausible. (Another hypothesis must be recognized as well: that both Marpeck and Schwenckfeld depend on a third source.[33]) At the very least there exists a surprising parallel and a

---

[33] One might ask: Was Michael Servetus the source of this way of distinguishing between the Testaments? George Williams notes that Schwenckfeld, Marpeck, and Servetus responded in this same manner to Bucer on this subject. See Williams, *The Radical Reformation*, 1st edition (Philadelphia: Westminster Press, 1962), 270. Schwenckfeld himself wrote: "I

fundamental agreement between these two men in regard to the historical function of the humanity of Christ.

William Klassen already noted in some detail these striking similarities between Marpeck and Schwenckfeld but did not address the question of possible influence.[34] This is probably due to his theory that Marpeck wrote the *Clear Instruction* against Schwenckfeld.[35] Following the lead of Heinold Fast, I have argued elsewhere that the *Klarer unterricht* was not directed primarily at Schwenckfeld, but rather at Christian Entfelder, who held to a more radical spiritualism than did Schwenckfeld during his Strasbourg years.[36] If this is the case, it is easier to imagine Marpeck's "borrowing" from Schwenckfeld. There were differences between the two when they were together in Strasbourg. But these differences were not yet totally apparent and would increase over the years. Theological differences with Luther did not keep Marpeck from using a similar anti-Spiritualist approach and nor did the bad reputation of Bernard Rothmann – one of the "fathers of Münster" – keep Marpeck from producing a revised translation of one of Rothmann's works.[37] Marpeck was in the habit of borrowing ideas that he found useful.

---

debated much with Servetus, a few years ago (1531) and I read his books…" In these books he says he found "many good things… but also many weighty and dangerous errors…" Cited in Husser, 516.

[34] Klassen, *Covenant and Community*, 165-169.

[35] For Klassen's position on this question, see "Pilgram Marpeck's Two Books of 1531," *MQR*, (January 1959), 21; *Covenant & Community*, 39; "The Legacy of the Marpeck Community in Anabaptist Scholarship" *MQR*, (January 2004), 13.

[36] Cf. "Pilgram Marpeck and Caspar Schwenckfeld: The Strasbourg Years," in Jean-Georges Rott & Simon L; Verheus, *BIBLIOTHECA DISSIDENTIUM, scripta et studia*, N° 3, *sixteenth-century Anabaptism and Radical Reformation, I* (Baden-Baden & Bouxwiller: Editions Valentin Koerner, 1987), 371-380. A careful literary comparison Marpeck's *Klarer unterricht* and Entfelder's *Von den manigfaltigen im glauben zerspaltungen* leads to the conclusion that Marpeck had Entfelder (and not Schwenckfeld) in mind. Cf. as well Heinold Fast's article, "'Nicht was sonder das' Marpeckhs Motto wider den Spiritualismus," in: *Evangelischer Glaube und Geschichte. Grete Mecenseffy zum 85. Gerurtstag*, hrs. V. A. Raddatz u. K. Lüthi (Wien 1984), 72;

[37] In response to my position, William Klassen ("The Legacy of the Marpeck Community," 17) thinks that I perhaps idealize too much the relationship between Marpeck and Schwenckfeld during the Strasbourg years and that it was this "glossing over of differences"

Soteriology and ethics: the work of Christ

With this section we begin an important sub-theme of our work. Up until this point, Marpeck's Christology has been dealt with in terms of the Incarnation. The "humanity of Christ" has been seen to have had two functions: as a way of arguing against the Spiritualist rejection of "outer means," and against Bucer's "leveling" of the testaments. Since the ethical and ecclesiological implications of the Incarnation are an essential part of Marpeck's theology, part of our task will be to trace the development of his soteriology and to ask how Marpeck's understanding of the Incarnation spoke to the themes of salvation and ethics.

Just as the notion of the humanity of Christ was constructed in a step by step chronological manner, we will attempt observe the different stages of Marpeck's understanding of the relationship between salvation, justification by faith and ethics. In the following section we will take a first look at how Marpeck formulated Anabaptist soteriology in contrast to Luther and Bucer.[38] In the following chapters we will continue to trace the development of Marpeck's thinking in this regard, leading to some conclusions in chapter 7.

The Death of Christ and Atonement

Regarding the redemption accomplished through the death of Christ, Marpeck's confession includes traditional understandings that are not subject to debate between him and other reformers. In the section above, it was observed that Marpeck emphasizes the cross and the blood of Christ to reinforce the idea that the humanity of Christ atoned for human sin

---

that led to my questioning that the *Clear Instruction* had been written against Schwenckfeld In reply, I would reiterate that this questioning first of all merely followed the lead of Heinold Fast ("Marpeckhs Motto wider den Spiritualismus") and in the meantime has been affirmed in subsequent studies by Stephen Boyd (Pilgram Marpeck, 59-63); John Rempel (*The Lord's Supper in Anabaptism*, [Scottdale: Herald Press, 1993], 153); W. O. Packull, (*Hutterite Beginnings*, 134; 146); Geoffrey Dipple, "Sebastian Franck in Strasbourg," *MQR* (October 1999), 786 and G. Williams (*Radical Reformation*, 3rd edition, 682).

[38] A critique of Lutheran exclusively "sola fide" soteriology was already implicit in the *Clear Refutation's* use of the "Gospel of all creatures."

at a particular time in human history. These same notions of suffering and death are also given prominence in the affirmation of the necessity of this death for the redemption of sinful humankind. Thus for example, Christ was sinless, he bore the sins of others, and his death is described as a sacrifice, etc.

> ... for he appeared in the form of a mortal and sinful body. Without sin, He bore our sin and our weakness, and fastened it to the cross.[39]

> ... we live in the righteousness of Christ, who became a sacrifice for us in his righteousness and innocence which is valid before the face of God.[40]

The death and sacrifice of Christ take away the sins of the world and render accessible forgiveness and salvation. In sum, Marpeck simply reiterates the basic biblical affirmations regarding Christ's death in an apparently "Anselmian" fashion.[41]

The Work of Christ and the Sin of Adam

Following Augustine, Western medieval theology understood Christ's death as necessary to remove original sin in such a way that rendered infant baptism necessary. An Anabaptist understanding of baptism obviously necessitated a reformulation of the question. It is thus not surprising that Marpeck drew conclusions about the work of Christ that do not affirm the traditional positions of the Church. For Marpeck, Christ, by his work, freed humanity from the guilt resulting from the sin of Adam. But this salvation cannot and should not be mediated through infant baptism. In other words, since the death and resurrection of Christ, Adam's sin has been redeemed for all of humanity. If guilt is to be attributed, it is no longer because of Adam's sin, but rather because of the conscious sin of individuals. Though all humanity inherits the necessary tendency to sin,

---

[39] *WPM*, 124.
[40] Ibid., 154.
[41] Finger (*Contemporary Anabaptist Theology*, 341) gives a list of texts where Marpeck speaks of Christ's death in substitutionary terms.

individuals no longer inherit the guilt of original sin, because the death of Christ has done away with it.

> From now on, therefore, since the man Christ Jesus, the Son of God, has appeared and restored the fall of Adam and Eve, every man himself takes and eats of the forbidden fruit, the knowledge of good and evil, and does not eat through the fault of Adam and Eve. Otherwise it would have to follow that the fall of Adam could not be restored in us [...] through Christ.[42]

George Williams has shown that this manner of conceiving of redemption and original sin is common to a number of Anabaptists.[43] His analysis is certainly confirmed in Pilgram Marpeck's *Confession of 1532*. A connection also exists between this soteriology and the Zwinglian notion of original sin.[44] Influences of Zwingli are already visible in the first article of the confession, where sin is tied to knowledge.

> First, that all sin, including the fall of Adam (Gen. 3:[7]), consists in the recognition of the knowledge of good and evil; where there is no knowledge, there is no sin (Jn. 15: [22]).[45]

Williams explains that understanding sin as a question of knowledge and affirming that the death of Christ eliminates the sin inherited from Adam requires the concept of a "double work" of Christ: a first work that universally eliminates original sin and a second that is experienced by each believer. An important source for this conception is medieval mysticism, including the *Theologia Deutsch*, in which the key elements are Christ's historical work on the cross and the action at the individual level when the believer is justified and sanctified.[46]

---

[42] *WPM*, 131.

[43] G. Williams, "Popularized German Mysticism as a Factor in the Rise of Anabaptist Communism," in: W. Muller & W. Zeller, *Glaube, Geist und Geschichte: Festschrift für Ernst Benz*; (Leiden, 1967), 295; *The Radical Reformation,* 1st edition, 799.

[44] *The Radical Reformation*, 1st edition, 799.

[45] *WPM*, 108.

[46] Williams, "Popularized German Mysticism," 296-299. One could also argue that all of medieval theology required a "double-work" of Christ, the first one mediated by the sacrament of baptism and the second a personal appropriation of satisfaction for individual sin via confession and penance.

The Work of Christ as a "Fromm-machung"
Polemical Function

In order to grasp Marpeck's understanding of the work of Christ, justification and sanctification, it is helpful to situate the position of the larger Anabaptist movement on these questions. Marpeck was part of a current of thought that did not originate with him, but was visible already in the beginnings of the Anabaptist movement in 1524-1525, if not earlier. Most Anabaptists accepted the Reformation premise of "justification by faith" but they never accepted this doctrine as formulated by Luther. For the Anabaptists, salvation by "faith alone" produces no fruit. H.-J. Goertz claims that the goal of the Anabaptist reformation was the reform or the improvement of life (*Besserung des Lebens*).[47] Where "justification by faith" was preached, the Anabaptists saw no changes in the way of life of those claiming "faith." This theme recurs quite often in Anabaptist writings. Two examples help situate Marpeck. The first is written by B. Hubmaier in 1527.

> In which time people had learned no more than two points, without any amelioration (*Besserung*) of life. The one point, that they could say: "We believe. Faith saves us." Second: "We can do nothing good of ourselves." Now both of these are true. But under the mantle of these half truths all kinds of iniquity, unfaithfulness, and injustice have completely taken over and fraternal love has meanwhile become colder among many, Matt. 24:12, more than in many thousand years.[48]

Hans Hut, in his *Von dem Geheimnis der* Taufe, offers the same critique, directly challenging the "preachers" of the Reformation.

> I therefore counsel all those who seek and love justice to beware of all the voluptuous, ambitious and hypocritical scribes who preach for money. They are not concerned about you but about their bellies. We can see nothing other in them than in all other worldly people and whoever trusts in them will be betrayed. We hear nothing other in their teaching than "Believe!" and

---

[47] H.-J. Goertz, *Die Täufer.Geschichte und Deutung* (Munich: C.H. Beck, 1980), 48.
[48] H. Wayne Pipkin and John H. Yoder, trans. and eds. *Balthasar Hubmaier, Theologian of Anabaptism* (Scottdale PA, Herald Press, 1989), 375.

it goes no farther.... Oh, how they deplorably betray the whole world under the pretext of a false and fictitious faith that produces no *Besserung*.[49]

In each case the criticism connects the lack of *Besserung des Lebens* (improvement of life) to the doctrine of justification by faith. The Anabaptists' polemics may well have been exaggerated, but they did have a foundation in fact. Luther himself wrote the following comments after an inspection of Lutheran churches in 1529.

> The deplorable, miserable conditions which I recently observed when visiting the parishes have constrained and pressed me to put this catechism of Christian doctrine into this brief, plain and simple form. How pitiable, so help me God, were the things I saw; the common man, especially in the villages, knows practically nothing of Christian doctrine, and many of the pastors are almost entirely incompetent and unable to teach. Yet all the people are supposed to be Christians, have been baptized, and receive the Holy Sacrament even though they do not know the Lord's Prayer, the Creed, or the Ten Commandments and live like poor animals of the barnyard and pigpen. What these people have mastered, however, is the fine art of tearing all Christian liberty to shreds.[50]

The Anabaptist doctrine of justification was formulated in such a context. The objective of their reformation was to create communities in which members lived differently from their contemporaries and in conformity with Christ's example and teachings. It was with this goal that they formulated the doctrine of justification in a different manner than Luther. In Goertz' view, the Anabaptists did not seek "to complete" the doctrine of justification; rather they replaced it with something else.[51]

Marpeck clearly stood within this young Anabaptist tradition. On the ninth of December 1531 when he appeared before the Strasbourg Council, Bucer reported that Pilgram criticized the Lutheran understanding of

---

[49] Heinold Fast: *Der linke Flügel*, 80-81.
[50] M. Luther, "Preface to the Small Catechism," found at http://www.lcms.org/graphics/assets/media/LCMS/smallcatechism.pdf
[51] Goertz, *Die Täufer*, 67-68. As we will see in chapter 7, it was actually Luther who changed the medieval doctrine of justification, to which the Anabaptists adhered fairly closely.

justification, saying that wherever the Gospel was preached in a Lutheran way he had seen "carnal freedom" and could not find peace.[52]

In his exposition of the work of Christ and of justification, Marpeck thus fought against this "carnal liberty" that he noticed in the churches of the Reformation. This is done by challenging and re-interpreting "justification by faith." The meaning of this doctrine therefore deserves close scrutiny. In an important way, Marpeck wanted to be part of the Reformation discovery of the doctrine of justification. This can be seen when he cites Romans 3: 22ff and adds a personal commentary:

> For here there is no difference: they are all sinners and lack the praise which God desires from them. They are justified [*from gemacht*] without any contribution on their part [Rom. 3:23 f.]; *understand clearly* that they were justified [*from gemacht*] through the redemption which took place through Christ...[53]

Here – as was generally the case – Marpeck follows the Zurich Bible (Froschauer) and not Luther's translation of the New Testament.[54] In relation to the English "justified," the Zurich Bible uses "*from gemacht*" (literally "made pious/just/righteous") whereas Luther translates "*gerecht werden*" (literally "to become just or righteous").[55] Understanding the significance of "*from gemacht*" is crucial, since certain historians see in the simple presence of these words in Anabaptist writings a formal and categorical rejection of any Lutheran terminology regarding justification.

As already noted, Marpeck himself identified with several important aspects of the Lutheran understanding of justification: humans are sinners and are in need of righteousness before God, a righteousness that flows exclusively from the work of Christ for those who believe. Via justification by faith, believers receive forgiveness along with a peaceful conscience.

---

[52] QGT VII, 352.
[53] *WPM*, 136.
[54] This has been verified using a 1536 edition. See also Klassen, *Covenant and Community*, 146 and Williams, *The Radical Reformation*, 1st edition, 816-817.
[55] In modern German, *fromm* means "pious." In the sixteenth-century, it was a synonym with *gerecht*, and both words could be rendered in English with either "just" or "righteous."

They [those baptized] know, to begin with, that Christ is the living power of God, and the end of the law, for the sanctification (*Frommachung*) of everyone that believes. They have the forgiveness of past sins, a certain comfort, security and rest through faith in Christ.[56]

For Luther, justification was forensic, i.e., God declares righteous those who are really not so. But this "declaration" does not make them capable of doing the will of God. In contrast Marpeck affirmed that humans can become "truly" righteous or just,[57] i.e., they can now please God by their actions. The thesis can thus be stated in the following manner: Marpeck formulated his understanding of justification (*Fromm-Machung*) in order to demonstrate that if humans are *declared* righteous before God, they also *are made* "just" (*fromm gemacht*) and capable of accomplishing the will of God. Such justice or righteousness does not arise from humans themselves, but is the consequence of the work of Christ and of the ensuing gift of the Holy Spirit, made possible by the Incarnation.

The connections between faith, justification, and "*Fromm-Machung*" are quite evident. The believer has a "just heart" or is "*from von hertzen.*"[58] Christ is the end of the law for the "*frumbkait*" (justification/righteousness) of the person who believes in him.[59] When human beings believe in Christ, their hearts are "*from gemacht.*"[60] Before Christ there was neither "*gerechtigkhait*" (justice/rigteousness), "*rechtfertigung*" (justification), or "*frommachung.*"[61] In order to better understand this "*Fromm-Machung*," the relationships in Marpeck's confession between faith, justification, and the circumcision of the heart/baptism by the Spirit must be highlighted.

---

[56] *WPM*, 217.
[57] In many European languages such as French and German, the English terms "righteousness" and "righteous" are synonymous with "justice" and "just."
[58] *QGT* VII, 447.
[59] (justification/righteousness/justice) *QGT* VII, p. 449.
[60] *QGT* VII, 432.
[61] *QGT* VII, 439.

Fromm-Machung: Circumcision and Inner Baptism

Those who believe in Jesus Christ are "circumcised in their heart" and "baptized by the Holy Spirit." This circumcision and baptism are part of the *Fromm-Machung*. Marpeck wrote:

> I fear that he whom Christ has not baptized into godliness with fire and the Holy Spirit can say little about the might and power of Christ.[62]

> When man believes in and confesses the revealed Christ, the heart is circumcised and made just (*"from gemacht"*)...[63]

The circumcision of the heart, not done by human hand (Col. 2: 11), takes place "in Christ, by the preaching of the Gospel."[64] The hearts of those who hear the Gospel and believe, are immediately circumcised and they receive the baptism of the Spirit and are made *"fromm."* This inner circumcision permits the "the covenant of a good conscience with God" (1 Peter 3: 21 following Luther's translation).[65] Since the circumcision of the heart and the baptism of the Spirit are given with personal faith, water baptism can only follow afterwards.

As in most Anabaptist writings on baptism, the order of events is also very important in this case: the proclamation of the Gospel, faith, circumcision of heart/baptism of the Spirit, water baptism. The priority of the Spirit is crucial, even though the Spirit works through "outer means."

> Since the Spirit of God to whom the elements and all creatures are witnesses, and since the greater rightfully takes precedence, it follows that the Spirit is the first witness...[66]

Since not everyone believes, children (who do not believe) cannot be baptized. The baptism is only a testimony (*zeug*), but nevertheless a necessary testimony to the inner baptism empowered by the action of the

---

[62] *WPM*, 127
[63] *WPM*, 116.
[64] QGT VII, 433.
[65] For the use of the concept of covenant (*Bundt*) for baptism in Marpeck's work, see Armour, *Anabaptist Baptism*, 118-119.
[66] *WPM*, 138.

Holy Spirit. Faith is thus a matter of personal commitment. Nevertheless Marpeck does not claim that this active participation originates primarily in the human will.

> Our covenant, which we make with God, is real only for him who is united with God and who has consented to it in the power of the Holy Spirit in faith...[67]

Fromm-Machung: The Power to Accomplish God's Will

From the perspective of Marpeck's covenant theology, the "ancients" sought to accomplish the law but could not. In contrast, those of the new covenant can. This capacity is a result of the baptism of the Spirit, which flows from faith. This gift of power is part of the *Fromm-Machung*.

> The baptism of water and the Spirit of Christ, which springs from faith in Christ ... adds power and action to the desire. Whoever does the will of the Father is a child of God.[68]

> ... the circumcision of the spirit took place through the revelation of Christ, the Son of God, who first gave this power to all.[69]

> I fear that he whom Christ has not baptized into godliness (*frommachung*) with fire and the Holy Spirit can say little about the might and power of Christ.[70]

It should now be more apparent why the Incarnation and the historicity of redemption are so important in this discussion. In relation to social and political ethics, the mainline reformers referred often to the Old Testament to justify participation in war, swearing of oaths, and Christian civil authorities (or government). Marpeck, for whom the teachings of Jesus Christ and of the New Testament are the basis of ethics,

---

[67] *WPM*, 142. Unfortunately Marpeck does not address the doctrine of election in this confession, even though, implicitly, he is challenging the reformed doctrine of election. The unique explicit reference in this document appears to affirm the person's coming to faith as a sign of his election. See *WPM*, 129.
[68] *WPM*, 110.
[69] *WPM*, 109.
[70] *WPM*, 127.

wishes to differentiate this ethic of Christ from that of the Old Testament. The Incarnation marks an important distinction between the Old and the New Testaments. Moreover the work of Jesus Christ offers the believer the power to live this new ethic.

This ethic is described in Pauline and Johannine terms: "to live in Christ," "being dead to sin," "to become children of God," "if the Son frees you, you will truly be free," "whoever does not rest in the doctrine of Christ has not God," etc. Marpeck also uses a vocabulary that emphasizes the believer's participation in the sufferings of Christ (already seen in *A Clear Refutation*).

> He that participates in the tribulations of Christ will also inherit the Kingdom of God.[71]

> The children of the Spirit are faithful men, full of love and patience, marching below the cross of Christ.[72]

The work of Christ can thus be summarized as follows. Through the Incarnation at a given moment in history, Jesus Christ brings about salvation within history by his life, death and resurrection. Those sinners who hear the Gospel and believe are freely justified before God, i.e., the work of Christ confers the justice that humans need in order to be righteous before God. Yet by faith, believers are not simply "declared" righteous but by the circumcision of the heart/baptism of the Spirit, they become truly righteous (*fromm*). They receive a power, accorded by the Holy Spirit that makes them capable of accomplishing the will of God. They now can obey, even if imperfectly. The first step of this obedience is manifested in the testimony of water baptism. Outer baptism is preceded by inner baptism. While outer baptism is essential, it is no more –but no less – than the first step in obedience to the words and example of Christ. What we have seen here certainly agrees with Stephen Boyd's observation.

> Having been put off by the fleshly freedom of Lutheran believers who had been justified by faith, but whose lives, in his opinion, did not manifest Christ's reordering, Marpeck

---

[71] Ibid., 112.
[72] Ibid., 128.

was drawn to this notion of justice which issued in a change of life, or "the obedience of faith."[73]

Fromm-Machung: The Context of the Reformation

Even though some historians and theologians have already briefly noted the concept of *Fromm-Machung* in the thought of Marpeck,[74] its role in his *Confession of 1532* has never been described in detail. Marpeck is not unique among Anabaptists in his use of *Fromm-Machung* to describe justification. For some interpreters, the very concept or the conscious use of these words was an intentional device to counter Luther's "forensic" formulation of justification.[75] Robert Friedmann affirms that Anabaptists did not use the term *Rechtfertigung* to describe justification because it was alien to their understanding.[76] G. Williams claims that the Anabaptists invented the terms *Gerechtmachung* and *Fromm-machung* to indicate that justification leads to a change of life for the believer.[77]

Historians increasingly agree that this unity of justification and sanctification originates in medieval thought and particularly in mysticism.[78] In Tauler's mysticism and in the *Theologia Deutsch*, salvation is conceived as a union between God and a person that depends on cooperation between the human being and God. Justification appears as

---

[73] Boyd, *Pilgram Marpeck*, 41. "This conjoining of justification and sanctification does not reject the *extra nos* character of grace or the historic, *pro nobis* character of Christ's work, but insists that that grace and Christ's justice come *in nos* to reorder the lives of those who receive it." Ibid.

[74] Williams, "Popularized German Mysticism," 302 addresses this topic, but based on later writings by Marpeck.

[75] See Robert Friedmann, *The Theology of Anabaptism* (Scottdale, PA: Herald Press, 1973), 87-88; K. Davis, *Anabaptism and Asceticism* (Scottdale, PA: Herald Press, 1974), 136; Williams, "Popularized German Mysticism," 294.

[76] Friedmann, *Theology of Anabaptism*, 87.

[77] Williams, "Popularized German Mysticism," 294.

[78] Williams, "Sanctification in the Testimony of Several So-Called Schwärmer," *MQR* (January 1968), 5-6. In chapter 6 below it will become clear that the joining of justification and sanctification is Augustinian and permeates all of medieval theology and not just mysticism.

a progressive divinization that is inseparable from sanctification.[79] This medieval mysticism is dependent on an anthropology that perceives a divine aspect in the soul of the human being, therefore permitting a divine-human cooperation in the salvation process.[80]

Luther's conception of justification was aimed against any notion of human intervention in the salvation process, to such an extent that Steven Ozment claims that Luther's theology can be explained as a polemical response to medieval mystical anthropology.[81] Indeed the Lutheran idea of *"simul justus et peccator"* is impossible if justification and sanctification are inseparable, as in medieval thought. In Packull's perspective, the Lutheran understandings of justification and of the Word of God are quite distant from medieval thought.[82]

Certainly in Marpeck's thought justification and sanctification are joined and the notion of *Fromm-Machung* is directed against Luther. But if the word-choices themselves were so "anti-Reformation" (as Friedmann affirms), we could expect Bucer to have reacted emphatically. Yet he did not. This then raises an interesting question: at what level is the polemic situated? Does it reside already in the word choice (*Fromm-Machung* against *Rechtfertigung*) or rather in the definition of justification (joining justification and sanctification over against a purely forensic understanding)? If it was already in the word choice, it would be a surprise to find the words *fromm machen,* and *fromm gemacht,* etc. in the magisterial reformers' vocabulary. Williams affirmed that the Anabaptists invented this terminology (*Frommmachung*) and Robert Friedmann claimed that Hubmaier was the first to use it.[83] In fact, these affirmations do not hold up to further examination.

---

[79] Packull, *Mysticism,* 25-26.

[80] See S. Ozment, *Mysticism and Dissent,* (New Haven & London: Yale University Press, 1973), 1-13; also Packull, *Mysticism,* chapter 1.

[81] S. Ozment, *Homo spiritualis. A comparative Study of the Anthropology of Johannes Tauler, Jean Gerson and Martin Luther (1509-16) in the context of their Theological Thought* (Leiden: Brill, 1969), 3. Mysticism was not Luther's only or exclusive target.

[82] Packull, *Mysticism,* 28-29.

[83] Williams, "Popularized German Mysticism," 294, and Friedmann, *Theology of Anabaptism,* 88.

It is true that the term *fromm machen* appears already in the first writing published by Hubmaier at the beginning of 1524, the *Eighteen Theses*.[84] The first article affirms: "faith alone makes us righteous before God" (*Der eynig glaub macht uns frumm vor Gott*).[85] But before confirming that there is here a typical Anabaptist formulation, the document in question needs to be investigated. It consists of a series of propositions that were to serve as the basis for a theological disputation in order to advance the reformation in Waldshut. These propositions in their form and content are quite similar to Zwingli's 67 Articles, which set the stage for the first disputation in January 1523 in Zurich. When Hubmaier wrote these propositions two disputations had already taken place in Zurich and he took these two as the models for his work.[86] Thus the theses advanced by Hubmaier are grounded in the Zwinglian reformation, with an emphasis given to the authority of the Bible and to justification by faith, even though the question of baptism is raised.[87] The term *fromm machen* is found in this document (and in Hubmaier's other writings), but at this point, Hubmaier still saw himself as an associate of Zwingli's and had not yet become "Anabaptist." In fact, adult baptism in Zurich had not yet taken place.

Thus it appears difficult to claim that the Anabaptists invented this notion as a polemical term. But the real argument against such a claim is that the presence of *fromm machen* and *fromm gemacht* reflect the simple fact that Anabaptists read and used the Zurich Bible and were merely using terms found in the German translation of the biblical text.[88] It is possible

---

[84] *Eighteen Theses* in Pipkin and Yoder, *Balthasar Hubmaier*, 30-34 and (T. Bergsten and G. Westin (eds.), *Balthazar Hubmaier Schriften*, 1962,) 69-74
[85] Pipkin and Yoder, *Balthasar Hubmaier*, 32; Bergsten and Westin, *Hubmaier Schriften*, 72.
[86] Bergsten and Westin, *Hubmaier Schriften*, 69.
[87] Ibid., 73, "wie ein yeder Christ fur sich selbs glaubt und getaufft wirt…"
[88] See in the Zurich or Froschauer Bible (1536) Romans 4:2 "Ist Abraham durch die werck fromm gemacht?", Galatians 3:8, "Die geschrift aber hatts vorhin versahen, das Gott die Heiden durch den glauben fromm macht." James 2:23-25 shows that "fromm machen" and "rechtfertigen" have the same meaning: "Abraham hat Gott glaubt, und ist jm zur gerechtigkeit gerechtnet, und ist ein freund Gottes geheissen. So sehen jr nun das der mensch durch die werck rechtfertig wirt, und nit durch den glauben allein. Desselben glichen die hur Rahab, ist si nit durch die werck fromm gemachet"…

that Anabaptists gave a specific theological meaning to *Fromm-Machung*, but the choice of the words themselves means nothing. Even Luther used the term *gerecht machen* in his translation of the Bible[89] and *fromm machen* in his writings.[90] This would make no sense if, as Friedmann, Davis, and Williams affirm, there exists a marked differentiation between Luther's and the Anabaptists' terminology regarding justification.

In terms of the context in Strasbourg, not only does Bucer not react to Marpeck's use of this terminology but he himself uses it in a positive manner in his response to Marpeck.[91] Indeed Bucer and Marpeck's theologies are not too distant from each other in their general approach to the work of Christ and justification. In the *Tetrapolitan Confession* (1530), presented to the emperor Charles at the same time as the *Augsburg Confession*, the article concerning justification affirms that humans become "frumm und gerecht" by the means of the work of Christ.[92] The relatively strong emphasis on sanctification and the ethical life of the justified believer is also notable. In the section entitled "*Was glaubens der Rechtfertigung zuegebenn*," the heart of the matter is a salvation and a "*frumbkeit*" that do not consist of fruitless thoughts or a faith without love.[93] The believer must become conformed to the image of the Son of God and must practice an "*unschuldigen und ganntz frummenn leben*" (blameless and totally just life)[94] because "we have been created in Jesus Christ for good works" (Eph. 2: 10).[95]

---

[89] In Luther's translation, see Romans 4:5: "Dem aber, der nicht mit Werken umgeht, glaubt aber an den, der die Gottlosen, gerecht macht"…; Galatians 3:8: "Die Schrift aber hat es zuvor gesehen, dass Gott die Heiden durch den Glauben gerecht macht…"

[90] For example, in WA 28, 96, commenting on Isaiah 53:11, Luther writes: "Durch sein erkendnis wird er (main knecht, der gerechte) viel gerecht oder frum machen…"

[91] See for example in "Bucers Widerlegung des Bekenntnisses von Pilgram Marbeck," QGT VII, 430: "Redet man aber von dem anfang des glaubens, der from machet…"

[92] R. Stupperich, *Martin Bucers Deutsche Schriften*, Band 3, (Gütersloh-Paris: Gerd Mohn-Presses Universitaires de France, 1969), 48.

[93] Stupperich, *Martin Bucers Deutsche Schriften*, 54. According to my notes from lectures by Richard Stauffer (at the Ecole Pratique des Hautes Etudes, Paris-Sorbonne) addressing the Tetrapolitan Confession (1978-1979), Bucer refers here to the medieval distinction "fides informis" and "fides formata." Stauffer claimed that most reformers did not value this distinction and that Bucer distanced himself from Luther on this point.

[94] Stupperich, *Martin Bucers Deutsche Schriften*, 54.

[95] Ibid.

In order to demonstrate the true Christological differences between Marpeck and Bucer or Luther, one needs to go beyond the simple use of "*Fromm-Machung*" and "*fromm gemacht.*" Marpeck certainly gives *Fromm-Machung* an anti-Lutheran or anti-Reform significance in his debates. But contrary to Friedmann, Davis, and Williams, the presence of the words themselves proves nothing. These same terms are found in Bucer's and Luther's writings and particularly in the Zurich Bible. This proves only that Marpeck (and the Anabaptists in general) preferred the Zurich Bible to Luther's. The fact that Bucer and Marpeck both describe justification as a *Fromm-Machung* requires us to study the web of meaning accompanying the words, not simply the word choice itself.

Marpeck and Bucer

Just as the anti-Spiritualist writings gave us important insight to debates going on in Strasbourg and Moravia, Marpeck's confession to the Strasbourg city council helps to situate the debates going on between Anabaptism and the "official" Reformation in Strasbourg. Marpeck was seen as a real danger by Bucer and the latter made the effort to refute the confession in great detail.

At first glance, what seems to most offend Bucer is the fact that Marpeck, under the pretext of offering something better, separates himself from the "official" church. The separation and the division implied by Marpeck's theology were indeed the real problems in Bucer's perspective. He often returned to these when speaking about his Anabaptist adversary.[96]

> O heresy! (which means seeking separation and rebellion in spiritual matters), you are a virulent and pernicious evil and, as you destroyed all piety in Paul and the apostles' time under the guise of rigorous piety, so you continue to act up until this day.[97]

Are there significant Christological differences between these two men? The basis for the problem seems first to be found in other areas: baptism and Church/State relations. Regarding the central doctrine of

---

[96] *QGT* VII, 341, 345, 410, 527.
[97] *QGT* VII, 410.

justification by faith, Bucer writes that Marpeck finds fault with him not at the level of doctrine but in terms of the order. The Anabaptist's position does not deny the doctrine's validity but calls first for the preaching of repentance and baptism only afterwards so that faith may bear its fruits.[98] In Bucer's view, Marpeck had heard "a good and sensible doctrine of Jesus Christ our Lord and a doctrine of true faith that cannot exist without good works"[99] in the church of Strasbourg. But he saw among the preachers and members of this church many things contrary to this doctrine. Thus, while forgetting his own faults, Marpeck left the "official" church to join the Anabaptists.[100] Due to Marpeck's abilities, the Anabaptist movement grew in Strasbourg, but Bucer was not convinced that his adversary had been called by God to teach Scripture. To strengthen his perspective, Bucer points out a number of errors in Marpeck's doctrine.

> He arrives at such frightful errors that he denies explicit Scriptures and encloses the work of Christ in time, that he accuses the faithful and innocent ecclesial practice of child baptism by affirming that it is a sacrifice to Moloch, a stealing of souls and a murder; that he dismisses the functions of the civil authorities, with many other errors too numerous to mention.[101]

Bucer's first theological objection indeed addresses Christology. The Strasbourg reformer refused the role of the humanity of Christ as the turning point for salvation history and thus attempted to refute the fundamental distinction that Marpeck made between the Old and the New Testaments. For Bucer the only difference between the faith of the patriarchs and the faith of the New Testament was that the former was more childish. Christ was preached veiled in the Old Testament but unveiled in the New Testament. Consequently the "ancients" needed more rituals, and after the ascension, the Gospel had to be preached to the pagans in order for the fruits of the Incarnation to be better known.[102] In Bucer's view,

---

[98] *QGT* VII, 521.
[99] Ibid.
[100] Ibid., 521-522.
[101] Ibid., 522.
[102] Ibid., 400.

which was bolstered by a strong sense of predestination, the Incarnation or the historicity of Jesus was not decisive in understanding the work of salvation. The "ancients" also benefited from the redemption accomplished by Christ without needing to wait.

> For Christ is a unique and eternal savior, who also offered to his own, before his Incarnation, the forgiveness of sins and all good things.[103]

To seek to limit God and his work in Jesus Christ in time is, in Bucer's view, a significant error.

> We only have one mediator between God and all humankind, Jesus Christ, and this by no other means than his bitter suffering and death. For God, Christ's work was as present before taking place in [historical] time, as it is now...[104]

All other disagreements between Marpeck and Bucer follow from this fundamental Christological difference, because the Incarnational and historical dimension was the foundation of Marpeck's thought concerning adult baptism and his christocentric ethic, made possible by the "*Frommmachung.*" It was precisely this understanding of a pneumatic and christomorphic ethic that called into question the right of the Strasbourg civil authorities to lead the reformation of the church as well as the Christian duty to unquestionably obey all that was commanded by the magistrate.

H-J. Goertz had remarked that the Christological differentiation made by the Anabaptists between the testaments cannot be considered an original foundation of their thought. According to Goertz, this differentiation is rather a reaction to the arguments of the reformers (first of all Zwingli) who compared infant baptism to circumcision in the Old Testament.[105] This is obviously the case, but one could also affirm that Zwingli's and Bucer's argumentation on this point developed as a reaction to the Anabaptist position that insisted on adult believer baptism. In any case, theology is never done in a vacuum, but rather in specific contexts

---

[103] Ibid., 417.
[104] Ibid., 440. My translation.
[105] Goertz, *Die Täufer,* 58-59.

in response to specific questions and issues. Thus, when we note that the opposition between Bucer and Marpeck results from a fundamental Christological difference, one cannot claim that each approaches the debate with a "pure Christology" from which the discussion begins. Christologies, here and elsewhere, are reflections (based in biblical texts and in other sources) arising in particular contexts in response to the issues at hand. It was in this precise context of baptism and Church/State relations that Christology became the point of contention for Marpeck and Bucer.

Bucer and Marpeck both shared a soteriology with an understanding of an active faith and a justification that conform the Christian to the image of Christ.[106] Yet active faith and conformity to Christ are given two different meanings. Marpeck, having rejected the Old Testament as an ethical norm for the civil authorities and their functions in the church, and having adopted and adapted Luther's theology of two-kingdoms,[107] left no room for the civil authorities to play a guiding role in the Reformation.[108] In addition, his ethic, which is based strictly on the words and example of Jesus, makes it difficult for Christians to participate in acts of violence.[109] For Bucer, the fact that the two testaments are essentially the same permits

---

[106] If we follow Alister McGrath's description of how Bucer understood justification, it is clear that he and Marpeck were fairly close together. "Bucer argued that there were two stages in justification. The first stage, which he termed 'justification of the ungodly'… consisted of God's gracious forgiveness of human sin. The second stage, which he termed 'justification of the godly,' consisted of an obedient human response to the moral demands of the gospel… Christ was regarded as an external moral example, graciously provided by God, which justified sinners were required, through the assistance of the Holy Spirit, to imitate." Alister E. McGrath, *Reformation Thought, An Introduction,* Third Edition (Malden Massachusetts, Oxford, Victoria, Australia: Blackwell Publishers, 1999), 124.

[107] QGT VII, 507-508. For an analysis of Marpeck's position on these questions, see J. M. Stayer, *Anabaptists and the Sword*, Second Edition (Lawrence Kansas: Coronado Press, 1976), 177-187. Stayer shows that Marpeck adopts a more moderated position than the Schleitheim Confession. Nevertheless the debate described here and the fact that Marpeck was asked to leave Strasbourg because of his convictions about the sword and the magistrate, question Stayer's affirmation that Marpeck is a "tame Anabaptist" and that his position would not be a menace to the religious and political authorities, Cf. Stayer, 187.

[108] Marpeck's use of Luther's two-kingdom theology will become clearer in the next chapter dealing with the *Aufdeckung*.

[109] QGT VII, 350. Bucer writes in November 1531 that Marpeck "die leute bereden, das schweren und weren unrecht sye…"

to a much greater extent the use of the Old Testament's ethics and examples to justify his conception of the civil authorities. In fact for Bucer the greatest Christian good work consists of obedience to the magistrate. And none can better fulfill the function of a magistrate than a Christian.[110]

Precisely this differentiation between the testaments allowed Marpeck to break the civil-religious unity that was so important to Bucer. The refusal of the latter to accept this distinction also entails a different understanding of the work of Christ in regard to "outer things." Marpeck conceived of the *Fromm-Machung* as a state of living a life guided by Christ's words. Marpeck's emphasis on the words (or letter) implied, in Bucer's perspective, that Marpeck did not grasp how Christ freed humankind; in other words, the Anabaptist had a false doctrine of the work of Christ. For the reformer, the liberation accomplished by Christ does not necessarily address outer realities. The norms for life in the outer realm (baptism, magistrate, etc.) are love and faith. Bucer writes of Marpeck:

> The fact of emphasizing so dramatically Christ's commandments towards outer realities demonstrates a misunderstanding of Christ. Because Christ has declared us free. His new commandment is that we love one another. He reigns over our consciences with his Spirit by true faith and a love without restraint, which is oriented toward improvement without particular rules or without dependence on outer things... One must remember that we have no commandment other than to believe in Christ and to love our neighbor in truth.[111]

This "rule of love" (*Regel der Liebe*) was a classic response by the reformers to Anabaptism, common to Zurich, Basel, Berne, and Strasbourg.[112] The notion can be found for the first time in a disputation between Zwingli and several Anabaptists (Grebel, Mantz, and others)

---

[110] See the Tetrapolitan Confession, "wess ains Cristen menschen thun sey" (Stupperich, *Martin Bucers Deutsche Schriften,* 62-64) and "von der welltlichen Oberkheit," Ibid, 162. Marpeck does not deny the role attributed to the authorities in Romans 13, but he insists that this role has nothing to do with the kingdom of Christ and believes that it would be difficult for a Christian to be a magistrate.
[111] *QGT* VII, 403.
[112] Yoder, *Anabaptism and Reformation,* 176-77.

towards the end of 1524.[113] Zwingli claimed that love meant that Grebel and Mantz should argue no further against him, even if they remained unconvinced by his position. In the *Elenchus* of 1527, Zwingli wrote to the reformers of Basel and Strasbourg that "love" may require ignoring a biblical command for the preservation of ecclesiastical and political unity.[114] In sum, "love" requires capitulation to maintain the unity of the Reformation.

Bucer was very close to Zwingli when he responded to Marpeck using this notion of love. Nor was it the first time Bucer used this approach, since at the end of 1526, his colleague Wolfgang Capito and he made the same argument against Michael Sattler.[115]

Bernd Moeller's analysis – offered outside the context of the debates between the mainline reformation and Anabaptism – also shows how important the notion of ecclesio-political unity was to Bucer and how this communal life "is guided by a single principle: love."[116] Thus "the rule of love" became a hermeneutical principle[117] in the defense of the Reformation and the city from the Anabaptist menace, which risked breaking this unity.

Though we are entering here into the political realm, it still appears possible to conceive of the distance that separates Bucer and Marpeck, as at least in part as a Christological issue. Bucer understands the work of Christ in a manner that permits the separation of the inner (the justice of God) and the outer (baptism or the unity of Strasbourg). In a situation where the application of the literal words of Christ risks breaking the unity of the Reformation, Bucer affirmed that love (and faith) did not

---

[113] Yoder, *Anabaptism and Reformation*, 45. Zwingli describes the use of this "rule of love" in a letter to the reformers in Strasbourg.
[114] Ibid, 177-182..
[115] QGT VII, 68.
[116] B. Moeller, *Villes d'empires et Réformation* (Geneva : Librairie Droz, 1966), 59.
[117] Moeller, *Villes d'empires*, 63: "Zwingli and Bucer placed the republican ideal as a dogma above all other considerations." See also 65: "The opinions of Zwingli… and of Bucer on the idea of the State resulted in great measure from the fact that they were both citizens of free cities and they were deeply attached to these cities and their structures."

address the outer realm. This concern to maintain the unity of the Reformation gave a specific interpretation to the notion of love.

For Marpeck, such a conception of love appears empty of Christological content. Love must be defined by Christ and the New Testament. Marpeck writes:

> When you say that the commandment of love is the principal tenet and work of Christians, which accomplishes every improvement [in man], I agree, but with this difference: In Christ we have a true God, and we must remain in His teaching and order. Whoever does not remain in the teaching of Christ has no God. Thus the beginning of love is to believe in and hold to God and His Word, as John 8 [:21 f.] advises: If you remain in my words, you will be my true disciples and you will know the truth, and the truth will make you free.[118]

This debate indeed fits well within the wider context of the discussions between the Swiss reformers and the Anabaptists studied by John Yoder. Concerning the differences between the Old and the New Testament and the historicity of the Incarnation, Bucer appears to start with an ontological and platonic framework, as did Zwingli; Marpeck is shaped by a more historical and eschatological vision, as were the Swiss Anabaptists.[119] Just as the Incarnation implies that God takes "outer means" seriously, it also means that time and history are also essential in the outworking of God's plan of salvation for humanity.

Therefore two distinct world-views clash and it would be difficult to keep the differences between Marpeck and Bucer at the Christological level without considering the philosophical assumptions at work. One might ask whether the Christological difference originates in the difference of worldview or vice-versa. But in such polemical situations, to establish what are "axioms" and what results from fundamental axioms is a difficult, if not impossible task. In any case the existence of these different thought systems reinforces the claim that Bucer and Marpeck display fundamental Christological differences despite the occasional use of similar language to describe Christ and his work. Marpeck's emphasis on the humanity

---

[118] *WPM*, 156.
[119] Yoder, *Anabaptism and Reformation*, 171;175.

of Christ and the historicity of redemption demonstrates a fundamental difference with Bucer and the Reformation in Strasbourg.

The debate is complicated by the fact that politics and theology are intertwined, and studying just the thought of both adversaries does not sufficiently address all that is really going on. The debate was between a person with a certain amount of power who sought to protect institutions (that were evidently in a fragile state) and a person who had no ecclesial or political authority. Bucer understood Christ from within his vision of the Reformation in a free imperial city. Marpeck developed his Christology in the context of a persecuted and increasingly illegal movement. On both sides, theological argumentation took place in a particular context, each seeking to interpret and justify his situation based on the biblical texts, and as H-J. Goertz affirms, a person without power reads the Bible differently than a powerful person.[120]

Final remarks

In his study of the hermeneutics of Pilgram Marpeck, William Klassen concludes that Marpeck's theology was addressing two fundamental problems: (1) that of the relation between the old and the new covenant, and (2) the problem of the letter and the Spirit.[121] The last two chapters have demonstrated how Marpeck sought to resolve these questions Christologically, particularly by means of the humanity of Christ.

Against the Spiritualists, Marpeck, drawing heavily on Luther, uses *die menscheit Christi* to prove that God always has used and still uses "outer means" to make himself known. In the same way that Christ, the man, leads humans to the spiritual reality of God, the church's sacraments are necessary to fulfill this same task. The Spirit is only known by the letter (and the opposite is also true). For Marpeck, as for Luther, these exterior means are the prolongation of the Incarnation, which explains why they are called "the humanity of Christ."

---

[120] Goertz, *Die Täufer*, 23.
[121] *Covenant and Community*, 149.

Against Bucer, the humanity of Christ signifies that God acted in history and that the promise of the Old Testament found its fulfillment in the Incarnation of Jesus Christ. That Marpeck and Schwenckfeld are in close agreement in this understanding of the Old and New Testaments has been demonstrated. A radical separation of the two covenants and a foundational Christological ethic are the consequences of Marpeck's view. The ethical life is a result of the work of Christ, a work that makes the believer just and pious, capable of accomplishing the will of God revealed in the teaching of Jesus. This break between the covenants is one of the fundamental differences between Marpeck and the Reformation in Strasbourg.

Thus in two specific cases Marpeck used the humanity of Christ as a theological starting point. It remains to be seen if these two ways of conceiving of the humanity of Christ could be joined by Marpeck to construct a coherent Christology.

Chapter 3

Widening the Debate Again:
Exposé of the Babylonian Whore

Any study of Marpeck's theological development in Strasbourg can no longer be complete without taking into consideration the *Aufdeckung der Babylonischen Hurn* (*Exposé of the Babylonian Whore*)[1] and what it contributes to our knowledge of Pilgram Marpeck and the development of his thought.

The sixteenth-century pamphlet that is the focus of this chapter was first made known and reproduced by Hans Hillerbrand in 1958.[2] In 1987 Walter Klaassen suggested Pilgram Marpeck was the most likely author of the document – a hypothesis that has been increasingly accepted by Marpeck scholarship.[3]

---

[1] English translation in Walter Klaassen, Werner O. Packull and John Rempel, trans. and eds., *Later Writings by Pilgram Marpeck and His Circle*, (Kitchener: Pandora Press, 1999), 24-44 (cited henceforth as *Exposé*). This chapter is a shortened and revised version of my article "*The Uncovering of the Babylonian Whore*: Confessionalization and Politics Seen from the Underside," *MQR*, (January 2001), 37-56.

[2] Hans Hillerbrand, "An Early Anabaptist Treatise on the Christian and the State," *MQR* (January 1958), 28-48.

[3] Walter Klaassen, "Investigation into the Authorship and the Historical Background of the Anabaptist Tract *Aufdeckung der Babylonischen Hurn*," *MQR* (July 1987), 251ff;

For reasons that will become clear, it is most likely that the *Exposé* was published late in 1531 or early in 1532, close to the time of Marpeck's expulsion from Strasbourg. The text is best read as an Anabaptist critique of the larger Reformation process of confessionalization – that is, the process by which churches joined forces with local political powers within the Empire to establish "confessional" territories and cities. In what follows we will pay attention both to the context in which the document was written and to its Christological and ethical focus.

Historical context: the beginnings of confessionalization

Marpeck's arrival in Strasbourg coincided with a crucial moment in the reformation of that city. In February of 1529 the Alsatian city formally abolished the Roman Catholic mass. Several months later, at the Diet of Speyer, the emperor attempted to revoke agreements reached in 1526 that had permitted Luther and his followers a range of freedom within sympathetic cities and territories. On April 19, 1529 six princes and fourteen German cities protested against this action and thereby became "Protestant." Four days later the Diet responded to the threat of Anabaptist dissidence by reinstating the death penalty for "rebaptism." Though Strasbourg was an imperial city, it did not enforce this imperial law, which could only be a sign of hope for Marpeck and others.

One year later Strasbourg participated in the Diet of Augsburg and, together with three other cities, presented its own confession of faith alongside the Lutheran Augsburg Confession, which was read on June 25, 1530. Of course, Charles V was not convinced by these confessions and demanded that the "Lutherans" abandon their faith. When they refused, the emperor gave them until April of 1531 to recant. The Protestants, however, responded in December of 1530 by forming a defensive alliance

---

Stephen Boyd, *Pilgram Marpeck*; Werner O. Packull, "Pilgram Marpeck: *Uncovering of the Babylonian Whore* and Other Anonymous Anabaptist Tracts," *MQR* (July 1993), 351-55; Werner O. Packull, *Hutterite Beginnings*: 133-58.

known as the Schmalkaldic League, with the Augsburg Confession as its official doctrinal statement.[4]

Two months later, in February of 1531, Strasbourg and several other south German cities became members of the League. Between June 26 and 28, 1531 a commission of Protestant theologians and jurists conferred in Torgau on the question of political and military resistance to the emperor and concluded that resistance could be "juridically justified."[5] Already in April of the same year, Luther wrote his *Warnung an seine lieben Deudschen*,[6] reluctantly accepting the possibility of political and military resistance to the emperor. As with many of Luther's writings, the *Warnung* was also printed in Strasbourg in 1531.

Strasbourg's decision to join the Schmalkaldic League could not have been good news to Marpeck and other Anabaptists. Moving closer to Luther meant, at least theoretically, a more strict anti-Anabaptist stance on the part of Bucer, given the five condemnations of Anabaptism in the Augsburg Confession, the official doctrinal basis for the League. It was, interestingly enough, during this same time, in July of 1531, that the city council of Strasbourg officially censured two of Marpeck's writings for containing "anabaptist doctrines."[7]

These remarks help clarify the much larger context of political tension that lay behind Marpeck and Bucer's meeting in the presence of Strasbourg's city council on December 9, 1531. The records of this conversation report that Marpeck accused Bucer of hiding behind the political power of either the "common man" or of "princes and cities"[8] – terms and accusations that

---

[4] Harold J. Grimm, *The Reformation Era* (London: MacMillan, 1965), 212.
[5] Klaassen, "Investigation," 253. "That same month Luther, Jonas, Melanchton and others made this decision public and identified themselves with it. In April 1531 Luther's *Warnung an seine lieben Deudschen* appeared. In this work he argued that military resistance to the emperor was self-defense and therefore justified. This work was reprinted four times during 1531. The Protestant Schmalkaldic League was established that same year on the basis of these arguments."
[6] *WA*, XXX , 254f.
[7] *QGT VII*, 335. These two censured booklets are commonly identified as Marpeck's two anti-Spiritualist writings, *A Clear Refutation* and *A Clear Instruction*.
[8] "Seye also erstlich uss den oberzelten ursachen die erst ursach und jrthumb der predicanten, dass sie in jren predigen entweder hinder dem gemeinen mann ober bey fürsten und stätten

would reappear in the *Exposé*. Shortly afterward, on December 18, 1531, the council decided to relieve Marpeck of his employment and to expel him from the city.[9] One last time, in January of 1532, Marpeck discussed his theology with the Strasbourg council, having previously sent a confession of faith directly to Bucer in order to justify his position. This confession also criticized any recourse to political structures to impose or defend the Gospel.[10] After this point in time, however, all traces of Marpeck in Strasbourg disappear.

If Marpeck was indeed the author of the *Exposé*, two reasons point to the strong possibility that he wrote it shortly before or just after his leaving Strasbourg in January 1532. First of all, the first edition of the *Exposé* came off Jacob Cammerlander's press in Strasbourg as did Marpeck's two other 1531 anti-Spiritualist writings.[11] Second, the *Exposé* refers to possible upcoming violence that might result from evangelical resistance to the emperor. That violence did not happen. The deadline of April 15, 1531 set by Charles V, came and went without any attack, and when the next diet met in Nüremberg in the summer of 1532, the Lutheran princes had become strong enough to force the emperor to make concessions.[12] At least for the time being, the Reformation had some breathing space. In other words, the political climate had changed enough by the summer

---

gesuch und nit frey zum creutz Christi geprediget haben." *QGT VII*, 352. See also 353: "Als er aber anzeigt, das sie, die predicanten, die obrigkeit anrueffen etc. (Pilgram) daruff sagt, das welcher schutz oder schirm der creaturen sucht, der sey verflucht."

[9] *QGT VII*, 360-61.

[10] *QGT VII*, 425: "Aller eusserlicher gwallt mag im reich Crissti nicht herschen, nutzen noch regieren."

[11] "Klaassen noted that one of these editions came off the same press as Marpeck's tracts of 1531, *A Clear Refutation* and *A Clear Instruction*. . . . This hypothesis of Marpeck's authorship can be strengthened by the identification of Jacob Cammerlander of Strasbourg as the printer of Marpeck's 1531 tracts as well as of the first edition of *The Babylonian Whore*." Packull, "Pilgram Marpeck," 351.

[12] Grimm, *The Reformation Era*, 213. According to Grimm, "The failure of Charles to act decisively against the Protestants during the years 1530 to 1532 permitted the Protestant estates to consolidate the churches in their territories."

of 1532 that the fears of bloodshed and violence expressed in the *Exposé* no longer made sense after this point in time.[13]

Read as a commentary on the course of the Reformation in late 1531 and early 1532, the *Exposé* – which Walter Klaassen calls "the most penetrating treatment of the subject of Christ and the sword that the sixteenth-century Anabaptists produced"[14] – provides a fascinating historical, political and theological commentary on the course of the Reformation and its growing dependence on political power to survive and develop. As we will soon see, the *Exposé* went beyond the Strasbourg context and took on Martin Luther directly. Given the strong possibility of Luther's influence on Marpeck's anti-Spiritualist pamphlets, the disappointment reflected in this writing is all the more poignant.

For readers familiar with Marpeck's other writings of 1531, the title page already gives a strong hint that the pamphlet was directed against Martin Luther. On the bottom of this page two different Bible verses are quoted:

> Give to Caesar what is Caesar's, and to God what is God's (Mt. 22:21).
>
> . . . do not join with the rebellious (Prov. 24:21).

When compared with another important writing by Marpeck, *A Clear Instruction* of 1531, these quotations give a clue to why the book was written. At the bottom of the cover page to *A Clear Instruction* is

---

[13] Packull mentions the fact that Marpeck's later presence in Augsburg meant that he was in a position to further the second edition of the *Aufdeckung*, which was printed by Philip Ulhart in Augsburg during the 1540's. Packull, "Pilgram Marpeck," 352. Given the historic references to the Schmalkaldic League, it is important to note that a second edition of this treatise would once again make sense at this very point in time, given the context of the Schmalkaldic war (to which Marpeck was a witness). He also wrote against this war in February 1547. See "Concerning the Lowliness of Christ" in *WPM*, 427-63. The Strasbourg edition corresponds to Marpeck's presence in Strasbourg, the Augsburg edition corresponds to his presence in Augsburg, and the timing of both makes sense given the respective political contexts.

[14] "This can best be accounted for by the fact that Marpeck possessed a level of ecclesiastical and political perception that was unusual in the Anabaptism of the early 1530s." Klaassen, "Investigation," 261.

the enigmatic statement, "Nit was/sonder das." We know that this was intended as a direct reply to a similar motto ("Nicht wer/Sonder was") which appeared on the cover page of the Spiritualist theologian Christian Entfelder's *Von den manigfaltigen im glauben zerspaltungen*. As already stated in the previous chapter and elsewhere, the contents of Marpeck's *A Clear Instruction* confirm that it was a direct refutation of Entfelder's work and a contribution to Anabaptist-Spiritualist debates in Strasbourg and beyond.

If Marpeck used this same strategy in the case of the *Exposé* – i.e., calling attention to his adversary's position already on the title page – it is interesting to note where and in what context one finds these different verses cited, especially in light of Marpeck's references to Luther in his other writings of 1531.

In other words, the *Exposé* confirms our suspicion that Marpeck had read Luther and even considered him to be an important influence on his theology. And indeed, the two verses cited at the beginning of the *Exposé* can be found at strategic points in Luther's writings related to questions of political power.

"Give to Caesar what is Caesar's, and to God what is God's" appears only once – at a very crucial point – in Luther's *Von weltlicher Oberkeit, wie weit man ihr Gehorsam schuldig sei* of 1523[15] as it does in the *Warnung an seine lieben Deudschen* of 1531. The Proverbs passage ". . . do not join with the rebellious" (Prov. 24:21), appears in Luther's *Ein sendbrief von dem harten Büchlein wider die Bauern*[16] of 1525 as part of his argument that rebellion against divinely ordained political authorities can never be justified. The pertinence of these references will become clear, since it appears that Marpeck was writing against Luther on the basis of what Luther himself had written previously. The *Exposé* appears to direct Marpeck's reading of *Von weltlicher Oberkeit* and *Ein sendbrief* against Luther as well as Bucer.[17]

---

[15] *WA* XI, 229-81.

[16] *WA* XVIII, 375-401.

[17] If one assumes that the *Exposé* was written against Luther, it is at least possible to imagine that the title is an implicit or even explicit reference to Luther's 1520 treatise on the Babylonian captivity.

Content and Argumentation of the Exposé

The basic argument of the *Exposé* is simple and consists of a theological and historical analysis of the Reformation process up until 1531. According to this Anabaptist reading of events, Luther began the necessary work of the Reformation by unmasking the Babylonian whore, i. e., the Roman Catholic Church, and continued to make several important theological contributions. Nevertheless, by allying itself to the political power of the princes and cities the Lutheran movement became a new manifestation of the Babylonian harlot by seeking out and availing itself of the protection of civil authority. Only by following Christ without recourse to political power can the cause of the Gospel move forward without compromise; forcing people to believe or imposing faith by political means is a betrayal that contradicts the very message of the Gospel. Confessionalization – the creation of churches under the auspices and the protection of civil authority – is a process in which all sides are wrong and the churches and the christianization that follow from it are doomed to failure.

The *Exposé's* understanding of the history of the Reformation has an eschatological starting point. Marpeck shared the general sixteenth-century assumption that the Reformation was a sign that history had moved into its final stage[18] – "this last and perilous time"[19] – during which God's judgment would become manifest.[20]

---

[18] "There is a consensus concerning the coming storm. In the 1500's people spoke and wrote about living in 'these last and perilous times'." Walter Klaassen, *Living at the End of the Ages: Apocalyptic Expectation in the Radical Reformation* (Lanham, MD: U. Press of America, 1992), 20. Heiko Oberman highlights the importance of the apocalyptic perspective in Luther's theology and understanding of the Reformation. H. Oberman, *The Reformation, Roots and Ramifications* (Grand Rapids, MI: Eerdmans, 1994), 24-32.

[19] *Exposé*, 24. Any references to the original text come from the reproduction in Hillerbrand's article in the MQR 32 (Jan. 1958), 34-47. This is the second (Augsburg) edition of the Exposé.

[20] "das ernsthafft gericht Gottes seines erschrecklichen tages/der kommen soll." *Aufdeckung*, 3.

It was clear to Marpeck that the Reformation had already uncovered the "red Roman Whore."²¹ But in "this last time," the Babylonian whore was no longer just Rome. Rather, she had made herself known and was attempting to seduce true Christians through a new disguise, i.e., the Reformation. Referring to Ezekiel 23 and the story of the two prostitute sisters, Ohola and Oholiba, the *Exposé* clearly put the Roman Catholic Church and the Reformation in the same camp. What Ezekiel 23 called "prostitution" was in fact Israel and Judah's lusting after Assyrian and Babylonian political power instead of trusting in God. The result was clear: political defeat and exile. Just as Israel (Ohola = Rome) had been taken captive by Assyria, Judah (Oholiba = Lutheran Reformation) would also fall to Babylon:

> You have gone the way of your sister, so I will put her cup into your hand . . . you will drink your sister's cup, a cup large and deep. It will bring scorn and derision, for it holds so much (Ez. 23: 31-32).

In other words, the *Exposé* was written so that the new forms of seduction (i. e., Luther) would be revealed, just as the old (i. e., Rome) had already been uncovered.²²

The Reformation began the "uncovering" of the harlot but it did not go far enough, since two of the papacy's errors – infant baptism²³ and the corporal presence of Christ in the Eucharist – had been maintained and made into the centrepiece (*fürnemsten stuck*)²⁴ of Luther's theology.

---

²¹ *Exposé*, 25. Marpeck was not the only Anabaptist in Strasbourg who dealt with this theme. Melchior Hoffman, who published an entire *Commentary on the Apocalypse* with Beck in Strasbourg, considered it his mission to reveal the identity of the Book of Revelation's "Babylonian Whore." See Packull, "Pilgram Marpeck," 351. Before Hoffman and Marpeck, Balthasar Hubmaier also wrote against "die Rott hür von Babylonen" in 1525, referring to the Roman Catholic Church. G. Westin and T. Bergsten, eds., *Balthasar Hubmaier Schriften*, 110.

²² "das die recht/war ainfalt des glaubens/all jr newe arglistigkait und falsche kunst auch erkennen/ als wol as jre alte Hürendick/Ezech. 23. erkent seind." *Aufdeckung*, 4-5. (*Exposé*, 27).

²³ In Marpeck's Confession of 1532 he also identifies infant baptism as "the root of the Roman harlot." *WPM*₁ 145.

²⁴ *Exposé*, 26.

Here the *Exposé* names Luther explicitly for the first time. In typical Anabaptist fashion, Marpeck denounced Luther's eucharistic theology for falsely assuming that giving communion in both kinds to the laity could somehow purify a defiled ceremony.

> In Martin Luther's eyes all who eat and drink the body and blood of Christ, regardless of whether they are adulterers or prostitutes, gluttons or drunkards, gamblers, murderers, betrayers, tyrants, deceivers, or whatever else are all a good community of his kind of godliness.[25]

At this point, the main argument of the *Exposé* begins to unfold. Luther's teaching was responsible for the Peasants' War and, in a similar manner, was currently inciting princes, lords and cities to rebel against the emperor, which would certainly lead to a bloodbath.[26] Against the backdrop of Protestant and Catholic persecution of Anabaptists, Marpeck then exhorted true Christians to be patient, not to resist, and to be willing to die if necessary.[27]

The *Exposé's* argument against political coercion in matters of faith is fundamentally Christological in nature, in the sense that Christ becomes the ethical model for disciples. Christ was subject to all authorities; he never resisted any authority, but "gave to Caesar that which is Caesar's and to God that which is God's." Thus, in an odd way, Marpeck, who represented a seditious rejection of civil authority in the eyes of the Reformers, justified and defended the emperor's authority. Since Charles V was the authority ordained of God, he must continue to exercise authority in temporal affairs until God's final judgment.[28] This parallels what Luther wrote in his *Von*

---

[25] Ibid.

[26] Ibid.

[27] "For the Lamb of Christ must suffer and be killed until the end of the world… Pilate, Herod, Annas, and Caiaphas will unite against it as they united against the head…. Christ was subject to all Authority and never responded with violence." *Exposé*, 27.

[28] "I know of no other Authority specifically appointed by God than the Emperor; all emperors hold the imperium even today and will hold it until the appointed time… For all flesh needs his authority and rule." *Exposé*, 27.

weltlicher Oberkeit of 1523, where he quoted Matthew 22[29] and then argued that the emperor has power over "body, goods and honor."

Like Luther, Marpeck presupposed the right of divinely ordained political authorities to fully act within the sphere of their jurisdiction[30] – all external (*eusserliche*) things were subject to earthly authority. However, no civil authority may impose true faith in Christ.[31] In his effort to distinguish between what belongs to God and what belongs to Caesar, Luther had also rejected the imposition of faith by temporal means.[32] Marpeck's argument quickly comes into focus: Luther – who in 1523 had drawn a sharp line between temporal and spiritual authority – had clearly changed his mind.

Against these "so-called evangelicals and their teachers and preachers,"[33] there could only be one argument: the example of the crucified, patient and loving Christ. A true understanding of Christ may be taught only under the cross, in patience and in love. Those who did not teach this Christ, Marpeck argued, whether Catholic or Evangelical, were new Antichrists who would come under the judgment of Christ.[34]

---

[29] "Sondern uber leib güt und ehre hat er wol solchs zuo thun, denn zolchs ist unter seines gewallt." Luther, *WA*, XI, 266.

[30] In 1523 Luther wrote that God ordained two kinds of government: spiritual government, which operates through the Holy Spirit and in submission to Christ, and temporal government, which punishes those who are not Christian. Luther, *WA*, XI, 245-80. Marpeck insisted quite similarly throughout the entire *Aufdeckung* that spiritual government operates through the Spirit in submission to Christ.

[31] "All external things including life and limb are subjected to external authority. But no one may coerce or compel true faith in Christ." *Exposé*, 27.

[32] "Denn wie gesagt ist, die Seele ist nicht unter Keisers gewalt. Er kan sie wider leren noch furen, widder tödten noch lebendig machen, widder binden noch lösen, widder richten noch urteilen, widder halten noch lassen. . . ." *WA*, XI, 266. For Luther (in 1523) it was up to each individual to decide what to believe without having to fear any sanction of civil authority. Temporal authority should take care of its own affairs and let each person believe as desired without any constraint whatsoever. Luther also quoted Matthew 22:21 at a key point in his *Warnung and seine lieben Deudschen* when trying to distinguish between submission to authority and sedition. *WA*, XXX, 282.

[33] *Exposé*, 27.

[34] *Exposé*, 27.

In a critique similar to the one he had leveled against Bucer in his discussions of December 1531,[35] Marpeck linked the impending judgment of Christ to the events of the Peasants' War. Through their writings and teachings, the Evangelicals had first of all put the sword in the hand of the common people.[36] This led to "Korah's rebellion" (Jude 1:11) and to death. Now these same "Evangelicals" were inciting princes and cities to "to take the way of Cain" (Jude 1:11) and were "hiding behind them," which certainly would lead to a bloodbath worse than the Peasants' War.[37]

Luther had also referred to Proverbs 24:21 ("Fear the Lord and the king, my son, and do not join with the rebellious") to justify repression of the peasants in 1525. This verse is now quoted on the cover page of the *Exposé*. To those who accused him of being too hard on the peasants, Luther responded by saying that he had supported the princes because the peasants had rebelled against divinely ordained authority.[38] It is not difficult to imagine that Marpeck was consciously and ironically using Luther's own earlier reasoning, turning it against the Schmalkaldic League's justification of "rebellion" against the empire.

At this point in the argument against Luther and the Reformers, Marpeck paused to express appreciation for what he learned from them. Through their writings, teachings and preaching, Marpeck had been led

---

[35] The record of Marpeck's position in this conversation with Bucer reads as follows: "Seye also erstlich uss den oberzelten ursachen die erst ursach und jrthumb der predicanten, dass sie in jren predigen entweder hinder dem gemainen mann oder bey fürsten und stätten gesuch und nit frey zum creutz Christi geprediget haben." *QGT*, VII, 352.

[36] *Exposé*, 28. This was of course the common Catholic explanation of the Peasants' War. Recent scholarship has shown that the peasants' movement can and should be understood as having been rooted in the Reformation. James Stayer, *The German Peasants' War and Anabaptist Community of Goods* (Montreal: McGill-Queen's U. Press, 1991).

[37] *Exposé*, 28.

[38] ". . . Salomo spricht: mein kind, furchte Gott und den könig und *menge dich nicht unter die auffrurischen*, Denn ihr umfall wird plötzlich komen, und wer weis seiner verderben? . . . Da sahen wir, das *beide, die auffrurischen und die sich unter sie mengen verdampt sind, und Gott kein schertz draus gemacht will haben*, sonder den könig und oberkeit soll man furchten. Die aber mengen sich under die auffrurisschen, die sich der selben annemen, klagen, rechtfertigen, und erbarmen, welcher sich Gott nicht erbarmet, sonder gestrafft, und verderbt will haben." Luther, *Ein sendbrief von dem harten Büchlein wider die Bauern 1525, WA,* XVIII, 385.

out of captivity to "the human laws of the papacy."³⁹ Lutheran criticisms of the medieval Church were true and should be accepted as such.⁴⁰ But this newfound freedom had quickly become a "liberty of the flesh" with which Marpeck was not at ease.⁴¹ What was missing in the Evangelicals' preaching and teaching, was the secret of the cross of Christ and the narrow way.⁴² Even worse, the Evangelicals were now persecuting those who taught "the secret of the cross of Christ," while defending themselves by taking refuge "behind princes, lords and cities."⁴³

In order to justify such harsh criticism of the Reformers, the *Exposé* devoted considerable effort to discerning what belongs to God and what belongs to Caesar, i.e., to describing and biblically justifying the civil authority and how it relates to Christian faith.⁴⁴ For Marpeck, God had ordained civil authority to keep the peace in the temporal sphere, i.e., to protect the innocent and to punish evildoers. But civil authority did not extend to matters of faith or conscience. The only legitimate means to "convert" someone was through the power of persuasion. When, as in the case of tensions between the reformers and the emperor, things were not going as desired, the only legitimate means of resistance was to

---

³⁹ *Exposé*, 28.
⁴⁰ Ibid.
⁴¹ This corresponds to what Marpeck had said to the Strasbourg Council. "Dann er (Marpeck) an orten, da man das evangelion uff lutherische wyss gepredigt, darin auch ein fleischlich fryheit gespürt werde, dan jne etwas hinderstellig gemacht, also das er in jme nit ru mögen befinden." *QGT*, VII, 352.
⁴² Once again, one is tempted to see a veiled reference to Luther at this point in the text. For Marpeck, this teaching of nonviolence (i.e., the cross of Christ) is necessary for true salvation. This is said in terms of the believer being led into the "liberty of Jerusalem." According to the *Exposé*, the Reformation (Luther) began this road to freedom (by liberation from the "Babylonian Captivity," i.e., Luther's treatise of 1520), but didn't go far enough: "But then as now the evangelical teachers said nothing about the mystery of the cross of Christ, and the narrow gate through which the flesh and the one who has been liberated from the Babylonian captivity could once again be led into the liberty of Jerusalem." *Exposé*, 28.
⁴³ *Exposé*, 28-29.
⁴⁴ One almost has the feeling that Marpeck had a copy of *Von weltlicher Oberkeit* on his table when writing the *Aufdeckung*, even though he had his own understanding of Luther's doctrine of the two kingdoms.

suffer injustice.[45] The introduction of temporal authority into Christ's kingdom was simply the work of Satan.[46] The reformers resorted to various justifications: it was necessary to protect Christians when they were being threatened; if no one helped governments to protect the innocent against evil, chaos would ensue. Marpeck accepted such justifications, but only to the extent that they remained within the temporal sphere and had nothing to do with Christ's kingdom or the imposition of a particular theology through political means.

For Marpeck, civil government had its origin in God's goodness and mercy, and functioned to keep peace and protect human property.[47] God has offered peace to all. If everyone were a Christian, there would be no need for civil government; but since not everyone is a believer or chooses to accept this peace, God ordained government to keep peace in the temporal

---

[45] "If the Authority, established by God (Rom. 13), bears the sword in accordance with God's bidding and command, you are physically under the protection of God. When that Authority does not bear the sword as it should, but rather protects wickedness, destroys godliness, lives the lie, and persecutes the truth, you must be content to admonish that Authority which is God's servant, to be converted and leave vengeance to God. No other sword or deterrence has Christ commanded his own to use." *Exposé*, 29.

[46] "Satan seeks to mix temporal power with Christendom by making it attractive through his prophets." *Exposé*, 30.

[47] "Even as God has offered peace to everyone, but not all have accepted it, likewise he has in his mercy also established and ordained divine Authority on earth to preserve temporal peace wherever the true peace of God, which is incompatible with self-seeking, is not accepted, in order that they don't destroy each other over their property." *Exposé*, 31. According to James Stayer, "The most original aspect of the *Aufdeckung* was its linking of property to the Sword." *The Anabaptists and the Sword*, 171. More recently, Werner Packull argues that Marpeck and the *Aufdeckung* represent a more "Hutterite" understanding of community of goods. Packull, *Hutterite Beginnings*, 137-38. This might be true, but we find no explicit affirmation of community of goods in the *Aufdeckung*, and references to "property" may also be understood as Marpeck following Luther's earlier distinction between civil and spiritual authority, where property is related to the *eusserlich* temporal sphere. For Luther in 1523, civil authority had to do with the corporal and with possessions (i.e., property) and other "outer things."

sphere.⁴⁸ Within this temporal sphere, Christians remain subject to civil authority, even at the cost of their lives.⁴⁹

Marpeck bolstered this argument theologically with the same distinction between the Old and the New Testament that he was also using against Martin Bucer with the help of Schwenckfeld's writings during this same period of time. According to this perspective, the Old Testament sword used by Moses, Joshua and David served to maintain temporal peace (*zeitlichen friden*). Christ, however, came to give another kind of peace, which is spiritual and not temporal, and which does not defend itself against temporal persecution.⁵⁰ The christological foundation at the heart of the difference of the Testaments here is practically identical with Marpeck's position in his other writings of 1531. The Incarnation fulfilled the promises of the Old Testament and released the Spirit of the new covenant, giving a peace that had never been known previously.⁵¹

In this context, Christ's teachings and example became the key for understanding how to discern what belongs to God and what belongs to Caesar. In a setting where Protestant princes and cities were seeking to justify political rebellion to further the cause of the Reformation, Marpeck's understanding of civil authority "disarmed" the Christian when it came to using political means to either protect or impose a given understanding of faith. Among his own, Christ rules only through his Spirit, even when outer or corporal things are concerned, for the Son of Man came not to hurt

---

⁴⁸ According to Luther in 1523, those who didn't have faith were not Christian and did not belong to Christ's kingdom, but to the worldly kingdom, where they were constrained and governed by the sword. Christians spontaneously do good, without any constraint, and need only God's word. *Von weltlicher Oberkeit.*

⁴⁹ "Because of this goodwill and love of God for everyone, all true Christians are, as God's children, obligated by love to obey and be subject to all temporal authority, even to death, but to give to God what belongs to him." *Exposé*, 31.

⁵⁰ "This peace does not complain about temporal persecution, however cruel it may be." *Exposé*, 32.

⁵¹ "No one had this peace before Christ who first redeemed us into this peace. His bodily departure was necessary, otherwise the Comforter would not have come … so that we may endure all temporal tribulation in this peace of heart without objecting." *Exposé*, 32.

people but to save them.⁵² Christians do not lord it over others or impose their views, but patiently suffer in obedience to God. The only judge or sword that Christians use (among themselves) is the word of Christ, which clearly teaches that Christians are servants and not lords. Even if it were a matter of protecting a friend or neighbour, the Christian may only love, not hate, his enemy, for true Christian love hurts no one, friend or enemy. If the corporal or bodily sphere interferes with the kingdom of Christ, Christ's obedience and death were in vain.

Not surprisingly, Protestant reformers since Zwingli had accused the Anabaptists of holding to a seditious and diabolical understanding of civil authority that could only lead to anarchy. The author of the *Exposé* was quite aware of this criticism and turned it back against the reformers themselves.⁵³ Who, he asked rhetorically, was now "contradicting" the emperor? Who was now justifying a refusal to obey divinely ordained political authority?

What the Reformers wanted, according to Marpeck, was the best of all imaginable worlds: a civil authority that protected them and acted only on their behalf. They wanted protection and security, but at the same time they did not want anyone to have authority over them if they should happen to disagree on theological matters.⁵⁴ For Marpeck, this came very close to Luther's definition of sedition (*Aufruhr*) in 1525.⁵⁵ Divinely ordained authority, Marpeck argued, may act justly or unjustly. When it

---

⁵² "He rules in his own through his Spirit alone also in temporal matters ... for the Son of Man has not come to destroy the lives of human beings but to save them." Therefore his own, also, may never destroy anyone. *Exposé*, 33.

⁵³ "Those who contradict us accuse Christ and his own of opposing the Emperor and forbidding payment of taxes, refusing him obedience, saying government is not necessary, wanting to be our own lords, and appoint ourselves a king of the Jews and the like. Observe the cunning and the tricks which Satan's own employ. Out of the surfeit of their own wickedness they accuse Christ and his own of that which they themselves do." *Expose*, 34.

⁵⁴ "These people demand only protection and security. However, no one wants to endure the authority that goes with the protection ..." *Exposé*, 34-35.

⁵⁵ In his *Warnung* of 1531, Luther comes close to saying the same thing: "Auffrur ist nicht, wenn einer widder das Recht thut, sonst Müsten alle ubertrettung des Rechten auffrur heissen, Sonder der heisst ein auffrürer, der die Oberkeit und recht nicht leiden wil, sonder

acts unjustly, as did Pilate in the case of Christ, the Christian may not rebel, but must suffer the consequences, even unto death.[56]

In this respect, the *Exposé* stands clearly within the Anabaptist tradition of using New Testament teachings to solve disagreements and disciplinary problems within the church.[57] In such a process, the worst treatment that a "heretic" could receive was excommunication. Neither physical punishment, imprisonment nor the death penalty may be applied when Christians disagree on theological questions or need to take disciplinary measures. By contrast, the confessionalization process against which Marpeck was arguing identified the "heretics" (i.e. Anabaptists) as "criminals" and assumed that differences among Christians could be solved politically and militarily. The *Exposé* clearly rejected such a strategy. Echoing the Luther of 1523, Marpeck claimed that, among Christians, there was no need for civil authority: "For the brotherhood of Christ is patience and love, does not have nor desires to have either Authority or subjects, but is one in Christ."[58]

Marpeck clinched his argument with a barrage of biblical texts presented in an Anabaptist hermeneutical perspective and a distinctive reading of church history which offers an interesting glimpse of his understanding of the historical context of these events and the Reformation itself. According to this reading of history, the early Church, from the time of the Apostles until the emperor Constantine, used neither political force nor the sword.[59] If someone would not listen to the admonition of the community and needed "disciplining," that person was considered a pagan or an unbeliever but was not "punished" by civil authorities. However, in the fourth century the Pope "married" the Leviathan (temporal authority) in the name of Christ, thus giving birth to the Antichrist. This "secret of iniquity" had only been recently revealed, along with the new Antichrist

---

greifft sie an und streit widder si un wil sie unter drucken und selbs Herre sein und recht stellen, wie der Müntzer thut. . . ." *WA*, XXX, 282.

[56] *Exposé*, 35.

[57] *Exposé*, 36.

[58] *Exposé*, 37.

[59] *Exposé*, 38. Stephen Boyd has shown that Marpeck is probably following Sebastian Franck on this point. Boyd, *Pilgram Marpeck*, 60.

(the Evangelical preachers and their union against the emperor). Referring perhaps to persecution of the Anabaptists, Marpeck commented that this terrible beast did a better job of killing innocent people than any pagan government ever had.[60]

The conclusion of the *Exposé* is devoted to one last major biblical argument against the intervention of civil authorities in spiritual and theological questions: the parable of the weeds (Mt. 13: 24-29; 36-43).[61] After citing the entire parable and its explanation,[62] Marpeck drew out its meaning in terms of how the church should respond to political coercion. Christ came to save and not to destroy, which means that all should have the possibility of being saved until the last day. In other words, the time that remains before the Last Judgment is a time when repentance should be offered to all people.[63] Civil government may judge outer (temporal) and contemporary questions (*das ausswendig unnd gegenwürtig*) during this time, but not future and inner (spiritual) questions. Otherwise, the grace of God is cut short and civil authority usurps the role of God's judgment.

The political meaning of the parable is that Christians are not to use the sword or coercion in theological and spiritual questions. Faith may not be imposed, and the only weapon to be used in this case is patience, i.e., nonviolence. Those who use the sword to judge in matters of faith will themselves be judged by the sword.[64]

Marpeck based this argument on a Lutheran theme – justification by faith – which he interpreted in an Anabaptist perspective. Having

---

[60] "No heathen tyrant ever murdered and killed so thoroughly. The most horrible monster, turning even against it own kind..." *Exposé*, 39.
[61] Erasmus used this parable to argue for tolerance in religious matters.
[62] *Exposé*, 39-40.
[63] "For as long as a person remains in this mortal life, no matter how wicked he may be, he may be converted to a better life through the grace of Christ and the patience and love shown to him by those around him." *Exposé*, 40.
[64] "He also instructs his own by the foregoing parable to wait. He commands no one to condemn and kill with the sword. Virtually the whole of Matt. chapter 5 testifies that no one is to be coerced or dominated. Rather, the disciples allow themselves to be forced and dominated and to submit to what is done to them with patience. Those who do the opposite are of the world and are not Christ's, are unbelievers and do not have faith. Those who fight with the sword will be condemned by the sword." *Exposé*, 41.

faith meant trusting in God and not in other powers, including civil authority. Outside of faith nothing is pure, nothing is acceptable to God.[65] Justification of one's cause comes through this faith alone and this trust finds expression in a patient refusal to impose one's position. Either one trusts God's word and allows that word to justify and defend the faith or there is no faith: "In Christ, through faith, the only sword is the Word; with this only Christians judge and are judged."[66] Using political coercion meant, for Marpeck, an absence of faith in God's power to justify and defend his cause and his people.

Conclusion

Strasbourg had been a city of hope for Anabaptists and Spiritualists in the 1520s. The course that the Reformation was taking in 1531 and 1532 clearly meant that even this small ray of hope would soon disappear. Marpeck's *Exposé* revealed a keen awareness of what was happening and attempted to respond to this new course of events. If, as appears to be the case, this document was indeed contemporary with Marpeck's debates with Bucer, it was one of the last examples of an Anabaptist trying to converse with the "official" Reformation before the final dividing lines had been drawn.

Marpeck left Strasbourg sometime in January 1532. By the end of February the statutes of the Schmalkaldic League had been prepared, the right to resist the emperor was accepted, and a war council and budget for war had been established.[67] The results of these preparations are well known. The princes assumed full control over the churches. Efforts to establish the political and confessional unity of Christian territories through the "interpenetration" of politics and religion dominated the second half of the sixteenth century. French historian Marc Venard suggests that Luther's tendency to consider questions of organization and power as secondary

---

[65] Ibid.
[66] Ibid.
[67] Luther's *Warnung* shows that he was not happy with this turn of events and that he only very reluctantly accepted what happened. Marpeck's criticisms did not always take this fact into account.

opened the door to this process.⁶⁸ Heiko Oberman goes even further to argue that "things could not have turned out otherwise."

> The Anabaptists excited attention at that time not so much for their beliefs . . . as for their activities in the realm of politics: they were rebellious conspirators, dangerous to the common good, who, quite simply, compromised the cause of the Lutheran Reformation. The Protestant Estates could not afford to be seen as rebels and schismatics – like the Anabaptists – under pain of death. In 1530, moreover, commitment to the unity of the Church was inseparable from the struggle for the unity of the empire.⁶⁹

On the other hand, Marpeck's critique of constantinian forms of Christianity made it possible for him to separate the unity of the Church from the unity of the empire. Regardless of whether or not things could have turned out otherwise, the *Exposé* makes clear that in the midst of the confessionalization process, dissident and critical voices found expression. Not only were these options expressed verbally, but they were also being embodied concretely in the lives of small communities of people who were willing to suffer exile or death for their convictions.

---

⁶⁸ Ibid, 41.
⁶⁹ Oberman, *The Reformation*, 163.

Chapter 4

The Christological Synthesis of 1542

Historical prologue

From 1532 to 1544, Marpeck resided in Switzerland and travelled to Tyrol, Moravia, South Germany and Alsace where he established congregations and had contact with the Hutterites and Swiss Brethren.

By 1544 (until his death in 1556) he was working in Augsburg's city forest near Füssen. Although warned three times to desist from Anabaptist activity, he participated in the leadership of a group which met in his home on public property. He continued significant correspondence with Anabaptist groups in Switzerland, Alsace, South Germany and Moravia.[1]

Marpeck's Admonition

No known writings further develop Marpeck's Christology until 1542, ten years after the presentation of his confession to the Council of Strasbourg and the *Exposé*. The rejection of Anabaptism by Strasbourg was a severe

---
[1] Stephen Boyd, "Marpeck, Pilgram" in *ME* V, 538.

blow only to be reinforced by the catastrophe of Münster in 1534-1535. The Empire-wide death penalty for rebaptism (1529) now seemed more than justified in the eyes of most European church leaders and politicians. Even if physical and geographical traces of Marpeck are hard to find during this period, the treatise examined in the following pages shows that his theological development was not put on hold, that he kept on reading and reflecting and that his concern for the unity of the Anabaptist communities with whom he related was quite real.

The greatest part of this chapter will examine the Christology of the *Admonition*,[2] an important book in Marpeck's career for its lengthy theological developments and for the reaction it provoked from Schwenckfeld. For quite understandable reasons, the text itself indicates no author, date, nor the city of publication. A letter from Schwenckfeld dating from the twenty-first of August 1542 indicates that Pilgram Marpeck was one of its authors.[3] This letter also allows us to date the text, because Schwenckfeld wrote a critique (*Judicium* or *Judgment*)[4] of this *Admonition*, and this critique is mentioned for the first time in the letter. Also in the *Judgment* itself, it is observed that the *Admonition* was written in 1542. Thus Marpeck's text had to be written relatively early in the year 1542 to give time for Schwenckfeld to write his response before the twenty-first of August.

The *Admonition* presents itself as a type of "corporate" confession of faith; i.e. that of the network of scattered and clandestine Anabaptist communities related in one way or another through their recognition of a common theological base.[5] The contents of the book display the influence

---

[2] Two copies of this work exist, one in London and the other in Stuttgart. Quotes from the original text will be made from the edition of Christian Hege, *Gedenkschrift zum 400 Jahrigen Jubilaum der Mennoniten oder taufgesinnten*, 185-282. It will be cited simply as *V*, using the page numbers of the *Gedenkschrift*.

[3] CS 8, 161. Elsewhere Schwenckfeld writes that he thinks that there are two authors. This other person was most likely Marpeck's colleague Leupold Scharnschlager. But in the letter cited here, Schwenckfeld mentions only the name of Marpeck.

[4] The title of Schwenckfeld's critique begins thus: "Ueber das new buechlein der tauffbrueder im 1542 iar ausgangen Judicium," see Loserth, 65.

[5] *WPM*, 38.

and the thought of Marpeck, but his role is more that of a translator-editor than of a primary author. In 1956, Frank Wray demonstrated that the *Admonition* was in fact a translation and revision of the *Bekentnisse Van Beyden Sacramenten, Doepe und Nachtmaele*, ("Confession concerning the two Sacraments: Baptism and Lord's Supper") written in 1531 by the Münsterite preachers in Westphalia.[6] Bernard Rothmann is considered the principal author of the *Bekentnisse*, but William Klassen underlines the fact that these two texts need to be seen as texts belonging to groups and not representing the thought of any single individual.[7]

The longest section of the *Admonition* is a direct translation of the *Bekentnisse*, with certain additions and revisions. These changes were made necessary by the events that took place at Münster in 1534-1535. The preface is mostly rewritten, as is a large part of the conclusion. Interestingly enough, two important sections of the *Admonition* address Christological questions. These are not found in Rothmann's text but were added by Marpeck.[8] Indeed the most important Christological passages are from Marpeck's pen and, though one must seek always to distinguish between Marpeck and Rothmann's work in our study, one can still affirm that the complete text represents Marpeck and his colleagues' point of view. The preface of the *Admonition* notes that other sources have been used without specifying which ones, adding that what was true in the other sources has remained; what was false has been corrected.[9]

The structure of the *Admonition* is quite simple. Following the table of contents and a preface, a short discussion of the understanding of sacrament leads into a long section on baptism (60 pages), a section on the Lord's Supper (20 pages) and a brief conclusion. The *Admonition* is the longest and most detailed Anabaptist text on the sacraments.[10]

---

[6] F. J. Wray, "The 'Vermanung' of 1542 and Rothman's 'Bekentnisse;'" *ARG* 47 (1956), 243-251.
[7] *Covenant and Community*, 136.
[8] The English translation of the *Vermanung* ("The Admonition of 1542," in *WPM*, 159-302) notes in italics where Marpeck adds to or changes Rothmann's text.
[9] *V*, 188.
[10] *WPM*, 159.

The stated purpose of this text is to unify and strengthen the diverse groups of Anabaptists. In the introduction, the *Admonition* is presented as a witness to all those searching for the truth.[11] The proclamation of the truth is necessary over against the recent and ancient errors that divide Christians and lead to the formation of harmful sects.[12] Marpeck's time in Strasbourg was extremely influential and decisive because he reflects on sects and divisions dating back twelve years prior (1530).[13] The reader is invited to read and judge what is presented. All who are convinced by this testimony and wish to join themselves to this covenant[14] in Christ are invited to do so. Perhaps the text can be read as an effort at Anabaptist theological regrouping after Münster parallel to what was going on in the Low Countries under the leadership of Dirk Philips and Menno Simons.

After analyzing and accepting the word "sacrament" in a more or less "Zwinglian" perspective (i.e. anything done in relation to an oath or to a similar obligation), the *Admonition* proposes to define baptism and the Lord's Supper in a purely biblical perspective. The misunderstanding and the misuse of these two sacraments are at the origin of all the problems in the Church. In fact, the *Admonition* claims there are three elements necessary for the reform of the Church: the preaching of the Gospel, true baptism, and true Lord's Table.

> And when the matter is placed in proper perspective, we can say that if these three things – the true proclamation of the gospel, correct baptism, and correct communion – are in doubt, there can be no true church of Christ. If one of these parts is missing, it is not possible outwardly to maintain and support a true Christian church.[15]

---

[11] Ibid., 166-168.
[12] Ibid.
[13] *WPM*, 163.
[14] The concept of covenant (alliance - bundt) is central in the *Vermanung*, to the extent that it is also called the "buchlein der buntzbezeugung" or the "bundszeugnus." See Loserth, 72, 77-78. Schwenckfeld calls it the "taufbuchlein," Kiwiet, 73.
[15] *WPM*, 292. One is tempted here to see an Anabaptist commentary on the Lutheran conception of the church as expressed in the Confession of Augsburg, article 7 (...the

The Lutheran principle of *fides ex auditu* (faith comes from that which is heard) becomes the basis for adult baptism. The logic is quite simple. As the Good News is preached, it brings about the recognition of sin and repentance. The function of baptism is to gather those who heard this Word, repented, accepted the forgiveness of sins, and henceforth walk in newness of life. Baptism is both the personal commitment of the individual and the doorway into the Christian community.[16]

> Then upon verbal confession of the sound faith, which he believes with his heart, he shall be baptized, in God's name, or in Jesus Christ. That is, he shall be baptized, in God's name and in Christ's, when he is cleansed of sin by repentance and faith, and enters into an unblemished, obedient way of life. So shall the holy church be gathered through baptism…[17]

In this perspective, the function of the Lord's Supper, in addition to commemorating the death of the Lord, is double.

> The one function is that the Holy Christian church shall be held together by it, and be maintained in a united faith and Christian love. The other that all evil and all that does not belong to the holy, pure church of Christ and is offensive may be cut off and banned.[18]

Marpeck's use of a Münsterite text in his attempt to unify the Anabaptists might be surprising. But in his adaptation he explicitly rejects any recourse to force or violence, which demonstrates his care to distinguish himself from the events of the "kingdom" of Munster.

---

assembly of all believers where the gospel is preached faithfully and the holy sacraments administered in conformity to the Gospel).

[16] This corresponds to what T. Finger writes about Marpeck's understanding of baptism: "Baptism involved co-witness among all the following realities: inner faith and outer ceremony, a spiritual reality and its material expression, individual and congregational commitment…" *Contemporary Anabaptist Theology*, 170.

[17] *WPM*, 294-295. This citation shows that G. Williams is mistaken to write that the *Vermanung* does not emphasize the ecclesiological importance of baptism (*Radical Reformation*, 1st edition, 474). The fact that baptism constitutes the entry into the church is one of the principal points of the *Vermanung*.

[18] *WPM*, 297.

The task of assessing the influence of the *Admonition* amidst the Anabaptists of the sixteenth century is quite difficult. Despite Marpeck's struggle against the Hutterite notion of a community of goods,[19] a copy of the *Admonition* was found in the Hutterite archives.[20] Around 1553, Marpeck wrote that he would send 20 copies to the communities in Moravia.[21] Martin Rothkegel has shown that the *Admonition* was also part of theological discussions going on in Moravia outside of Anabaptist circles at about the same time.[22] Another non-Anabaptist reference to the *Admonition* is found in the writings of Heinrich Bullinger in 1560. Zwingli's successor in Zurich affirms that the Anabaptists peddled this book and valued it as *das allerhochwurdigste Heiligtum* (the most high and worthy holy thing).[23] Bullinger's remark takes on new credibility given Arnold Snyder and Hanspeter Jecker's recent findings about Marpeck's probable influence among the Swiss Brethren in the second half of the sixteenth-century.[24]

---

[19] For Marpeck the community of goods cannot be required systematically as a mark (sign) of the church as the Hutterites demanded. If it exists, it must be a freely given choice.
[20] *WPM*, 159. One must also recall Marpeck's visit to the Hutterites in 1541 and the report that he left them disgruntled and somewhat bitterly.
[21] In a letter (that is not dated, but is probably from around 1553) and sent to Anabaptist communities (not Hutterites) Marpeck wrote "Weiter schicken wir euch hiemit 20 bundtzeuknussen…" *Kunstbuch*, 166 v.
[22] Martin Rothkegel, "Benes Optat, 'On Baptism and the Lord's Supper': An Utraquist Reformer's Opinion of Pilgram Marpeck's *Vermahnung*," *MQR*, (July 2005), 359-381.
[23] H. Fast, *Heinrich Bullinger und die Täufer* (Weierhof: Mennonitischen Geschichtsverein, 1959), 126.
[24] Cf. C. Arnold Snyder, "The (Not-So) 'Simple Confession' of the Later Swiss Brethren. Part I: Manuscripts and Marpeckites in an Age of Print" *MQR* (October 1999), 677-722; "The (Not-So) 'Simple Confession' of the Later Swiss Brethren. Part II: The Evolution of Separatist Anabaptism" *MQR* (January 2000), 87-122 and Hanspeter Jecker, *Ketzer-Rebellen-Heilige. Das Basler Täufertum von 1580-1700*, (Verlag des Kantons Basel Landschaft, 1998), 599-600. Cf. Claude Baecher, "Le jugement eschatologique des puissants chez les anabaptistes," in N. Blough, *Eschatologie et vie quotidienne* (Cléon d'Andran: Editons Excelsis, 2001), 40 and *Les eschatologies anabaptistes de la haute vallée rhénane en débat avec les réformateurs (1524-1535)*, (Villeneuve d'Ascq: Presses Universitaires du Septentrion, 1996), 543.

The Humanity of Christ: The Material Function
The Unity of Inner and Outer Baptisms

In the section of the *Admonition* that addresses baptism, Marpeck explains the relationships that exist between the inner and outer baptisms. He responds at the same time to two different positions: the first that makes of baptism the necessary act to save children from original sin and the second that sees no necessary relation between the two baptisms. Marpeck's theology of baptism here helps develop his understanding of the humanity of Christ that was noted in *A Clear Instruction*. Due to their importance, a number of passages will be cited at greater length to portray the function of Marpeck's Christology in the argumentation about baptism. In the following passage, Marpeck explains "inner" and "outer" baptism.

> Moreover to dunk into water or to pour water over someone in baptism is a sign, namely, a sign of the burying of the flesh, of the laying aside and washing of sin, and of the putting on of Jesus Christ. *Whoever has the truth in the heart, the truth, which is pointed to and signified by the external sign, for him it is no sign at all, but rather one reality*[25] *with the inner.* If however, I receive the sign and do not have the reality[26] in my heart, what would this sign benefit anyone? Would it not be a mockery of Him in whose name I receive it? Accordingly if one desires to receive the external sign correctly, he must certainly bring with him the inner and the outer reality[27] (*wesen*) together; *wherever and whenever that happens, then the signs are no longer signs, but are one in Christ, according to the inner and the outer being. For that which the Father does, the Son does simultaneously: the Father, as Spirit, internally; the Son, as Man, externally. Therefore the external baptism and the Lord's Supper in Christ are not signs; rather, they are the external work*

---

[25] I have replaced *WPM's* "essential union" and translated *wesen* as "reality." The original reads *ein wesen mit dem innwendigen* (*V*, 207). When citing the original, we will leave "wesen" as it is in the text and not modernise with "Wesen."

[26] For reasons that will become clear as Marpeck's thought develops, I prefer to translate *wesen* by the English term "reality" rather than essence or substance, so I will continually modify the translation of *WPM*. Marpeck is not talking about "substance" but about intention, meaning and action. Cf Boyd, *Pilgram Marpeck*, 119.

[27] *wesen* in the original.

> *and the reality*[28](*wesen*) *of the Son. For whatever the Son sees the Father doing, the Son also does immediately.*[29]

In this passage, inner and outer baptism are unified to create one single baptism. We saw in the Confession of 1532 that Marpeck understood water baptism as the necessary testimony to the initial baptism of the Spirit. Here Marpeck returns to this foundation and develops it in a fascinating manner in that baptism receives both a Trinitarian and a Christological foundation. The inner and outer acts correspond to the work of the Trinity. Marpeck bases himself on John 5:19 ("for whatever the Father does, the Son does likewise"). He apparently follows the Zurich (Froschauer) Bible but modifies the German text slightly to reinforce his point. In German Marpeck writes: "dann was der vatter thut, das thut auch zugleich der sun des menschens."[30] In English "likewise" is the word that translates the Greek term "ὅμοιος." In the German Bibles of the sixteenth century (Zurich and Luther) one finds the word "gleich," which does correspond to "likewise" and which renders well "ὅμοιος." Marpeck changes "gleich" into "zugleich," which can be translated "immediately." Changing "gleich" to "zugleich" emphasizes the temporal unity of the Father and Son's actions.

In this perspective, the outer sign is not valid without the inner witness of the Holy Spirit, and at the same time, the action of the Holy Spirit always needs an outer testimony. When this dual action takes place, however, the outer sign is no longer a sign but becomes a new reality because of the Spirit's presence. Inner and outer baptism thus correspond to the working of the Trinity. The Father acts internally by the Holy Spirit in the heart of humans and the Son acts externally, through water, "at the same time." The Trinitarian link strengthens what we previously saw in relation to the humanity of Christ, where "ceremonies" are an extension of the Incarnation. The ceremonies accomplished by believers in the power of the Spirit correspond to the work of Christ and "prolong" his humanity on earth.

---

[28] *wesen* in the original.
[29] *WPM*, 194-195. The italics show Marpeck's additions to Rothmann's text.
[30] Zurich Bible: "Dann was der selb thut / das thut gleych auch der sun." Luther: "Denn was derselbige thut, das thut gleych auch der Sohn."

Thus the children born of the Spirit and nature of Christ also do that which the Father, through the Spirit, performs in the inner man; they also perform externally as members of the body of Christ in baptism and the Lord's Supper. [...] Thus, in Christ, no longer does any sign exist, only reality (*wesen*), one baptism, one faith, one God, one Father of us all. Therefore baptism is done in the name of the Father, the Son, and the Holy Spirit, for the Son of Man cannot be without the Father and the Spirit, nor can the Spirit and the Father be without the Son of Man. Consequently the external reality (*wesen*) of the Son is one in reality (*wesen*), and works in the Father and the Spirit. Therefore, whenever a spirit comes who does not bring with him the external things, such as teaching, baptism, and the Supper of Christ the Man, whatever he has spoken, acted, done are denials of the Son of Man and not the Spirit of the Father. Furthermore, whoever would merely steal external teaching, speech, deeds, baptism, and the Lord's Supper out of the Scriptures ... without true faith ... in him the truth does not exist. It is evident now that, in Christ, no longer is a sign a sign, but only pure reality (*wesen*) through faith.[31]

Thus the sacraments and all outer actions receive a Trinitarian foundation. The Father takes the initiative in the heart of the believers and those touched by the power of the Holy Spirit act and witness externally. This outer action becomes the "humanity of Christ," the body of Christ on earth, i.e. the Son of Man who always acts externally. Marpeck uses Ephesians 4:5 ("one Lord, one faith, one baptism") and Matthew 28:19 ("Go therefore and make disciples of all nations, baptizing them in the name of the Father and of the Son and of the Holy Spirit") in order to reinforce his argument for the unity of the inner and outer baptism, but the fundamental logic displayed here is applicable to any outer action and not only to baptism.

---

[31] WPM, 195-196. (This section is entirely from Marpeck and not Rothmann).

The Notion of "wesen" Clarified

What did Marpeck mean when he affirmed that the outer sign is no longer a sign when the Spirit and faith are present? On account of the Trinitarian context of this passage, one can assume that in the same way that the Son of Man is part of the Trinitarian reality, each outer action accompanied by the inner reality also participates in the being of the Trinity. A letter written to Helena Streicher,[32] dating from the same period as the *Admonition* helps clarify the above citations.[33] This letter addresses the same subject, but Marpeck is yet more explicit than he was in the *Admonition*.

---

[32] Helena was a widow from Ulm, and an follower of Schwenckfeld. Cf. C. Arnold Snyder and Linda A. Huebert Hecht, eds. *Profiles of Anabaptist Women. Sixteenth-Century Reforming Pioneers* (Wilfred Laurier University Press, 1996), 112-113.

[33] This letter was written by Marpeck, but circulated under the name of a certain Magdalena Marschalck von Pappenheim. See Kiwiet, *Pilgram Marbeck*, 59-61; T. Bergsten, *Pilgram Marbeck und seine Auseinandersetzung*, 47-51; and G. Williams, *Radical Reformation*, 1st edition, 468. Magdalena sent it to Schwenckfeld's friend, Helena Streicher, who passed it on to Schwenckfeld himself. Kiwiet, *Pilgram Marpeck*, dates the letter from the summer of 1542 (60), which places it at the same period as the *Vermanung*. The text of the letter can be found in Loserth, 179-188 and in *WPM*, 376-389. What is important to note is that this letter dates from the period before Schwenckfeld's critique. Williams (468) believes that this letter as well as the *Vermanung* provoked Schwenckfeld's critical response in the *Judicium*. The preface of the letter from the sixteenth-century manuscripts confirms this timeframe and reaction: "Dise nachvolgende epistle ist der frau Helena Streichern gen Ulm geschriben worden und wider den brueder Billgram Marpeck und der junkfrau Magdalena Marschalckin von Bappenheim geschriben, und im buech des Judiciums findt mans, was den Schwenckfelder bewegt hat, so die warhait an tag ist kummen und die unwarhait hat weichen müessen." Loserth, 179.

These affirmations are cited because the English translation does not take note of them and dates the letter from about 1544 (and not 1542), stating "Although no date is assigned to this letter, it must be after 1542. The tone and the language suggest that relations between Marpeck and Schwenckfeld had deteriorated." *WPM*, 581, note 1. The criteria used for dating the letter by Klassen was that there had not been any conflicts between the two men in 1542. This point is contradicted by Schwenckfeld himself. On August 21, 1542, he wrote to Magdalena: "Allain das ich ainen brief unnd als sichs lest ansehen, des Pilgrams gedichte under eurem Namen, welchen auch die Brueder getragen, gelesen, auss deme ich wol hab vernemen megen, das mein auch drunder gedacht unnd alls das schreiben aussweisset, ich euch nicht mit dem freuntlischten bin eintragen worden…" CS 8, 217. This proves that the relations had already deteriorated in 1542 and (contra *WPM*) the letter mentioned here is indeed the letter to Helena, which proves that it was written

Because he is more explicit, Marpeck begins to develop his thought in a way that will cause some difficulties. That is he founds his notion of "*wesen*" not only on the doctrine of the Trinity, but also on the two natures of Christ, which means that he sometimes confuses the Holy Spirit and the divine nature of Christ, something that is not "theologically correct" in the Christological tradition of the early and medieval Church.

In the letter to Helena Streicher, Marpeck writes that the physical voice of Christ is the means by which the Spirit acts on earth. Thus, as there is one baptism (which consists of two different elements), "there is one single teaching, outer and inner, and not two, in Christ."[34] The physical voice of Christ without the Spirit is not his true voice. In the following texts the term "Spirit and life" (cf. John 6:63, "the words I have spoken to you are spirit and life") conveys the same meaning as "*wesen*" in the *Admonition*.

> First, I would question whether the physical voice of Christ the Lord can be separated from the Spirit and life. That voice is an outer, physical, magnificent voice, for the same physical voice of Christ enabled the Holy Spirit to have its sovereign movement. ... But, even though it was, admittedly, an external, human, and audible voice, the physical voice of Christ never simply came from Christ without Spirit and life. Whatever the Son sees the Father doing, the Son of the Father will also do, and He will act both as the Son, who has God and the Spirit in Him, and as the man, who comes from the flesh of the children of man.[35]

This passage clarifies the meaning of the sign that becomes "*wesen*." The Spirit joins itself to the outer and both things become one complete reality. What is new in the letter to Helena Streicher is that the doctrine of the two natures of Christ becomes the source of this idea. The physical voice of Christ is "truth" because Christ is at once both "Son of the Father, Spirit and God" and "flesh of the family of humankind." The humanity

---

before August 21, 1542. For this reason we use it in this chapter as a text that reinforces and interprets the *Admonition*.
[34] Loserth, "Letter to Helena Streicher," 180.
[35] *WPM*, 378.

of Christ is divine because the Spirit is present, but the Spirit cannot act without this humanity. When by faith the Spirit is joined to the outer elements, this same element becomes "Spirit and life," or a "*wesen*" with the inner realm.

> But, where the Holy Spirit moves and creates life, there, too, the same physical reality becomes Spirit and life through faith in Christ; it remains elemental for the sake of comprehension, sensitivity, and endurance, which man has according to his nature. Does it not follow that, if one uses the physical elements for the sake of Christ's command, these elements would also be Spirit and life, but not merely because of their physical nature? Otherwise, it would have to follow that, although he was the word, Spirit, and life from eternity, and became flesh, of the seed of David, the physical and earthly, but now heavenly and glorified, Son who is the same as the Father in essence, had not been Spirit and life. Far be it from us that we ourselves should divide the Lord in such a manner that the outer is separated from the inner, and the inner from the outer; we, still being earthly creatures, have been made spirit by God, through the faith in Christ. We are, and remain, human as long as we have not discarded the earthly, which only occurs in physical death.[36]

In this passage Marpeck explicitly uses the example of the person of Jesus Christ to explain how the inner and the outer become a single "*wesen*" or "Spirit and life." If, on the one hand, there is no union of the divine and human natures in Jesus Christ, the unity of the inner and the outer cannot subsist. But, on the other hand, if this union of the two natures does exist, it is not possible to separate the inner and outer realities in the lives of Christians.

This principle is necessary for human beings because of our material and corporal nature. We can only know God by that which is sensible and tangible. Just as God, who is Spirit, became flesh and blood in order to reveal divine reality, revelation continues throughout history in a way that is simultaneously a spiritual and material reality, both inner and outer. The Trinity is the guarantee that God continues to work both outwardly and inwardly as was the case in the Incarnation.

---

[36] *WPM*, 379.

The Influence of Luther

What was examined above is new insofar as Marpeck explicitly refers to the Trinity (in the *Admonition*) and to the doctrine of the two natures of Christ (in the letter to Helena von Streicher). We have seen above that Marpeck reasoned in a manner parallel to Luther in relation to the humanity of Christ. Is he now developing this key idea in an original fashion? In his study of baptism in the thought of Marpeck, R. S. Armour observes that the synthesis of inner and outer is the most interesting contribution to an Anabaptist theology of baptism,[37] and that thus Marpeck's doctrine of baptism is the most profound of the many diverse Anabaptist theologies.[38] Hans-Jürgen Goertz describes the manner in which Marpeck describes the inner and outer relations as original.[39] In an article that discusses Marpeck's understanding of church discipline, Walter Klaassen observes that through his synthesis of inner and outer, Marpeck was the most creative and original of all the Anabaptist theologians.[40]

Armour suggests that Marpeck's starting point can be found in the Gospel of John.[41] This may well be true but again there exists an interesting parallel with Luther. First of all, the Gospel of John is foundational for Luther in regard to his conception of the humanity of Christ and to the relations between this humanity and the Holy Spirit.[42] In addition, those who have studied Luther's thought arrive at very interesting conclusions when compared with what was seen above in Marpeck's writings. Regin Prenter claims that the foundation for the inner/outer relations in Luther's theology finds its starting point in the doctrine of the Trinity. Could one not make a similar affirmation about Marpeck?

---

[37] Armour, *Anabaptist Baptism*, 160.
[38] Ibid., 134. "This was, without question, the most perceptive and profound of the theologies of baptism in our study."
[39] Goertz, *Die Täufer*, 92. "Der Gedanke, wie beide Werke miteinander verknupft werden, ist originell und so bei Rothmann nicht zu finden."
[40] Walter Klaassen, "Church Discipline and the Spirit in Pilgram Marpeck," in Irvin Horst, et al., *De Geest in het Geding* (Willink: H.D. Tjeenk, 1978), 180.
[41] Armour, *Anabaptist Baptism*, 124.
[42] See for example, J. Atkinson, "Luthers Einschätzung des Johannesevangeliums," in V. Vajta, ed., *Lutherforschung Heute* (Berlin: Lutherisches Verlagshaus, 1958), 49-56.

> In his writing *Wider die himmlischen Propheten*, Luther spoke of the fact that God acts toward us in two different ways; externally by the oral Word of the Gospel and the living signs, i.e. baptism and the Lord's Supper, internally by the Holy Spirit and faith as well as by other gifts. These inner and outer actions correspond to the Spirit and to Christ. The fact that the outer signs and the inner action of the Spirit are paired is founded on the Trinitarian doctrine. The Spirit that Luther speaks of here is the Spirit that proceeds from the Father and the Son. His action consists in the fact of leading us in Christ to the Father. But this cannot happen by any other means than outer signs, because we find in them, and only in them, the humanity of Christ, under the protective cover by which the Father seeks to meet us.[43]

Describing unity between outer signs and inner actions via the doctrine of the Trinity is thus in no way original. Once again, Marpeck is quite close to Luther's thinking here. Even if he does arrive at different conclusions, the theological foundation is the same. The concept of a sign that becomes "*wesen*" or "Spirit and life" is not too far off from the thought of Luther either. Marc Lienhard writes:

> We will never emphasize enough Luther's insistence not only on the flesh of Christ, but also on the bodily element in general. Lutheran thought never admitted the strict dualism that western thought has affirmed since Saint Augustine. In fact, the fundamental dualism is not that which opposes the spirit to matter or the body; but is that which opposes faith to sin. *There where there is faith, all becomes "spirit."*[44]

"Where there is faith, all becomes 'spirit.'" Marpeck writes: "where the Holy Spirit moves and creates life, there, too, the same physical reality becomes Spirit and life through faith in Christ."[45] Luther writes: "All that our body does externally and corporately, in the measure that the Word of God is added and accomplished by faith, all that is and is called a spiritual event."[46]

---

[43] R. Prenter, *Spiritus Creator*, 285
[44] Lienhard, *Luther Témoin*, 216. My italics.
[45] *WPM*, 379. Loserth, "Letter to Helena Streicher," 181.
[46] *WA* 23, 189, cited by Lienhard, *Luther Témoin*, 216.

Since this logic leads Luther to the doctrine of the real presence, one might ask if Marpeck arrives there as well, as Schwenckfeld maintained that he had. In the next chapter it will become even clearer that Marpeck values the sacraments and all outer aspects of the Christian life in a way unique among sixteenth-century Anabaptists. Nevertheless he does not arrive at the same conclusion as Luther in regard to the real presence of Christ in the Lord's Supper. William Klassen thinks that Marpeck, in formulating his thought in the *Admonition*, feels himself caught between the positions of Luther and Zwingli.[47] Why does Marpeck not adopt the notion of the real presence? Perhaps the answer to this question can be found in his conception of the two natures of Christ and in the fact that he will let go of his Trinitarian foundation for the inner/outer relations (a foundation that is close to Luther's thought) in order to base himself more fully on the doctrine of the two natures of Christ. The next chapter will examine in greater detail the manner in which Marpeck conceives of this inner/outer "reality." In so doing, the answer to this last question will be addressed with greater clarity.

THE HUMANITY OF CHRIST: THE HISTORICAL FUNCTION

Not only did Marpeck expound on and develop the "material function" of the humanity of Christ in the *Admonition*, he also reinforced the "historical function" by conceptually integrating it with the "material function." In the first section on baptism, Marpeck added a long passage to Rothmann's text presenting the humanity of Christ more or less in the same way as in his *Confession of 1532*.[48] As he had done ten years earlier, Marpeck challenged the comparison of circumcision and infant baptism. The debate with Bucer had apparently affected Marpeck enough for him to begin this passage with a summary of Bucer's position on infant baptism.[49] Marpeck reiterates

---

[47] *Covenant and Community*, 66.
[48] *WPM*, 222-224.
[49] Compare *WPM* 222-224 with article 19 of "Bucers Apologie der Kindertaufe gegen pilgrim Marbeck," QGT VII, 400. In the *Admonition* he does not name Bucer, but the close citation suggests that he had kept Bucer's refutation of his confession.

what he wrote in his confession but also seeks to clarify his thought and strengthen his arguments in light of his opponent's objections.

The central argument is the same as ten years earlier. The Old Testament is presented as a covenant of promise, a promise fulfilled in the Incarnation. The humanity of Christ, through his death and resurrection, makes available the Holy Spirit, which was not present in the same way before the Incarnation. All the same arguments are made here in the *Admonition* but the way in which Marpeck further develops a few of them is significant. In the Strasbourg text, Bucer had noted that Marpeck's position did not account for the biblical texts that affirmed that the patriarchs were justified (Romans 4:3; Galatians 3:6).[50] The *Admonition* responds to this criticism.

First Marpeck offered the image of someone who promises to reimburse a debt, while at the same time waiting for the guarantor to reimburse it.

> Similarly Abraham's belief is reckoned to be righteousness, which, as Paul speaks of it, is first found in Christ and is the fullness of time in Jesus Christ (Gal. 4:4). At that time God took pleasure in the ancients, and they in him. Similarly the debt of a lost evil debtor is borne patiently until the guarantor himself comes to pay the debt. Christ is a guarantor of a better testament than that of Abraham, Moses, David, and all the ancients, who had merely a physical foretaste.[51]

Second, Marpeck distinguishes between faith and justice in the two testaments with a series of contrasts.

> In summary, the ancients had a sketchy, figurative, yet symbolic faith, which focused on hope. Such faith was reckoned as a figurative righteousness, which all the ancient believers as followers of Abraham and his righteousness had. Just as a shadow points forward to the light and the figure to the *wesen*, the faith of the ancients pointed forward to Christ and his true believers, and pointed to the regenerate righteousness; it became really *wesslich* only in the righteousness of Christ, when he had become justified and when, in His true

---

[50] *QGT* VII, 417.
[51] *WPM*, 236.

glorified humanity, He took His seat at the right hand of the Father.[52]

These contrasts (shadow/light, figure/*wesen*) will be discussed in further detail in the next section on the "order of God." But first a brief examination of Marpeck's use of the contrast between figure and *wesen* will show how he brought together the material and historical functions of the humanity of Christ.

Bringing Together the Material and Historical Functions

As we saw, the terms "*wesen*" and "Spirit and life" play a crucial role in establishing the inner/outer relations in the discussion of baptism. These same concepts are now used to describe the historical function of the humanity of Christ. The notion of "*wesen*" strengthens the coherence of Marpeck's Christology, while keeping the humanity of Christ as the fundamental category.

An external act becomes "*wesen*" when this action originates in the inner action of the Holy Spirit. The Son acts externally as the Father acts internally through the Spirit. Both together (material and spiritual) become a single "*wesen*" (reality) or "Spirit and life."

The *Admonition* affirms that this "wesen" was not present before the Incarnation. The new reality that came with the humanity of Christ is now called a new "*wesen*."

> The old covenant is merely a covenant of promise. It is the prediction of God's pointing forward to a new being (*wesen*) in Christ Jesus, for in Christ Jesus all things, consciousness, feeling, and the heart of the believing man, have been made new. What was promised in the Old Testament is fulfilled in the humanity of Christ.[53]

Marpeck is totally convinced of the importance of the Spirit. Even though the humanity of Christ is fundamental in his theology, it is not an end in itself, but rather the means by which God reveals "spiritual" reality (*wesen*) to humanity. The Incarnation allows the definitive self-revelation

---
[52] Ibid, 233.
[53] Ibid, 225.

of God. Nevertheless Jesus' physical words and outer actions are not valid or true unless accompanied by the Holy Spirit. The Son alone, as a human being, can reveal nothing of the Father.

> Christ Himself, through His human physical speech, did not place this revelation into any one's heart without the revelation of the Father. After all, flesh and blood could not reveal the Son of God in truth.[54]

Even the disciples who were with Jesus could not understand the revelation of the Father before the Holy Spirit came to light and guide their way.

> This knowledge of the Father first began only in the Son, and in the Holy Spirit. For even the physical speech of Christ could not be endured by the apostles until they had been instructed by the Holy Spirit, until the physical sayings of Christ were brought to their remembrance.[55]

Marpeck relies strongly on the Gospel of John's promise of the gift of the Spirit after the resurrection (John 7:39; 14:26).[56]

Thus the Church of the New Testament depends as much on the Holy Spirit as on the humanity of Christ. The new "reality" (*wesen*) inaugurated by Christ establishes the new "community of the Spirit."

> ... the new church of Christ was built, but it was built only afterward, through the Holy Spirit, which was prophesied ahead of time and which Christ, the Man, achieved through his death.[57]

Now that the new "reality" (*wesen*) is present in history, it continues its work through the external reality of the humanity of Christ which is the Church.

> Here, it can be clearly seen how the Lord has built His church on His body and the body of believers. He built it first through the resurrection, and took His place with the resurrected

---

[54] Ibid., 228.
[55] Ibid., 228.
[56] Marpeck is aware of the problem he faces in stating that the Spirit was not present in the Old Testament. The next chapter addresses this question in greater detail.
[57] Ibid., 230.

body at the right hand of the Father. It is only then that the Holy Spirit could build His temple and church in the hearts of believers.[58]

With these concepts of "reality" (*wesen*) and Spirit, Marpeck integrates two different ways of understanding the role of the humanity of Christ. He was thus able to construct a Trinitarian and Incarnational Christology that allowed him to argue for the necessity of both water baptism (against the spiritualists) and adult baptism (against the Reformers and Catholics). The humanity of Christ brings a new "reality" (*wesen*), the Holy Spirit, into history, and the visible prolongation of the humanity of Christ in the Church's history implies that this *wesen* manifests itself visibly in the external and material realm. When the Spirit is present, material reality is transformed (without being "transubstantiated").

The humanity of Christ and the Ordnung Gottes

As noted above, the *Admonition* distinguishes between the two testaments using a series of oppositions. The fundamental contrast is between "figure" and "reality" (*wesen*) but others build on this one. The following pairs are found in the *Admonition*.[59]

Old Testament	**New Testament**
Figur (figure)	*Wesen* (reality)
Verhoffen gerechtigkeyt ("anticipated" justice)	*Wiedergebornen gerechtigkeit* (justice of new birth)
Knechtisch (servile)	*Kindlich* (filial)
Leiblich (corporeal)	*Geistlich* (spiritual)
Leiblich (corporeal)	*Wesenlich* (real)
Schatten (shadow)	*Liecht* (light)
Figurhen (figure)	*Warheit* (truth)

---

[58] Ibid., 232.
[59] Ibid., 231-241.

The main point of these contrasts is to establish a clear distinction between the covenants and to show how God acts according to the order (*Ordnung*) established by His Word. God's order (*ordnung Gottes*) includes the notions of time, space, and creaturehood. God acts by means of this order and not outside it. God could act in other ways, but doesn't. Thus, for Marpeck a distinction exists between the way things are before God in his divine essence and the way God acts within the framework of created reality. In medieval theology, this distinction was between the *potentia Dei ordinata* and the *potentia Dei absoluta*, that which God has ordained in distinction to God's absolute power.[60]

With this distinction in mind, Marpeck returns to the notion of "creatures" that he used in his anti-Spiritualist writings in Strasbourg and integrates this notion more fully with his understanding of the Incarnation. God is eternal, omnipotent, omniscient, etc., but has bound himself to the order established by his Word. This order is found in history and in creatures (or in the created order).[61] After affirming the eternal nature of God, the text continues:

> The providence of God, however, we allow to remain in its place, unperverted in the will of God itself. Yet, it would be a mockery of God, who has given order to all creation, and a contradiction of His divine will and order, to say that it follows that His providence has this form and has no order of time, place, or person of divine will. All creatures are ordered and disposed through the Word. Creatures, time, essence, place, and person must remain, and nothing can come to the fulfillment of the will of God without this means, for he has disclosed His will in His order of the creatures.[62]

The will or the order of God is found in the order of the creatures and this order originates in the Word of God. Thus, none can know the will of God without relying on "*das mittel*" that is found in the creatures

---

[60] Ibid., 233-234. For these medieval concepts, see Ozment, *Mysticism and Dissent*, 2.
[61] A relationship between God's order and creatures exists also in the thought of Thomas Müntzer. See H.-J. Goertz, *Innere und äußere Ordnung in der Theologie Thomas Muntzers* (Leiden: Brill, 1967), 40, note 1.
[62] WPM, 233-4.

and in all that is created by God, including time and space. Since God ordered the world in this manner, it was necessary for the Word to become a creature with all that is implied by that state of being.

> Thus, it was ordered that Christ, the Son of Man and seed of Abraham, must come as a creature of God, as a person and *wesen*, within history...[63]

As in the case of the earlier Strasbourg writings, the creatures are associated here with the outer realm where the humanity of Christ functions. In the *Admonition*, with the help of the notion of "God's order," the previously noted "Gospel of all creatures" becomes more intentionally related to the humanity of Christ. God chose to be revealed through the creatures, or in that which is created, and most fully in the "humanity of Christ."

The concept of God's order is in fact a polemical response to the Reformers' doctrine of predestination. In speaking of the "*potentia Dei absoluta,*" it is possible to affirm that everything is "present" before God and that God knows everything before events take place in history. But, using this affirmation to deny the important role of history in God's plan for salvation bypasses what God has ordained within history.[64]

In summary, with the help of the concept of "God's order," Marpeck affirms that God created the world, all creatures, and history. In order to become known and to save, God takes seriously his created order and is thus "bound" to this very created reality through his Word. The humanity of Christ is the means by which God's ultimate design in this order is accomplished.

---

[63] My translation, *V* 233: "Und also ist es auch mit Christo dem sun des menschens und samen Abrahams geordnet, das es nach der zeit, nach wesen und person, als ein creatur Gottes, fürüber muss gehen..."

[64] The *Admonition* states, "Otherwise, there would be no difference between Creator and creature, and everything would be merely a monkey show, an aping such as the world does when it puts on a play or an act... If it had taken place according to the election and providence of God, creation would have been adequate without a process of becoming real essence, and work would be an oversight. The despicable preachers of God can be accused of thus despising election and the providence of God without the order of history..." *WPM*, 234.

The Order of God: Marpeck and Schwenckfeld

Some have wondered if Marpeck's use of the concept of God's order was original with him. In 1957, without having access to more recently discovered works of Marpeck, Jan Kiwiet claimed that the notion of "*Ordnung Gottes*" was the key to Marpeck's thinking and that Marpeck had found his inspiration for the notion in the writings of Hans Denck.[65] Our analysis of writings not known to Kiwiet shows that Marpeck's use of the "humanity of Christ" takes him too far from the thinking of Denck for Kiwiet's thesis to be plausible.[66]

Since Marpeck's *Admonition* synthesizes various important elements of his thinking, one could imagine that he is being original on this point. However, the evidence does not point toward this conclusion. A very similar line of reasoning can be found in Schwenckfeld's writings where he uses the notion of God's order in his polemic against the doctrine of predestination. Schwenckfeld wrote repeatedly against predestination during his time in Strasbourg. In most of the documents previously cited that demonstrate Schwenckfeld's influence on Marpeck's idea of the humanity of Christ, Schwenckfeld also debated predestination similarly to what is noted in the *Admonition*.

Indeed, the series of contrasts distinguishing the two testaments, observed in the Marpeck's Circle's *Admonition*, can all be found in Schwenckfeld's writings from the Strasbourg period.[67] These oppositions are found precisely where the Silesian theologian addresses the differences

---

[65] Kiwiet, *Pilgram Marbeck*, 84.

[66] A more detailed argumentation on this point can be found in *Christologie anabaptiste*, 127-130.

[67] Compare Marpeck and Schwenckfeld's contrasts:

Marpeck (V, 232-238)	Schwenckfeld (writings from Strasbourg)
Figur/wesen	
Figur/warhait	Figur/warhait (CS 4, 414-443)
Leiblich/geistlich	Fleischlich/geistlich (CS 4, 549)
	Leiblich/geistlich (CS 4, 440)
Schatten/liecht	Schatt/liecht (CS 4, 531)
Knecht/kind	Knecht/kind (CS 4, 527)

In addition, Kiwiet uses these oppositions to explain his analysis of Marpeck's theology. Kiwiet, *Pilgram Marbeck*, 94-102.

between the testaments and as he debates predestination. In this period of Schwenckfeld's life, this polemic was a foundational element for his thought. He even claimed that many persons were pushed toward Anabaptism because of the Reformation doctrine of predestination. On March 14 1531, Schwenckfeld writes:

> I believe that this article alone is the reason for which many simple and pious men have become Anabaptist and have sought rebaptism.[68]

As with Marpeck, the difference between the covenants is the key to understanding the way God acts toward humans. Schwenckfeld also distinguishes between God "in-himself" and God bound to God's Word and to history.

> It is necessary to understand that God acts in two different ways towards men. First it is in the way in which things are before God and in God in his all-powerful essence, and second it is in the way God comes to us in the fullness of time. The first way concerns predestination or providence in terms of the hidden and secret will of God. The second concerns the Word and all action that God attributed to Christ in the flesh.[69]

Exactly as for Marpeck, for Schwenckfeld, God binds himself to the Word, to time and to space.[70]

Once again Marpeck's thought is extremely close to Schwenckfeld's, and since the notion of God's order is in the same documents where there is similarity concerning the humanity of Christ, the influence of Schwenckfeld here is also highly probable. Certainly Marpeck did not copy Schwenckfeld's words in an unthinking way, but he did use Schwenckfeld's ideas whenever they could help him make a point. For example, Marpeck emphasized the outer and the creatures in a way that can't be found in Schwenckfeld's writings. But the basic progression, i.e. the manner of conceiving of God's order beginning with creation and the Incarnation and the affirmation that God is "bound" to work within the framework of the created order, is the same with both men and is found in Schwenckfeld's

---

[68] *CS* 4, "De Praedestinatione," 93.
[69] *CS* 4, 108. See also 550-554, 439, 442.
[70] Ibid., 108, 442.

thought already in 1530; it only appears in Marpeck's writings in 1542. In addition since Schwenckfeld quite probably influenced Marpeck's conception of the humanity of Christ and since for Schwenckfeld the concepts of the humanity of Christ and God's order are intricately connected, it is logical to suppose that Marpeck would also be influenced by Schwenckfeld in his understanding of God's order.[71]

It might even be the case that Marpeck's notion of *wesen* ("reality") that is of such great import in the *Admonition* was a result of his reading Schwenckfeld.[72] Such influence cannot be proven definitively, but a comparison of the following two citations point to the strong parallels of thought and language.

> (Marpeck) *Das alt testament, ist alleyn ein testament des verheyssens und der zuzag Gottes, eines newen wesens in Christo Jesu… das in den alten allein verheyssen ist worden,…*[73]

> (Schwenckfeld) *…Christus der samen Abradhe, welchem die verheissung geschehen war, keme… und ein gantz neuw wesen… durch das Evangelium erfurer brechte.*[74]

---

[71] This thought pattern is not unique or original to Schwenckfeld but fits clearly within the medieval theological backdrop; cf. Klaus Deppermann, *Melchior Hoffman Soziale Unruhen und apokalyptische Visionen im Zeitalter der Reformation* (Göttingen: Vandenhoeck & Ruprecht, 1979), 197. The claim is simply being made that Marpeck probably learned of it by reading Schwenckfeld, given Marpeck's documented close reading of Schwenckfeld's writings.

[72] Bergsten, *Pilgram Marbeck und seine Auseinandersetzung*, 102 notes that Rothmann's text contrasts "zeichen/wesen" and that Marpeck might have simply taken the "wesen" terminology from there. Klassen, "The Relation of the Old and New Covenants in Pilgram Marpeck's Theology," (*MQR*, April 1966), 106, also shows how Marpeck uses certain biblical verses to describe the differences between the testaments with the adjective "wesentlich." These affirmations do not exclude Schwenckfeld's possible influence because we find not only the same term but also its same logical use in argumentation against the doctrine of predestination. That use is not the case when Rothmann uses the term nor for the biblical verses cited by Klassen (Col. 2:17; Heb. 10:1).

[73] V, 227, 28. See *WPM*, 225: "The old covenant is merely a covenant of promise. It is the prediction of God's pointing forward to a new being in Christ Jesus, for in Christ Jesus all things, consciousness, feeling, and the heart of the believing man, have been made new. What was promised in the Old Testament is fulfilled in the humanity of Christ." (my emphasis)

[74] *CS* 4, 530.

The following affirmations can be made in summary. (1) The concept of God's order is not the central axiom of Marpeck's theology, as Kiwiet thought. Rather, the concept of God's order was integrated at this point into Marpeck's Christology and functioned particularly to establish the historical function of the humanity of Christ. (2) This understanding of God's order was not drawn from Hans Denck, but rather appears to be the fruit of Marpeck's reading of Caspar Schwenckfeld's writings on the subject.

The Humanity of Christ and the Celestial Flesh of Christ

One final aspect of Marpeck's use of the humanity of Christ in the *Admonition* addressed a very lively debate between Anabaptists and Spiritualists concerning the Incarnation. Several theologians, such as Melchior Hoffman, Menno Simons, and Schwenckfeld (later in his life), adopted a more or less monophysite Christology that privileged the divine nature of Christ.[75] It was through Clement Ziegler and Melchior Hoffman's influence that the "celestial flesh" Christology was taken up by other Anabaptists.[76]

According to this line of thought, Jesus Christ was conceived *in* Mary by the Holy Spirit but was born without receiving any flesh from his mother. The human nature of Christ is thus considered the same as Adam's before the fall. Jesus therefore did not have human flesh but "celestial" flesh.[77] This celestial flesh makes Jesus' perfect sacrifice possible, which would have beeen impossible for someone having any part in sinful human flesh.[78] In Rothmann's *Bekentnisse*, the doctrine was absent, though he adopted it in 1534.[79]

---

[75] Concerning Schwenckfeld, see P. Maier, *Caspar Schwenckfeld on the Person and Work of Christ* (Assen: Royal Van Gorcum, 1959), 55.

[76] G. Williams, *The Radical Reformation*, 1st edition, 488-500.

[77] For another analysis of the concept of the celestial flesh at the time of the Reformation, see H. J. Schoeps, *Vom Himmlischen Fleisch Christi* (Mohr, 1951), 25-56.

[78] See A. Beachy, *Grace in the Radical Reformation*, (Nieuwkoop: B. de Graaf, 1977), 84-86; Cornelius Krahn, "Incarnation of Christ," in ME III, 18-20; Schoeps, *Himmlischen Fleisch*, 25-47.

[79] Wray, "The *Vermahnung* of 1542, " 247.

Marpeck strongly opposed the "celestial flesh" reading, but the question of to whom Marpeck was aiming his arguments remains open. Perhaps Hoffman, who was in Strasbourg at the same time as Marpeck, or Schwenckfeld, but insufficient evidence limits any certainty. In any case, since the doctrine of the celestial flesh was spreading in various contexts, Marpeck felt obliged to take a position on the matter.

Marpeck openly attacks this doctrine on a number of occasions in the *Admonition*. For him, Jesus had truly human flesh that he received from Mary. Jesus was conceived without male "seed" through the Holy Spirit, but did receive his flesh from his mother, which meant that he had a completely human nature.[80] At the same time as it highlights Mary's participation in the Incarnation, the *Admonition* underscores the fact that Jesus fully participated in human life and that the Word made flesh is also the eternal Word of God. This eternal Word

> is also heard from the mouth of the corporeal, earthly man, Jesus Christ, as a physical, earthly, glorious, tangible, visible, perceptible, suffering, mortal, natural Word, which is with the Father eternally, one Word and equal to God forever.[81]

The unique conjunction of eternal Word and human flesh in Jesus Christ contributes to the coherence of Marpeck's theology centred on the concept of the humanity of Christ.

The work of Christ: salvation and ethics

In this section we continue tracking Marpeck's understanding of salvation in Christ and its relation to ethics.

The Death of Christ

In the *Admonition* as was the case in the *Confession of 1532*, Marpeck spoke without difficulty concerning the sacrificial dimension of Christ's death

---

[80] V, 262, 7. "…das er durch den weibs samen als vom samen der menschen, on mans samen und sunde empfangen hat, und dadurch das wort fleisch worden ist," *WPM*, 274. See also *WPM*, 211-2 and 233.

[81] *WPM*, 302. Once again, the italics indicate Marpeck's addition to Rothmann's *Bekentnisse*.

as a necessary event for the redemption of sinful humanity. Most of the formulations in this regard are drawn directly from Rothmann's text.

> Christ had been sacrificed for the sins of the whole world, had assuaged the wrath of the Father, had repaid unrighteousness with his blood and saved men from eternal death.[82]

Indeed, most of these affirmations are direct quotes or paraphrases of biblical texts concerning Christ's death.[83] The *Admonition* also uses "Lutheran" atonement language to describe the justification that flows from the death of Christ.

> ...faith and knowledge of Christ come out of teaching and hearing the divine Word.[84] (*fides ex auditu*)

> ...we actually confess by faith that God has been gracious to us through Christ, who has forgiven us all our sins and has reconciled us to God...[85]

Marpeck appears to be comfortable with the atonement language being used in the wider Reformation, for he allows these passages to stand without editorial amendment.

The Work of Christ and the Sin of Adam

Nevertheless, apparent commonalities quickly give way to important differences with the Reformers. In the *Confession of 1532*, Marpeck affirmed that the death of Christ cancels original sin and that thereafter all persons are responsible for their own sin. In the *Admonition* further clarification is given to what this means. Because of Christ's death, the guilt from original sin is taken away from children until they, of their own volition, gain knowledge of good and evil.

---

[82] *WPM*, 175.
[83] For example: "God had atoned for sin through Christ," *WPM*, 175; "...through Christ, who has forgiven us all our sins and has reconciled us to God," *WPM*, 184; "Show that Christ died for you, giving His body and spilling His blood for you, and show that, in the death of Christ, all your solace and life is directed," *WPM*, 274.
[84] *WPM*, 211.
[85] Ibid., 184.

Original sin is inherited only when there is knowledge of good and evil. Adam and Eve, our father and mother, inherited it when, contrary to the command of God, they ate the fruit of the knowledge of good and evil. Such is the inheritance of all men. But, prior to the knowledge of good and evil, neither inherited sin nor actual sin is reckoned before God.[86]

Before the knowledge of good and evil a child is in the same state as Adam and Eve before the fall.[87] Children are protected from original sin by the promise of Christ (Matt. 19:14) "Let the little children come to me, and do not stop them; for it is to such as these that the kingdom of heaven belongs."

In medieval thought and practice, Christ's death was understood to take away the guilt of original sin. Infant baptism removed the "stain" and Christians then became guilty of their own individual sins, for which they needed to do penance and be forgiven. Marpeck's understanding of Christ's death and original sin is similar, but removes the necessity of a sacramental mediation of forgiveness for children. The notion of promise replaces the sacrament and baptism can then function as a response to God's grace, a commitment to follow Christ and an entry into the new community of the Church.

The Conjunction of Justification and Sanctification

Despite Marpeck's relatively Lutheran (in fact simply Pauline) language describing Christ's death and justification, he continued to emphasize the concrete change that occurs in the believer's life because of Christ's work. The *Admonition* continues to engage the Radical Reformation's polemic against a uniquely "forensic" justification. Faith needs to produce a transformed life, and such a change does not appear to be a fruit of the faith preached in the wider Reformation.

---

[86] Ibid., 206.
[87] Ibid., 208. "Let the children remain in the promise of Christ until they can be instructed, and until they can believe, confess, and desire baptism. Prior to their belief and confession they are like Adam and Eve before the transgression."

> ...For it is not enough to be purified and united through faith. The old life must also be removed and buried...[88]
>
> All of Germany boasts about the gospel, all wish to be called Christians and evangelicals, and all wish to be considered as such. But the purpose of the proclamation of the Gospel, to be attained here upon earth, is that a holy community of God or church be founded in which all dealings and actions may be guided, to the praise of God, according to the proclamation of the gospel. Such is not to be found anywhere nor is to be seen. To be sure Christ is proclaimed everywhere, and many people take it quite for granted. In life, however, one has a feeling that everywhere the Antichrist or the opponent of Christ is present.[89]

The Child of God Similar to Christ

In the *Confession of 1532*, the notion of "*Fromm-Machung*" was highlighted to show how Marpeck brought together justification and sanctification. The "Christological synthesis" of the *Admonition* allows now for a new conceptualization of this question, one more directly tied to the concept of the "humanity of Christ."

As we have seen, the new reality (*wesen*) brought into history by the humanity of Christ includes two different elements, the one, inner, and the other, outer. God became known in the union of these two elements in Jesus Christ, completely human and divine, "Spirit and life" at the same time. An important consequence of the work of Christ is the gift of the Spirit to believers. Thus the humanity of Christ extends in time and space wherever the Spirit joins the outer element. In the *Admonition*, Marpeck begins to consider the believer as one of these "outer elements," allowing the "logic of the Incarnation" to continue in history.

In other words, the work of Christ and the sending of the Spirit make the believer similar to Christ. In this perspective those who have faith receive the Holy Spirit and thus a "second nature." By the flesh one

---

[88] *WPM*, 190.
[89] Ibid., 201-202.

is a child of humanity and by the Spirit one is a child of God. The believer becomes "Spirit" while remaining in the flesh.

> Thus, here and there, the children of God and of men are spirit, flesh, and blood, and they are also eternal after the resurrection.[90]

The believer now has a two-fold nature that will remain forever. The model for this dual nature is Jesus Christ himself, as is shown in continuation of the previous citation.

> Just as Christ is the Word, Spirit, and God, so, too, is He a man born from the seed of woman, but without the seed of man, born of a generation of human flesh and blood...[91]

The difference between Jesus and the believer has to do the difference in their flesh. Human flesh remains sinful and "divinization" will never be complete in this life. What is most interesting (and that which provokes a lively reaction from Schwenckfeld in his *Judicium*) is that Marpeck insists that the child of God truly is so in the flesh and that this material aspect is inescapable. Marpeck insists on this last point.

> So, too, we are spiritual and physical children of God and of men; we are included in the Spirit and Word derived from God, but we are also flesh and blood, derived from man, and we remain such with Christ eternally.[92]

The origin of this "*kindtschaft Gottes*" is the eternal Word brought by the Christ incarnate.

> This childhood comes, not from corruptible seed but, rather, from incorruptible seed, through the Word of the living and eternal God; that Word, however, has come to us *through the humanized word from the seed of woman*, and it is to be proclaimed through the gospel.[93]

Evidently if the believer becomes (almost) identical to Christ in his two natures, the capacity for obedience becomes much larger than if one

---

[90] Ibid., 212 (V, 219:13)
[91] Ibid.
[92] Ibid.
[93] Ibid. The italics are Marpeck's addition.

understands justification in purely forensic terms. By means of the work of Christ and the faith of the believer, the Holy Spirit lives in believers, giving them "new" natures similar to Jesus Christ's. The two natures of Christ become the model for what happens to the believer in the process of justification.[94] This understanding of justification is all the more fascinating in that it contributes to the Christological synthesis of the *Admonition*. Thus in Marpeck's thought, the doctrine of the work of Christ flows directly from the concept of the humanity of Christ. The humanity of Christ and the sending of the Spirit is aimed at "divinizing" the human being, which corresponds to the "*Fromm-Machung*" noted in the confession of faith from Strasbourg.[95] Christian life becomes sacramental, a vehicle for God's presence within the world.

Summary

Marpeck may not have consciously systematized his Christology but the *Admonition* represents a real bringing together of important elements of his theology. First the Anabaptist theologian merges two ways of understanding the humanity of Christ; the one found in Luther, the other found in Schwenckfeld. This synthesis is made possible by the notions of "*wesen*" (reality) and "Spirit and life."

Secondly, the idea of God's order, considered by Kiwiet as the foundation of Marpeck's theology is best understood in relation to Marpeck's understanding of the humanity of Christ. Outer means and history are part of the created order respected by God in his dealings with humanity through the Incarnation.

In relation to soteriology, Marpeck restates many of the expressions used by Rothmann to express the connection between justification and

---

[94] Finger makes the same point quite well. "Marpeck's ...view flowed from his Christology. Since Jesus' human corporeality was not opposed to divine Spirit but designed to be its vehicle, so is ours..." *Contemporary Anabaptist Theology*, 215.

[95] When using "divinisation" language, it is important to use the distinction found in T. Finger: "Divinisation does not mean 'transformation of human reality into another kind of reality' (divine) but transformation by divine reality of those who remain fully human." *Contemporary Anabaptist Theology*, 114.

sanctification. The concept of "Fromm-Machung" used in the *Confession of 1532* is left aside, but the concept of "child of God" is used to build a more explicitly theological connection to Marpeck's doctrine of the humanity of Christ.

Chapter 5

Marpeck's Christology and the Controversy with Schwenckfeld

Schwenckfeld responds to the Admonition

Historical Context of the Dispute

Even though the *Admonition* does not appear to have been aimed directly at Schwenckfeld, he reacted strongly to its publication. Schwenckfeld's written, but never-published critique and the response by the Marpeck Circle represent an extremely significant (and voluminous) milestone in the development of Marpeck's Christology.[1]

This exchange includes various documents and a number of authors, not only Schwenckfeld's critique (*Judicium-Judgment*)[2] and Marpeck's

---

[1] For other descriptions and analyses of this dispute, see T. Bergsten, *Pilgram Marbeck und seine Auseinadersetzung*; Williams, *Radical Reformation*, (3rd Edition), 681-722; Boyd, *Pilgram Marpeck*, 118-125; Blough, "Le Christ glorifié et le Christ humilié: le débat christologique entre Pilgram Marpeck et Caspar Schwenckfeld," in N. Blough (ed.), *Jésus-Christ aux marges de la Réforme* (Paris : Desclée, 1992), 141-162; Rempel, *The Lord's Supper in Anabaptism*, 119-142.

[2] *CS* 8, 168-214. "Ueber das new buechlein der Tauffbrueder im 1542 iar ausgangen Judicium."

response (*Verantwurtung-Response*).³ Nevertheless this chapter will focus primarily on these two texts and also briefly on a few of Schwenckfeld's letters written between the *Judgment* and the *Response* in order to help describe the context and issues of the controversy.

As we have already seen, Marpeck and Schwenckfeld had met in Strasbourg and had been on apparently friendly terms.⁴ They met again in 1540 without any signs of significant conflict.⁵ Nevertheless as time went on, Marpeck came to consider Schwenckfeld's spiritualist and individualist tendencies more and more dangerous. At this time, especially in the region of Augsburg, choosing between the Anabaptist and the Spiritualist options was a struggle for many believers, and the controversy between Marpeck and Schwenckfeld was imbedded in a broader discussion involving various people from both camps, especially a series of theologically interested and articulate women.

Magdalena Marschalk von Pappenheim, a former Benedictine nun, had contacted Schwenckfeld because of her interest in his theology.⁶ But prior to meeting him, she had encountered Marpeck and was influenced by his thought. Magdalena also knew Helena Streicher from Ulm, a follower of Schwenckfeld.⁷ It was under the name of Magdalena that Marpeck had written to Helena (the letter used in the last chapter) in the summer of 1542. Magdalena herself sent a letter of her own and parts of Marpeck's letter to Helena Streicher, who then passed them on to her friend Schwenckfeld. It is from Schwenckfeld's reaction in a letter addressed to Magdalena on the twenty-first of August 1542 that we learn

---

³ *Verantwurtung uber Caspar Schwenckfelds Judicium* in Loserth, 61-578. For the English translation see "Pilgram Marpeck's *Response* to Caspar Schwenckfeld's *Judgment*," translation by John Rempel in *Later Writings by Pilgram Marpeck and his Circle*, 76-157 (henceforth cited as LW). This English translation is not of the full text, thus occasionally I will translate passages from the original.

⁴ D. Husser, "Caspar Schwenckfeld et ses adeptes," 514; Bergsten, *Pilgram Marbeck und seine Auseinadersetzung*, 67.

⁵ Ibid., 46.

⁶ Cf. "Magdalena, Walpurga and Sophia Marschalk von Pappenheim," in C. Arnold Snyder and Linda A. Huebert Hecht (eds), *Profiles of Anabaptist Women*, 111-123.

⁷ Kiwiet, *Pilgram Marbeck*, 59.

that he had written a critique (*Judgment*) of the *Admonition*.⁸ Apparently Schwenckfeld had received a copy of the *Admonition* from another aristocratic Anabaptist woman, Helena von Freyberg, in exile from the Tyrol and living in Augsburg.⁹

Schwenckfeld's Letter to Magdalena, August 21, 1542

In this letter, Schwenckfeld notes first that he received a letter that Marpeck wrote under Magdalena's name.¹⁰ The fact that Marpeck had influenced her apparently annoyed Schwenckfeld, given the fact that she had previously expressed interest in his theology. He writes that Marpeck still needs to go to the school of the Lord, because even if he is seeking the Kingdom and loves Christ, he does so in a clumsy and error-prone manner.¹¹ According to Schwenckfeld, Marpeck teaches that Christ could have sinned¹² and to refute this error, sent him a letter with a treatise written by a colleague named Valentin Ickelsamer.

Schwenckfeld also mentions that he had read the *Admonition* and presumes that Marpeck was the author.¹³ He lists a series of errors that he found in the *Admonition*, mostly of a Christological nature. More specifically, these errors concern Christ, original sin, the word of God, the Church, communion, what it means to be a child of God, and the faith of the ancients.¹⁴ Schwenckfeld highlights two additional errors in Marpeck's writings: first that Christ is born of a woman without the seed of man and secondly the notion that the Father acts internally whereas the Son acts externally as a man in the flesh.¹⁵ Finally, Schwenckfeld claims that others had asked him to refute the *Admonition*.

> After some brothers requested it of me, I wrote a book against that man. I did so for their improvement and to gently show

---

⁸ *CS* 8, 217-222.
⁹ Snyder and Hecht, *Profiles*, 114. Concerning Helena von Freyberg, see ibid., 124-139.
¹⁰ *CS*, 217.
¹¹ Ibid., 219.
¹² Ibid., 220.
¹³ Ibid., 221.
¹⁴ Ibid.
¹⁵ Ibid. Also, 222.

them their mistakes and errors. I believe Pilgram will receive it in due time.[16]

Schwenckfeld's Letter of September 15, 1542 to Marpeck

Evidently Marpeck quite rapidly received a copy of the *Judgment* and responded by letter explaining to Schwenckfeld the he had misunderstood the *Admonition*. Marpeck's letter has been lost but Schwenckfeld's response remains.[17]

> Dear Pilgram, I received your letter in which you accuse me regarding the *Judgment* (that I wrote in response to a publication that exposes your doctrine).[18]

As already seen in his letter to Magdalena, Schwenckfeld thought that Marpeck believed that Christ – in his human nature – could have sinned, had he so desired. This accusation is also found in the *Judgment* and apparently angered Marpeck. Thus in his letter he demanded an apology from Schwenckfeld for such a claim and asked him to prove it.

To defend his *Judgment*, Schwenckfeld responded that all Christians are free to judge all doctrine (following 1 Thess. 5:21) and that moreover a number of brothers had asked him to write it.[19] The letter lists yet more reasons that compelled him to write: 1) the narrow-mindedness of Marpeck who affirms that those who do not accept baptism as described in the *Admonition* deny the Son of God; 2) Schwenckfeld is often accused of being an Anabaptist, and thereby associated with their theological errors, which necessitated a clarification of the differences between himself and Marpeck; 3) last but not least Schwenckfeld claims to have written simply to make known the truth and glory of the Lord.[20]

In this letter he goes on to ask Marpeck to reread the *Judgment* and to demonstrate point by point how the *Admonition* was misunderstood. He also asks Marpeck to clarify the following ideas: 1) the fact that Christ was

---

[16] Ibid., 222.
[17] *CS* 8, 271-279.
[18] Ibid., 271.
[19] Ibid., 272.
[20] Ibid., 272-273.

born of woman without the seed of man and 2) the fact that the Father acts internally while the Son acts externally. Schwenckfeld also affirms having received a tract in which Marpeck claims that Christ in his human nature could have sinned like the first Adam. For the Spiritualist, Christ did not have the capacity to sin, even if he had so desired.[21]

Schwenckfeld's Letter of September 25, 1542 to Magdalena

In yet another letter to Magdalena,[22] Schwenckfeld continued to pronounce judgment on the theological errors of his new adversary. The letter could be seen as a summary of the *Judgments*'s content. Over against the Anabaptist, Schwenckfeld claims that: 1) Christ never could have sinned, 2) Christ did not suffer in hell,[23] 3) the Spirit of Christ is the Spirit of the Father, 4) the ancients were saved before the Incarnation, 5) original sin was a fault leading to condemnation (*verdamliche Last*) and not only a matter of knowledge of good and evil, 6) Christ was born of the seed of Abraham and David and not only of the seed of Mary, 7) the inner and outer baptisms are not one single reality (*wesen*), 8) Anabaptists (*Tauffbrueder*) are not the only Christians, 9) Christians are not known by their baptism, but by the love and knowledge of Christ, 10) true communion is not a sign nor a ceremony but a true eating and drinking of the real flesh and blood of Jesus Christ, 11) the fact of eating and drinking externally is not the true inner communion with the body and blood of Christ. Christ in his human nature is no longer our servant, thus, one cannot affirm that the Father acts internally by the Spirit and externally by the Son (Marpeck is accused of Sabellianism in this regard), 12) Christ is not and never was a creature.[24]

---

[21] Ibid., 274-275.
[22] *CS* 8, 281-285.
[23] Evidently Schwenckfeld knew that Marpeck taught the opposite. See *CS* 8, pp. 277, 282.
[24] These points summarize Schwenckfeld's thought in *CS* 8, 283-284.

Letter to Pilgram Marpeck, September 29, 1542[25]

In another letter, written only four days after the previous one, Schwenckfeld sought to prove to Marpeck that his accusations were well-founded and that he had the proof that Pilgram held to a faulty Christology.

> Salutem dear Pilgram. Precisely as I was sending to Augsburg my response to your letter, I found the letter wherein is stated the error that Christ had the freedom of choice to sin. Your name is upon it and it dates from September 26 1540 from the Grisons...[26]

This series of letters demonstrate clearly that Christology was at the centre of the controversy. As will be shown, questions of baptism and communion depend to a great extent on the understanding of Christ and the relationship between "inner" and "outer," "visible" and "invisible." In this final letter Schwenckfeld expressively recognized the Christological distance between the two of them.

> I always believed that you possessed more righteous thoughts concerning Christ and I respected you much more than many brothers, until I observed that you contradict our revelation and teaching of the glory and knowledge of Christ... For this reason I had to examine in greater detail what you knew of Christ and what you say about it all.[27]

Schwenckfeld: The Dispute with Marpeck in Relation to Other Christological Controversies of the Time

The purpose of this perusal of Schwenckfeld's letters was to show the Christological stakes in the debate created by the *Admonition*. If the *Admonition* was not aimed at Schwenckfeld, if there had been no previous occasions of serious controversy between the two, why did Schwenckfeld feel attacked to such a great extent and why did he react so energetically? Was it only because of Marpeck's growing influence on persons close to

---

[25] *CS* 8, 291-294.
[26] Ibid., 291.
[27] Ibid., 291.

Schwenckfeld?²⁸ Certainly, the three women mentioned (Magdalena, Helena Streicher and Helena von Freyberg) played important roles in this debate and the *Judgment* was probably written for them.²⁹ George Williams calls this episode "the war of the ladies of the Radical Reformation."³⁰ Clearly, the competition between Marpeck and Schwenckfeld's groups contributed to the dispute. Nevertheless the broader context of what was going on in Schweckfeld's life helps to better understand his strong reaction to the *Admonition*.

Christology was the heart of Schwenckfeld's theology³¹ and he was particularly under attack by the magisterial reformers on this point beginning in 1535. On May 28 1535, during a colloquium at Tübingen, Schwenckfeld met Martin Bucer, Martin Frecht (a pastor at Ulm) and Ambrosius Blaurer from Constance. There these reformers agreed to no longer persecute Schwenckfeld and his followers in southern Germany. But Frecht still questioned Schwenckfeld's Christology without the group coming to a final resolution.³² His adversaries claimed that Schwenckfeld denied that Christ's human nature implied that he was a "creature." In July 1539, Bullinger wrote his *Orthodoxa Epistola* in opposition to Schwenckfeld's Christology. Frecht also continued his opposition, which led to the condemnation of Schwenldfeld's Christology by the Schmalkaldic League in March 1540. Conrad Grebel's brother-in-law, Vadian, reformer in St. Gall, twice wrote against Schwenckfeld on this topic (1540 and 1541).³³ In response to these attacks, the Silesian Spiritualist

---

²⁸ See Bergsten, *Pilgram Marbeck und seine Auseinandersetzung,* 48-49.
²⁹ Ibid., 49.
³⁰ Williams, *Radical Reformation,* (1st edition) 466.
³¹ P. L. Maier, *Caspar Schwenckfeld on the Person and Work of Christ,* 2. "The central concentration in Schwenckfeld's theology is neither his concept of the Eucharist, nor the Church, nor 'Word and Spirit,' but the doctrines concerning the person and work of Christ. Christological and soteriological themes clearly bulk largest in the some fifteen thousand pages of the latest critical edition of his work."
³² See R. L. Harrison "Schwenckfeld and the Tübingen Colloquy," *MQR* 52 (July 1978): 237-247.
³³ Maier, *Caspar Schwenckfeld on the Person and Work of Christ,* 39-40 and E. J. Furcha, *Schwenckfeld's Concept of the New Man. A Study in the Anthropology of Caspar von Schwenckfeld as set forth in his Major Theological Writings* (Pennsburg: Board of Publications

wrote two important books: *Vom Fleische Christi*[34] and *Confession und Erclerung vom Erkandnuss Christi und seiner Gottlichen Herrlicheit.*[35] In light of these controversies, it was probably very difficult for Schwenckfeld to consider Marpeck an isolated adversary. It also helps explain why most of Schwenckfeld's writings up until 1553 focus on Christological issues.[36]

Summary of Schwenckfeld's Christology

Several scholars have elaborated on Caspar Schwenckfeld's Christology.[37] The following seeks to highlight a few aspects of this Christology in order to better understand the perspective from which Schwenckfeld critiqued the *Admonition*.

As with Marpeck, Schwenckfeld's Christology cannot be separated from the question of how the inner and outer realms are related. Schwenckfeld's thought is most notable for a fundamental dualism at this point. This dualism is so pronounced that no possible bridges exist between these two realms of reality.[38]

From this point of view, only one "*wesen*" exists: the eternal one that is none other than "the Christ and God himself in his Holy Spirit."[39] The

---

of the Schwenckfelder Church, 1970), 98-100. For Schwenckfeld's condemnation, see Maier, 39; Bergsten, 46; Schultz, *Caspar Schwenckfeld von Ossig (1489-1561)* (Pennsburg: Board of Publications of the Schwenckfelder Church, 1977), 253.

[34] *CS* 7, 281-361.

[35] *CS* 7, 484-884.

[36] Maier, *Caspar Schwenckfeld on the Person and Work of Christ*, 40.

[37] For example, Maier, *Caspar Schwenckfeld on the Person and Work of Christ*, and André Sciegienny, *Homme Charnel, Homme Spirituel. Etude sur la Christologie de Caspar Schwenckfeld* (1489-1561) (Wiesbaden: Franz Steiner Verlag, 1975). See also Williams, *The Radical Reformation*, 3rd Edition, 692-694.

[38] Maier, *Caspar Schwenckfeld on the Person and Work of Christ*, 14. "It cannot be overemphasized how Schwenckfeld's entire theology, particularly his anthropology, Christology and his doctrines of the Word and sacrament are indelibly stamped with this dichotomy and its implications. Since the inner and the spiritual can affect only something else within the spiritual realm, and the outer and the material are limited to the physical, these two orders or spheres are independent of each other and there is no necessary correlation between them."

[39] Loserth, 122, 43.

notion of "*wesen*" is opposed to that of "*zeichen*" (sign). This contrast can be seen in the following table:⁴⁰

Wesen	*Zeichen*
Eternal	passing
Invisible	visible
Perceived by faith	perceived by the senses
Reign	service
Truth	image

It was because of this dualism that Schwenckfeld concluded that the term "creature" cannot be used to designate the humanity of Christ. As the years went on, he developed a notion of the progressive divinization of the humanity of Christ, until he finally rejected the term "creature" in 1538. The doctrine of the divinization of the humanity of Christ thus became the focal point for his soteriology. The logic is similar to what we will see in Marpeck's *Response*: that which happens to Christ, happens to the believer. In other words, the divinization of Christ permits the divinization of the believer.⁴¹

Already at the beginning of the Incarnation, Christ received a "celestial," i.e. non creaturely flesh. After the ascension, all the aspects of the humanity of Christ related to finitude, time and space, cease to exist and function. Christ is glorified and his activities in this state of glory cannot contain the notion of servitude as when he was humiliated on earth.⁴²

In light of Schwenckfeld's letters and this brief sketch of his Christology, his critiques of Marpeck become obvious. The fundamental

---

⁴⁰ Ibid.
⁴¹ Maier, *Caspar Schwenckfeld on the Person and Work of Christ*, 67. "The soteriological significance of the Incarnation in Schwenckfeld's theology derives from the fact that with the Word's assuming flesh, God's plan of salvation for mankind - that is a sinless non-creaturely flesh should redeem a sinful, creaturely flesh and enable its participation in the divine nature - was initiated. In fact Schwenckfeld's entire system is an extended commentary on the phrase 'God became man in order that man might become God or what God is.'"
⁴² Ibid., 75.

point of Marpeck's *Admonition*, i.e. the unity of the inner and outer baptisms centred in the Trinity, founded on a specific understanding of "*wesen*," was inadmissible for Schwenckfeld.[43] In his eyes, Marpeck had no knowledge whatsoever of the "*neu hymlisch wesen*" of Christ.[44] The Anabaptist also confused the inner and outer,[45] thereby connecting salvation to outer things, i.e. to the created order.[46] Baptism was an idol for Marpeck.[47] In sum, their perspectives were based on two very different Christologies.

Marpeck Responds to the Judgment

The very length of the *Verantwurtung über Casparn Schwenckfelds Judicium* (over 500 pages in Loserth's critical edition) indicates that Marpeck felt stung and challenged by Schwenckfeld's critique. The *Response* is divided into two parts, which will be studied separately in the following analysis.[48] The first part (113 pages) was probably finished towards the beginning of 1544, whereas the second part appeared after May 1547. Additionally, as noted earlier, it is important to remember that the Marpeck Circle, not only Marpeck himself, composed the text, or at the very least, stood behind the text. A note accompanying the manuscript affirms that a number of brothers worked many years to finish this response to Schwenckfeld.

> The elder witnesses of God of the entire community and brotherhood, namely Pilgram Marpeck and Leupold Scharnschlager, Sigmund Bosch, Martin Blaichner, Valtin Werner, Annthoni Müler, Hans Jakob, together with other elder brothers and believers in all lands, judged and answered concerning this.[49]

---

[43] Loserth, 111.
[44] Ibid., 123, 10.
[45] Ibid., 115, 14; 117, 18.
[46] Ibid., 117, 5.
[47] Ibid., 140, 25.
[48] Since the Judicium is reproduced in its entirety in the Verantwurtung, the two texts will be cited exclusively from Loserth's edition.
[49] Loserth, 50; translated in Snyder and Hecht, *Profiles*, 118.

The development of Marpeck's Christology in the first part of the Response

It goes without saying that the Christological developments in the *Response* were made in direct response to Schwenckfeld's criticisms. Much of the text is not explicitly Christological but most of the arguments developed depend directly on Christological themes and reflect the profound difference between Marpeck and Schwenckfeld's Christologies. Marpeck summarized the problem in the following manner:

> He (Schwenckfeld) teaches only the inner Christ, glorified, non suffering and magnificent who is in heaven and not the one who suffers on earth. He speaks only of his glory and majesty and not of the cross and the tribulation that he bore as the head before the glorification and ascension... [50]

While accepting the importance of the inner and glorified Christ, Marpeck underlined all the outer aspects of the Christian life that he had previously associated with the humanity of Christ. An examination of his thought on three themes 1) the sacraments (inner/outer union), 2) the Church, and 3) the ethical life, illustrates this point. These three themes are intimately interconnected and any division is artificial, for in Marpeck's view, ethical acts are as sacramental as communion, and the presence of the Church on earth is as much humanity of Christ as is baptism.

Sacraments and the Inner-Outer Wesen

In order to respond to Schwenckfeld, Marpeck was forced to clarify his conception of the relationship between the inner and the outer realms. The *Response* introduces a series of arguments to justify the notion of a "*wesen*" that consists of the union of inner and outer elements of reality. His arguments are both theological and biblical in nature and attempt to show that the rituals of the church are more than symbols while refuting the accusation that he arrives at a theory of transubstantiation.

---

[50] Loserth, 160, 34.

The Two Natures of Christ as Basis for "Inner-Outer" Union

In Marpeck's letter to Helena Streicher, introduced in the previous chapter, the author referred to the two natures of Christ to demonstrate that the divine (inner) and the human (outer) can coexist in one person. Marpeck thus founded his concept of "*wesen.*" This same type of reasoning continues in the *Response.*

The inner and outer elements are unified in the believer in the same way that they were in Christ; they are one and undivided (*ains und unzerthailt*).[51] In his "unglorified" (*unverklart*) body on earth, Jesus was at the same time both God and human, and his human nature was part of the divine and Trinitarian reality. Because of this, the same possibility is offered to humans and to other earthly realities. In other words the Incarnation is the basis for a certain divinization of believers and of their activities.

> Christ, as the unglorified head on earth was part of the invisible reality of the Word (as the third [sic] person of the divinity) even though he was a bodily and visible *wesen*. Thus it is possible in the same way that his unglorified body, i.e. his members on earth, also participate in the reality of God in Christ as a bodily *wesen*...[52]

At the same time Marpeck insisted on the fact that the Kingdom of Christ concerns the complete human being, inner and outer[53] and, contrary to Schwenckfeld who claimed that salvation meant the transformation or abandonment of all outer things, the Anabaptist emphasized that "without the flesh of our bodies we will not be saved."[54]

Inner-Outer Union Made Explicit

In his *Judgment*, Schwenckfeld cited Augustine to argue that sacraments are a sign and not divine reality itself.[55] In contrast, for Marpeck a sacrament

---

[51] Loserth, 76, 21.
[52] Ibid., 137, 2.
[53] Ibid., 139, 21.
[54] Ibid., 126, 28. "...und mag der mensch ausserhalb des fleisch seines leibs nit selig werden..." I prefer this more literal translation than *LW*, 82, which says "without our creatureliness we will not be saved."
[55] Ibid., 111, 35.

is a sign only for the unbeliever. When faith is present, the union between human reality and God which takes place during the sacrament is called "*wesen.*" At the same time, Marpeck insists that the elements do not change at all.

> In the following manner we affirm that the sign becomes reality. As soon as the signs and the elements cease to signify, that is when man is unified with God and God with man in such a way that that which is signified or represented is present, the sign is no longer one and becomes *wesen*. Nevertheless water remains water, wine, wine, and the bread, bread.[56]

The elements do not change, i.e; trans-substantiate, but rather the divine unites itself with the human spirit and in the sacramental unity the human will is transformed to accomplish the divine will.

> Concerning baptism and all outer and spiritual actions, we claim that when it happens properly, the outer serves the inner and the inner is witnessed to and revealed by the outer. The two are one in Christ according to the inner and outer man. The divine (as inner) unites with the inner man (as creature) to accomplish the will of God. Therefore what God demands inwardly, the inner man demands the outer man to do outwardly.[57]

Marpeck does not always use the same terms to describe the inner or divine reality. Thus it is not always easy to know precisely to what he is referring. Sometimes the divine or inner element is described as the Holy Spirit. In that case the Holy Spirit and faith play the central role in the inner/outer union. Indeed without faith the "*wesen*" is not present and the ritual remains a sign.

> External (*eusserlich*) teaching about faith cannot be active in our heart without the Holy Spirit, who recalls to us, and leads us into all truth. It is through faith that God gives us the Spirit (Gal. 3[:3-5]). Through this outward teaching, truth is presented and offered to the heart and to the whole person. For whoever believes and is not contradicted, to him the outward teaching is a co-witness and a truth with the

---

[56] Ibid., 124, 29.
[57] Ibid., 125, 40.

internal (*innerlich*) truth in the believing heart. Whoever doesn't believe the outward truth of Christ, to him it becomes a sign of contradiction leading to a fall.[58]

In light of this citation the previous one can be interpreted to indicate that the Holy Spirit (the divine element) unites itself to the human spirit (in faith) by outer means (baptism, preaching) which represent and proclaim the inner truth. These two aspects together shape a single reality (*wesen*) or truth (*warheit*). Interestingly, Marpeck now begins to clarify the notion of "*wesen*" with the term "truth."[59] Thus by "*wesen*" he is not referring to "substance" (as Schwenckfeld suspects) but rather to human will and intention and to the manner by which these inner aspects of the human reality translate themselves into outer actions.[60]

Nevertheless, the Holy Spirit is not the only way Marpeck describes the divine and inner reality that unites itself with the outer. He also uses the notion of the Word joined with the elements. For Marpeck the Word is associated in particular with baptism. The Church of Christ possesses a single baptism which occurs "through the Word, in the Word and with the Word" (*durchs wort, im wort und mit dem wort*).[61] The "*wesen*" in baptism is not water but water and the Word.[62] Here Marpeck may well be following Luther who writes "baptism is not simple water only, but it is the water comprehended in God's command and connected with God's Word."[63]

---

[58] LW, 75. (Loserth 125, 40).
[59] In the *Verantwurtung* Marpeck uses the two words "*wesen*" and "*warheit*" to express the same notion. See for example Loserth, 135, 48 and 169, 44.
[60] Stephen Boyd's discussion of *wesen* is quite helpful in clarifying these issues. See *Pilgram Marpeck*, 118-120.
[61] Loserth, 162, 7.
[62] Loserth, 167, 11.
[63] M. Luther, *The Small Catechism*, http://www.bookofconcord.org/smallcatechism.html. Bergsten, *Pilgram Marbeck und seine Auseinandersetzung*, 107-108, recognizes that Marpeck's position is quite similar to Luther's but excludes the possibility of a direct and conscious influence. However this study has shown that Marpeck was familiar with Luther's thinking and nothing excludes a possible dependence on the Wittenberg reformer, even if Marpeck, in contrast to Luther, promotes adult baptism.

Marpeck's simultaneous identification of the divine element with the Holy Spirit and the Word in the inner/outer union is at times rather confusing. This confusion is a result of Marpeck's tendency to identify the Holy Spirit with the divine nature of Christ, which will become even more apparent in the second part of the *Response*. George Williams attributes this clumsiness to Marpeck's lack of a firm grasp of the ancient theological categories and to the fact that he worked more directly from Scripture.[64] John Rempel and Thomas Finger both argue that what Marpeck was trying to say was more important than his awkward manner of saying it.[65]

The most important point here is that Marpeck's concept of *"wesen"* must be understood in terms of "truth" and not of substance. Thus he can claim that the outer elements of manifestations change in no substantial way. It is not a question of water but of baptism. Baptism includes of course an outer element, but the truth or the reality of baptism is much greater than water. When the inner and spiritual reality is present along with water, this water is part of the spiritual reality (or truth) that is the baptism of Christ. This is why Marpeck denies, explicitly and repeatedly, attributing any importance or transformation to the elements in themselves.

> It is not the elements of bread and wine but the action (*werk*) in which Christ's members make use of them, which is the witness and meaning of the word of God. We don't mean water, bread, and wine, but baptism and communion.[66]

---

[64] Williams, *The Radical Reformation*, 3rd Edition, 684. Such a point of view is also supported by John Rempel who writes: "The relatively unfixed and undifferentiated roles of the Trinity in the New Testament, particularly those of the ascended Son and the Spirit, account in part for those characteristics in Marpeck's Trinitarian scheme." Rempel, *The Lord's Supper in Anabaptism*, 159.

[65] "Marpeck's Trinitarian language is awkward and unorthodox but makes a profound confession. In his conflation of two and sometimes even three members of the Trinity, he is saying that to have communion with the body and blood of Christ is to participate in love, which is to participate in God." Rempel, *The Lord's Supper in Anabaptism*, 134. "Remember that Marpeck ... was not trained theologically. But despite this he wrestled more than any other Anabaptist to articulate many insights in dialogue with classical theology. Perhaps his convoluted concepts will yield meaning if we ask what he intended to say with them." Finger, *Contemporary Anabaptist Theology*, 192.

[66] *LW*, 85. Loserth, 137, 16.

The act of baptism performed in terms of its intention and its meaning is truth and reality.[67] Marpeck seeks to avoid an *ex opera operato* understanding of the sacraments. Baptism requires more than simply a priest or pastor's pouring of water over the head. The believer's faith must accept the divine reality offered in baptism. In this sense the act is more than a symbol. Since the believer trusts or has faith in the presence of the divine reality, the act itself becomes "*wesen.*" The event occurs at the level of will, intention, and meaning. Thomas Finger's description of the Lord's Supper as an "activity" in sixteenth-century Anabaptist thought and practice is a helpful way to conceptualize what Marpeck was trying to say.[68]

> So we don't ascribe any special holiness to the elements, but much more, to the action. It's the action, involving the heart, the soul, the understanding and to which the element is drawn which is ritualized (*gehandlet*). It is only the understanding and meaning of the action which makes a sacrament valid.[69]

Biblical Arguments

Though Marpeck exposes a careful biblical basis of his argumentation (indeed his arguments are filled with biblical references), the preceding points are more theological than biblical insofar as much depends on the concepts of the dual nature of Christ, the Word, and the inner/outer "*wesen,*" which go beyond the biblical framework as such. Nevertheless the most important biblical texts upon which Marpeck founds his theological arguments are worth noting.

In the *Admonition* John 5:19 ("...whatever the Father does, the Son does likewise") was central. This verse is an important key for the

---

[67] Loserth, 137, 44. "Solch werk, der mainung, nit dem element nach, haissen wirs ein wesen mit dem innerlichen..."

[68] "Especially since they experience Christ communally, and not simply in the elements, Anabaptists implicitly understood the Supper as an activity.... Historic Anabaptism's implicit awareness of the Supper as an activity can help contemporary theology explicate the connections of its spiritual and material dimensions." Finger, *Contemporary Anabaptist Theology*, 197.

[69] *LW*, 86. Loserth, 138, 20. The word "sacrament" used in the English translation cited here is not in the original text.

Trinitarian foundation of the inner/outer relations in Marpeck's thought and is found again in the *Response*.[70] Nevertheless in the first part of the *Response*, the person of Jesus and his two natures become more important than the Trinitarian foundation. It is in this way that Marpeck cites John 6:63: "The words that I have spoken to you are Spirit and life." For Marpeck this verse means that the audible words from the mouth of the man Jesus, i.e. something outer or external, can also be "*wesen*" or "*warhait*." The influence of the Gospel of John cannot be overemphasized in Marpeck's work (as with Luther).

Ephesians 5:30-32[71] also becomes an important text to demonstrate the continuity between the flesh of Christ and that of Christians.

> What is the unglorified body of Christ on earth (i.e. His community) a bodily and real (*wesentlicher*) temple, or the real (*wesentlich*) people and priesthood of God if not a bodily reality (*wesen*)? Thus we need to understand the words of Paul: "Are we not members of his body, of his flesh, of his bones?"[72] What's more: "The two will become one flesh: this is a great mystery; and I am applying it to Christ and the church." (Ephesians 5)

In addition to these efforts that take the biblical texts very seriously, Marpeck, like most theologians, sometimes goes too far in adapting certain texts to his theological convictions.[73]

The Humanity of Christ and the Church

In *A Clear Instruction* (1531), Marpeck identified the visible church with the humanity of Christ, thus considering the presence of the Christian community on earth as a prolongation of the Incarnation. While small

---

[70] See Loserth, 127-178.

[71] Loserth, 136, 42. Marpeck frequently cites this text.

[72] Marpeck follows here the standard sixteenth-century translations of Eph. 5:30 that add "von seinem fleisch und von seinem gebainen," a phrase found in Erasmus' 1516 Greek New Testament, but not used in modern translations. See K. Aland, M. Black et. al. (ed.) *The Greek New Testament* (Stuttgart: United Bible Societies, 1966), 677 note 8.

[73] See for example Loserth 138, where Marpeck tries to ground his concept of "*wesen*" by simply citing texts where the word can be found.

groups of Schwenckfeld's disciples met in diverse parts of southern Germany, these groups did not consider themselves as "church" nor did they practice the sacraments. Marpeck was extremely annoyed by these spiritualist tendencies in which he saw a rejection of what Christ asked of his disciples. He accused Schwenckfeld of placing too much importance on the "glorified" Christ. In order to have a "complete" Christology the unglorified life of Christ on earth needed equally significant consideration. With a change in terminology to counter Schwenckfeld, Marpeck now proposed that the "unglorified" Christ still exists on earth, in the form of the church. Christ also functioned as "head" on earth, during the Incarnation, not only after the Ascension.

> If Schwenckfeld recognized Christ truly, not only by his glorified, reigning head, but how he lived and worked on earth as head before his glorification and works today through his unglorified body on earth, he might understand our language better...[74]

Indeed the sacraments and the ceremonies are actions of the unglorified Christ. Christ glorified, in heaven, always acts on earth by means of his unglorified body, the church. All that the church does is part and parcel of the unglorified humanity of Christ.

> Schwenckfeld rejects our affirmation that Christ the Lord reigns today bodily (i.e. externally) by means of the unglorified body that continues to exist on earth (i.e. his community). This concerns every commandment, word, teaching regarding outer actions that serve the common good, such as teaching, baptism, the Lord's Supper, exhortation, excommunication, discipline, evidence of love, laying on of hands, improvement... The glorified and reigning Christ acts by these means through His and the Father's Holy Spirit.[75]

Schwenckfeld, who only wants to hear of the glorified Christ, denies the importance of the visible Church. Consequently Marpeck's *Response* affirms that Christ is not yet completely glorified.

---

[74] Loserth, 134, 40.
[75] Loserth, 135, 5.

> Schwenckfeld ... represents Christ uniquely in his glorified countenance, denying the existence of his unglorified body that is his community. Christ is not yet fully glorified. His unglorified body still needs to be glorified upon his return (Phil. 3).[76]

Marpeck associates the believers' transfiguration on the last day with the complete glorification of Christ.[77]

The logic of the humanity of Christ is thus found again in the *Response* and is used in the same way as in the *A Clear Instruction*. The difference is this new distinction between the unglorified and the glorified body of Christ, used to counter Schwenckfeld's Christology.

The Humanity of Christ and Ethics

Just as Schwenckfeld's emphasis on the glorified Christ appeared to ignore the importance of the visible church, so Marpeck believed that a spiritualist Christology had little room for an ethic of discipleship or "*Nachfolge Christi*." Maier affirms that Schwenckfeld's Christology may be characterized by the term "*Erkenntnis Christi*," that the goal of Schwenckfeld's thought was to come to the *knowledge of Christ*.[78] This same notion of the "knowledge of Christ" played an important role in the discussion between these two adversaries. For Marpeck true knowledge of Christ consisted in the following in his footsteps and keeping his commandments. Without such obedience, speculation concerning the divine nature and the glory of Christ had little value. He attacked the heart of Schwenckfeld's Christology.

---

[76] Ibid., 154, 25.

[77] See also 141, 11. Marpeck based his argument on Phil. 3:20-21. "But our citizenship is in heaven, and it is from there that we are expecting a Savior, the Lord Jesus Christ. *He will transform the body of our humiliation that it may be conformed to the body of his glory...*"

[78] Maier, *Caspar Schwenckfeld on the Person and Work of Christ*, 13. "The guiding principle of Schwenckfeld's theology ... was 'die Erkenntnis Christi,' the genuine knowledge of Christ and the true faith apprehending this knowledge. In fact he summarized his entire theology as 'Erkenntnis Christi' (CS 13, 985) and even amended the reformation formula to include the phrase: 'Justification derives from the knowledge of Christ through faith.'"

> We have no knowledge of Christ (who is light for life eternal) apart from obedience to his commandments and to his teachings. For a person who obeys them and does them, in such a one Christ is glorified and he in Christ. Apart from this presence of Christ in us, the knowledge of Christ (of his glory and light, of his being seated at the right hand of God in a majesty equal to God's, and of all that the Christ is) serves no purpose.[79]

In emphasizing this point, Marpeck connected it to the concept of inner/outer reality (*wesen*). The most important goal and result of the union of the divine/human and inner/outer elements was the changed lives of believers. Such a life is possible because the divine unites itself with the believer's spirit and thus opens the possibility of accomplishing God's will. Through faith and a transformed life resulting from union with Christ, the believer "knows" Christ. The union between believers and Christ is similar to that which exists between Jesus Christ and God. In the following citation, Marpeck alludes to John 5:19 to reinforce his point.

> What the inner man by faith in Jesus Christ sees God do, the outer man does likewise. Thus we know Christ in his new celestial reality...[80]

> ...The divine as inner reality unites itself with the inner man as creature in order to accomplish the will of God. Thus what God requires inwardly, the inner man requires of the outer man so that the latter can act externally.[81]

Marpeck sought to take seriously the ethical life of the believer without falling prey to the legalism that characterized some Anabaptist groups. Changed lives were the result of the work of Christ and not of human effort.[82] The Holy Spirit fills human hearts and thus renews the human spirit. This renewal is revealed in obedience which, in the language of Marpeck and Schwenckfeld's debate, remains an outer reality.

---

[79] Loserth, 66, 26.
[80] Ibid., 126, 31.
[81] Ibid., 125, 44.
[82] Loserth, 156, 14.

Marpeck used New Testament texts that describe Jesus as a model to follow but for him, these texts concern the unglorified Christ, before the resurrection and ascension. Thus it is clearly stated that one needs first of all to "know" the unglorified Christ before coming to knowledge of the glorified Son of God.

> When Paul exhorts us to be of the same spirit as was in Jesus Christ, he is not referring to Christ as he currently is (i.e. in heaven in his glory), but of Christ as he was before (i.e. on earth and unglorified). He first humbled himself before God raised him. (Phil. 2)[83]

In this perspective Christology is not only something theoretical but is actually lived. A "low" or "unglorified" Christology is needed before a "high" or "glorified" Christology.[84] In this context, Marpeck began to use a word that was already well-rooted in the Anabaptist tradition, *Gelassenheit* or "yieldedness." Jesus (and particularly his death) is the model of "yieldedness" and of the "low" Christology for the believer who must:

> ...Take up the cross of Christ and follow the example of Christ that he offered...
>
> ...in the depths of his yielding (*gelassenheit*) unto death.[85]

Marpeck observed a great divergence between Schwenckfeld and himself on this subject and severely judged his opponent.

> In summary, the spirit who presents Christ as the glorified head and denies his unglorifed body, i.e. the community ... who teaches salvation and seeks the magnificence and the light of Christ ... before descending with him into the depths of the true yielding (*gelassenheit*) of humility and of the obedience to his will, his teachings, and his commandments and to the Word of God (which concerns all visible and outer realms) ... cannot be from God.[86]

---

[83] Ibid., 156, 14.
[84] See Loserth, 135, 22; 140, 38; 154, 40.
[85] Ibid., 154, 40.
[86] Ibid., 155, 23.

The Human Christ and Sin

Marpeck hardly responded to Schwenckfeld's accusation that he had claimed that Christ, in his human nature, could have sinned if he had so desired. The *Response* simply notes that such an affirmation cannot be found in the *Admonition* and that Schwenckfeld must first prove that such is truly his thought on the matter. Marpeck denied any such thoughts, claiming that such an accusation merely demonstrated the biased character of the *Judicium*.[87]

Mary and the Conception of Jesus

In the *Admonition* Marpeck countered the doctrine of the celestial flesh of Christ by affirming that Jesus received the flesh of his mother. Schwenckfeld was not satisfied with Marpeck's formulation of Jesus' birth, that he was human from the "seed" of woman but not from the "seed" of man. (*Christus sey ein mensch von weibsamen aber one manssamen.*) The Silesian argued that Christ was a physical descendant of Abraham, which would mean that it was incorrect to say, as did Marpeck, that Jesus was born without the "seed" of man.[88]

Marpeck's response to this criticism was quite simple. The words "*one manssamen*" (without the seed of man) were meant to underline the virgin birth of Jesus. At the same time he buttressed his argument on traditional doctrinal formulations about Christ, which probably indicated his desire to remain christologically orthodox.

> We know that the origin of Christ's flesh resides in all the generations of patriarchs up until the pure and chaste virgin Mary. In her virgin body the Holy Spirit conceived the eternal word. It is in her body that he became flesh and is a true fruit of this body, having participated in its flesh and blood. As written in Luke 1, she knew no man. He (Jesus) is the Son of God and of men, with a divine and a human nature, whom we confess to be of woman's "seed." We know thus Christ – the eternal

---

[87] Ibid., 131, 23.
[88] Loserth, 130, 19. See also Schoeps, *Himmlischen Fleisch*, 29-30; Maier, *Caspar Schwenckfeld on the Person and Work of Christ*, 48-49; Furcha, *Schwenckfeld's Concept of the New Man*. 80.

Word of the Father and the third (sic) person of the divine unity – as well as the origin and reality of his humanity.[89]

Marpeck apparently wanted to formulate his thought on the birth of Jesus so that his concept of the humanity of Christ would flow directly and logically from it. Jesus received true human flesh from his mother, and with this flesh, as the Son of God, he made known the will of his Father. Marpeck's description of the humanity of Christ became a criterion of orthodoxy in his debate against Schwenckfeld.

> Christ himself is the Word of God ... by whom all things were created (John 1, Col. 1). He descended from the heights of God to come into this world (Luke 1, John 16, 17) and was conceived by Mary, the pure virgin, by the Holy Spirit. He was born from the blessed body, flesh and bones of Mary. He was a true man, without spot, natural, tangible, visible, capable of suffering and mortal. He was of the family, manner, and nature of earthly men, and created, possessing flesh, blood and bones. This very man and Son of God made known to us by his human mouth the will, teachings, and the commandments, i.e. the Word of God, that are Spirit and life (John 6)... He who does not confess but denies this humanity of Christ is to us an anti-Christ and denies the truth.[90]

The Christology of the second part of the Response

Our analysis of the second part of the *Response* will follow the textual divisions of the author which deal with original sin, the state of being a child of God, the Word of God, the Lord's Supper, and the faith of the ancients.

Original Sin

George Williams has aptly summed up Marpeck's theology of sin up to the debate with Schwenckfeld.

> In the *Bekenntnis* (Strasbourg 1532) he had said simply that infants were freed from the guilt of original sin ... by the

---

[89] Loserth, 131, 1.
[90] Ibid., 144, 44.

command of Christ, who said, "Of such is the kingdom of heaven." In the *Vermahnung (Admonition)* he had dropped this argument, but says that infants enjoy a countervailing inherited grace (*Erbgnade*) and are in a state of "creaturely innocence."[91]

In the second part of the *Response*, Marpeck felt the need to develop his thought regarding sin given the fact that Schwenckfeld had accused him of pelagianism, i.e., of the view denying that the fall of Adam affects in a profound way the being of each and everyone and of affirming that human beings can do good by their own means.[92] In addition, since Marpeck only considered humans accountable to God at the moment when they consciously acted against the divine will, Schwenckfeld accused him of limiting sin to outer acts instead of also including sin within the inner or spiritual realm of human existence.[93]

Original Sin and Knowledge

Even though Marpeck "localized" sin at the level of knowledge, he claimed not to deny the universal consequences of Adam's fall.[94] Original sin is "inherited" when one becomes conscious of good and evil and chooses evil. Everyone inherits this sin, but God does not count it against us until we come to the knowledge of good and evil and act upon it.

> Original sin is transmitted only in the knowledge of good and evil. Adam and Eve, our father and mother, inherited it when they ate the fruit of the knowledge of good and evil in disobedience to God's interdiction. By that, all humans inherit it. Before the knowledge of good and evil and before humans leave good and do evil, neither original sin nor actual sin count before God.[95]

---

[91] Williams, *The Radical Reformation*, 3rd edition, 719.
[92] Loserth, 189-190.
[93] Ibid., 227-227.
[94] For Marpeck, sin could not be located in the flesh as such, otherwise salvation would be impossible. "Wie hetten sy dann selig kunden werden oder wie mocht noch heute oder in ewig ein ainiger mensch selig werden, so fleisch und blut selbs die sünd were?" Loserth, 192, 41.
[95] Loserth, 194, 30. (Marpeck restates the *Vermanung*, 215).

Marpeck thus conceives of sin in relation to conscious knowledge. Moreover he uses the terms "intelligence" and "reason" in this discussion.

> Concerning our response regarding sin and original sin, first one must note what is truly and fundamentally sin. We first find an answer in the fall of the devil and in that of Adam. Both these falls take place in and through the intelligence of intelligent creatures...[96]

> Sin and unbelief originate ... in reason and not in the unreasonableness of humans.[97]

Unfortunately Marpeck does not precisely define these terms. However he was probably attempting to demonstrate that intelligence and reason are not yet functional among children and that infant baptism is falsely understood as the remedy for original sin. He also believes to have answered the accusation that he only sees sin in outer actions. Consistent with the broad strokes of his theology, he writes that sin is both an inner and outer reality.

> In Adam's transgression there is only one sin and not two, because there cannot be any outer sin without inner sin. No one can sin before the corruption of the human spirit.[98]

Sin and the *Theologia Deutsch*

To reinforce his position on sin, Marpeck introduces in this section a dozen citations from the *Theologia Deutsch*, a medieval mystical text that had been put back into circulation in the sixteenth-century by the young Luther.[99] The *Response* chose in particular a series of citations that define sin as disobedience.

> It is written in the 14th chapter of the *Theologia Deutsch*: Disobedience and sin are one and the same thing. There

---

[96] Ibid., 212, 47
[97] Ibid., 237, 26.
[98] Ibid., 251, 13. See also 213, 5; 251, 5 and Bergsten, *Pilgram Marbeck und seine Auseinandersetzung*, 75.
[99] For a history of the *Theologia Deutsch*, see Ozment, *Mysticism and Dissent*, 14-60.

exists no other sin than disobedience and that which results from it.¹⁰⁰

Disobedience consists of willing something other than the divine will.

> All willfulness outside the will of God (i.e. all self-will and that which flows from it) is sin.¹⁰¹

By citing the *Theologia Deutsch* Marpeck probably did not improve his situation in Schwenckfeld's perspective. By wanting to emphasize that sin is a question of will (disobedience), Marpeck cited a few texts which implied that salvation depends also on this same human will and not only on the grace of God revealed in the work of Christ.

> Whoever is disobedient is living in sin. Sin cannot be expiated or healed without a return to obedience. Thus as long as man lives in disobedience his sin is never expiated or healed, no matter what he does. Note well that disobedience itself is sin. If one returns to true obedience, all is healed, expiated and forgiven; otherwise not.¹⁰²

This text definitely implies that forgiveness depends on obedience, which was not the position of the Reformation, of Marpeck in general or even of medieval Catholicism. Previously it was noted that obedience was seen as the fruit of the Holy Spirit's labour and does not precede it. Here in his attempt to demonstrate that sin cannot be identified with material reality, but that it should rather be located in human intention, Marpeck does leave himself open to the charge of pelagianism.

The Death of Christ Cancels the Sin of Adam

In the defense of adult baptism, Marpeck continuously affirmed that since the work of Christ, humanity is no longer guilty of Adam's sin (original sin) but only of conscious (actual) sin.¹⁰³ Catholic theology affirmed as

---

¹⁰⁰ Loserth, 213, 37. See also 214, 3; 213, 41.
¹⁰¹ Ibid., 215, 38. See also 214, 32; 215, 25.
¹⁰² Ibid., 215, 2.
¹⁰³ "Die schuld Ade und Eve ist durch Christum widerbracht, nit allein an Adam und Eva sonder auch an allen menschen…" Loserth, 205, 5. See also 199, 14; 236, 36. Cf. Finger,

much, but posited infant baptism to mediate the taking away of guilt. In Catholic theology, after baptism and the healing of original sin, Christians became responsible for the sins they committed, for which they needed to confess and do penance. Marpeck (and Anabaptism) claimed as much, i.e., that the work of Christ cancels original sin, but they did away with the sacramental mediation of infant baptism. Baptism was then free to take on a radically different meaning than in the medieval tradition.

Sketch of an Anthropology

Pilgram Marpeck needed to strengthen his anthropology in response to Schwenckfeld's *Judgment*. How does one claim the universality of sin while at the same time positing human responsibility? How does one posit human responsibility without being "pelagian," i.e. without denying salvation by grace? Schwenckfeld used the example of a young fox. The fact that the young fox has not yet eaten a chicken does not change the nature of the fox; he still is a fox and someday he will eat a chicken. The analogy is self-evident. For Marpeck, the fox is not guilty before he eats the chicken, whereas for Schwenckfeld the fox is already guilty before he eats it. Marpeck replied that a comparison between a human being and an animal was not very helpful.

The Light of Nature

Since the fox has nothing to help him resist evil and see the good, he will necessarily eat the chicken. This is not the case for humans. Humans simultaneously possess *"erbbresten"* (Zwinglian term for original sin) and a certain "original grace" (*erbgnaden*)."[104] Humans have both an inherent tendency toward evil and a tendency toward good. God gives this tendency toward good to humans.

> We discover thus two tendencies in children. First a good tendency, divine and pure (the inbreathed spirit and the law of

---

"…Most Anabaptists thought that though children were affected by sin, they were cleansed through Christ's atonement." *Contemporary Anabaptist Theology*, 169.
[104] Loserth, 206, 44.

God that is written on the heart) and second a bad tendency, diabolical and impure...[105]

The *Response* describes this "*erbgnad*" with several other descriptive terms: the light of nature, the inner eye, the inbreathed spirit. Marpeck went to great lengths to ground his thinking in biblical texts. This grace was given to humans in creation and precedes the fall; nor does the fall completely destroy it. Marpeck describes this "light of nature" by referring to many biblical texts.[106]

The "*erbgnad*" is first of all the spirit breathed into man at creation (Gen 2:7: "God... breathed into his nostrils the breath of life; and the man became a living being"). This very spirit is that which makes humans intelligent. (Job 32:8: "But truly it is the spirit in a mortal, the breath of the Almighty, that makes for understanding" and Sirach 17:6-8: "Discretion and tongue and eyes, ears and a mind for thinking he gave them. He filled them with knowledge and understanding, and showed them good and evil). Marpeck calls this spirit "*der unsterblich geist*" in which the divine law is written. This law is a light for the eyes (Ps. 19:9). The *Response* identifies these eyes with "the inner eyes of the intelligence" (Eph. 1:18).[107] Next the eyes of the intelligence are associated with Matt. 6:22: "The eye is the lamp of the body. So, if your eye is healthy, your whole body will be full of light." This is the eye that can understand the will of God as Paul affirms in Rom. 2:14-15 "When Gentiles, who do not possess the law, do instinctively what the law requires ... they show that the law is written on their hearts." In sum, this light of nature was given to humans by God and makes them intelligent creatures,[108] different from animals, capable of knowing the law of God. This light does not function before the age of reason (which is not specified).

---

[105] Idid., 219, 25.
[106] All biblical references noted are from the pages 218-219 (quoted here from NRSV).
[107] Marpeck's exegesis is interesting but at times somewhat forced. For example he changes Eph. 1:18 from "die augen euwerer verstentnuss" into "die inneren augen des verstands."
[108] Loserth, 221, 12.

> Prior to the Fall, nature's light shone bright in Adam without any obstacles but the Fall darkened the light's brilliance, for "its light is obstructed by our own perverse life and will."[109]

At first glance Marpeck appears to present a perspective that recognizes complete freedom of choice. One of the important functions of "nature's light" is to resist disobedience and in a number of passages, whether the light shines or not seems to depend on the human will.

> Still today, it shines in all who admit it and creates such light or law in people in whom the fear of God dwells and leads them to natural holiness.[110]

Human beings do indeed have a certain choice in this matter – this is true. They may obey with the aid of the light of nature, but only in the meaning and manner of Old Testament obedience. The human can attain what the *Response* calls a "natural holiness" (*zu naturliche frommkeit*)[111] which however is not yet salvation in Christ. The ancients in the Old Testament who lived in the hope of Christ lived this natural piety.[112] In the *Confession of 1532*, Marpeck ascribes a certain obedience and piety to these ancients, but it was not the obedience and piety of the new covenant in Christ.[113] Thus this natural piety is important but the light of nature plays a yet more fundamental role for humankind.

It is by means of this light that God may lead humans to Christ.[114] The first step of this process is consciousness of sin. The light simultaneously shows the divine law and the fact that human beings do not accomplish it. Thus comes a consciousness of the need for Christ.

> It is by this light of nature (if we let it shine) that God draws men to Christ. This light brings the knowledge of sin by means

---

[109] *LW*, 92. Loserth 220, 24.
[110] *LW*, 92. Loserth, 220, 22.
[111] The English translation cited previously speaks of natural "holiness." *Fromm* or *Frommigkeit* in the sixteenth-century could also be translated as just or righteous, justice or righteousness. It must be remembered that the *Fromm-Machung* language was used in the context of Pauline justification passages.
[112] Ibid., 220, 19.
[113] See the article 4 of Marpeck's Confession of faith, *WPM*, 108-109 or *QGT* VII, 417.
[114] Loserth, 222, 33.

of the law. By this knowledge of sin and condemnation, the human being is broken and wounded. He becomes sick and needs Christ, the healer.[115]

This knowledge of sin is the first element of God's grace.[116] Once sin is recognized and one repents and believes in Christ, salvation and the Holy Spirit are accorded.[117] This process transforms human beings; they pass from the "natural" to the "supernatural" and become "spiritual" beings,[118] which means that obedience becomes possible through the power of the Holy Spirit.[119]

Observations

Marpeck's anthropology is an obvious attempt to undercut the doctrine of predestination as taught by the Reformers. For the Anabaptist theology of baptism to make any sense whatsoever, human repentance needed to be the result of a possible choice and not of an "eternal decree."[120]

As did Hubmaier, Marpeck uses medieval theological categories to argue that sin did not totally eradicate the *imago Dei* in the human race. We have seen that Marpeck was familiar with the *Theologia Deutsch*. That text puts forth the idea that the human being's soul has two eyes; one to see and understand the eternal and the other that keeps one from doing so.[121]

---

[115] Ibid., 234, 14
[116] Ibid., 234, 27: "das erst stuck gnad gottes."
[117] Ibid., 234, 39.
[118] Ibid., 234, 48.
[119] Ibid., 235, 9.
[120] Thomas Finger seems not to take this "anti-predestination" element of the natural light into account when discussing it in relation to mission. ("Marpeck went further. An incomplete kind of salvation involving repentance and hope for Christ's fullness could result from openness to God's breath or light or natural law infused into everyone... This implied that this salvation could be mediated epistemologically by features of other religions." *Contemporary Anabaptist Theology*, 270). Exclusivism or inclusivism of salvation was not the issue Marpeck was wrestling with here. The "natural light" was that very element that allowed humans to respond to the preaching of the Gospel (over against an "eternal decree" of salvation). Finger takes into account neither the larger context of Marpeck's argumentation nor of the contemporary debates with which he was dealing.
[121] Boyd, *Pilgram Marpeck*, 7.

The continuity seems evident. At times, the *Response* designates nature's light as "an eye," and presupposes the same two functions as does the *Theologia Deutsch*. Echoes of Tauler (1330-1361), are present, for whom man possesses a "light of grace" that helps him enter into relationship with God.[122]

In the eyes of the Reformers, Marpeck's thought obviously displays a certain synergism. Those who choose to let the "natural light" shine, "cooperate" with God in the process of salvation. Marpeck would reply that humans cannot save themselves by their own power but need the possibility to "want" to be saved and to repent before being "justified."[123]

In other words, the natural light does not allow humans to please God by their actions. But it gives them the possibility to refuse or accept grace. In fact, by calling the light "*erbgnad*" (inherited or original grace over against "*erbsund*," i.e. inherited or original sin) Marpeck could also claim that even the desire to want to be saved is the product of God's grace.

Finally as noted above, Marpeck's concept of sin in more consciously formulated in relation to his understanding of salvation. The notion of a single inner/outer "*wesen*" addresses particularly the dimension of human will and intention. Sin means that the human will needs to be changed, to will God's will and not one's own will. It is for this reason that Marpeck speaks of sin in terms of knowledge of good and evil, spirit, reason, i.e., in the realm of intentionality. Stephen Boyd describes this quite well:

> Marpeck says that "sin, death and hell and their rule and mastery consist purely of self-enclosed knowledge"... This self-enclosed knowledge was introduced through Adam and Eve, in whom the human nature became "an enemy to his own life."... Falling from the mind and will of God in unknowing, the human was snared by the cunning deceit, and will of the snake. Therefore, the ensuing knowledge of good and evil

---

[122] See H.-J. Goertz, *Ordnung in der Theologie Thomas Muntzers*, 95. See also A. Beachy, *The Concept of Grace in the Radical Reformation*, 202-206.

[123] Stephen Boyd apparently misunderstood my interpretation of *erbgnad* as a natural tendency toward the good (*Pilgram Marpeck*, 148). The "natural tendency" comes first of all from God via creation and secondly has the function of allowing one to respond to the Gospel, rather than being a tendency toward the good.

reflected a selfish reason ... bent on self rationalization and self control.[124]

Just as sin expresses itself first of all in intentionality, but also in outward, physical and bodily life, salvation is a healing of the human will (inner) that results in a renewal of the outer. The humanity of Christ is the very embodiment of the inner/outer *wesen* in which divine intentionality produces visible and outward newness of life in the realm of the created world.

The Child of God

In the *Admonition* Marpeck consciously related his soteriology to his doctrine of the humanity of Christ by means of the concept of "child of God." Those who believe become "children of God" through the reception of the Holy Spirit made available by the work of Christ. In other words the believer receives a "divine" nature similar to that of Christ, which means that the "child of God" is spirit and flesh as Christ was.

Schwenckfeld could not of course accept such a definition of a child of God. For him, Marpeck was guilty of confusing the spiritual and the material. In Schwenckfeld's eyes, a child of God is a completely spiritual being since it is impossible to be a child of God in the flesh. This criticism flows logically from Schwenckfeld's Christology, which claims that Jesus was never a creature and that flesh cannot be related to the divine.[125]

The State of Child of God as the Goal of the Incarnation

As always, we can observe an ethical concern and a critique of an exclusively forensic doctrine of justification by faith at the heart of Marpeck's thought. Christ became human so that humanity may become as Christ (particularly in behaviour).

---

[124] Boyd, *Pilgrim Marpeck*, 69-70. Boyd has shown how this notion of sin is rooted in the *Theologia Deutsch*. Cf. ibid., 26-30.
[125] This criticism is found in the statements by Schwenckfeld in Loserth, 284, 39.

> Christ, the Word, became flesh of our flesh and bone of our bones, so that our flesh may become pure flesh of his pure flesh and bones.[126]

To become a child of God means more than simply a spiritual change in the believer. It is a complete transformation of the human being. For Marpeck, the work of Christ transforms the very flesh of the believer, so that sinful flesh becomes conformed to Jesus' holy flesh.[127]

In addition to the individual aspect, becoming a child of God implies a social dimension, i.e. the incorporation into the Church. To have a purified flesh means participation in the body of Christ. Thus Marpeck can emphasize the importance of the visible church, a key emphasis for most Anabaptists.

> For God made a woman from the first, or figurative, Adam in a supernatural bodily form; thereby Eve became bone of his bone and flesh of his flesh. Even so, out of the flesh and bone of the second *wesentlichen* Adam, God made a woman, the church, Christ's bride in a supernatural form … Thereby she was made pure by his pure flesh and bones. So Christ the head and the church his bride are both one flesh (Eph. 5).[128]

The Purification of the Flesh: Spiritual Transformation

The affirmation that becoming a child of God meant the purification of human flesh obviously leads to the question of how Marpeck understood this purification. By highlighting first of all the double nature of the child of God, the *Response* insists that the believer remains in this world of things, flesh and bone. Salvation does not withdraw the believer from the world,

---

[126] Loserth, 287, 17. Marpeck is here (as is Schwenckfeld) indebted to the theological tradition of the medieval period, for which God became human so humans could become divine. See Ozment, *The Age of Reform*, 1250-1550 (New Haven and London: Yale University Press, 1980), 242. This is not an exclusively Orthodox or Eastern concept, as Thomas Finger seems sometimes to claim throughout his *Contemporary Anabaptist Theology*.

[127] Loserth, 287, 20: "das unser fleisch dem rainen heyligen leib und flesich Christi wie in anderen dingen in disen…gleichförmig ist."

[128] Loserth, 287,3.

it concerns his entire being. "Children of God are such in spirit, soul, and body, i.e. in terms of their full humanity."[129] But the question remains: how does this "purification of the flesh" take place? As in the case of the water of baptism and the bread and wine of the Lord's Supper, the material aspect or element is not directly transformed, or "transubstantiated." The transformation or purification of the flesh is also a "spiritual" change, i.e. it takes place first of all at the level of the will and of intentionality.[130] A true change of (outward and bodily) behaviour can only be the product of a spiritual transformation and a change of the (inner) will.

> The Church or the community of Christ is composed inwardly (spiritually) and externally (bodily before the world) of humans born of God. *They are children of God with their flesh and blood purified in the unity of the Holy Spirit with spirits and hearts purified.* Each is purified before God by the Holy Spirit in Jesus Christ and bears his treasure in an earthen vessel...[131]

Being a "child of God" means receiving a transformed will and intentionality through the Holy Spirit. Such a description stays completely within the bounds of the inner/outer union, where *"wesen"* still means *"geistlich"* or spiritual. But that which is *"geistlich"* never excludes the material realm. A transformed will "purifies" the body.

The Two Natures of Christ

Given that the concept of an inner/outer *"wesen"* is founded, at least in part, on the doctrine of the two natures of Christ, it is not surprising that Schwenckfeld called Marpeck to task on this important question. Two long sections expose Marpeck's thinking on this subject in two distinct contexts: 1) the two natures of Christ in light of the humanity of Christ as key to salvation; 2) the two natures of Christ in relation to the Lord's Supper.[132] The following analysis of these two passages will be accompanied

---

[129] Loserth, 291, 27.
[130] Ibid., 286, 22.
[131] Ibid., 294, 9. Our italics for emphasis.
[132] "Of the Word of God," Loserth, 294-316; "Of the Lord's Supper," Loserth, 427-584.

by references to the *Explanation of the Testaments*, the Marpeck circle's extensive biblical commentary.[133]

The Humanity of Christ and the Old Testament

Marpeck clarified his doctrine of the two natures of Christ in response to Schwenckfeld's accusation that he did not consider the biblical texts that speak of the pre-existence of Christ (prior to his Incarnation, 1 Cor. 10:3-4 for example). In short, the *Response*'s position is that all affirmation of Christ's presence in the Old Testament concerns his divine nature, not his humanity. Marpeck holds to the traditional position here: Christ was God from eternity, but had not yet been born in his humanity.[134] This was apparently an attempt to be in harmony with the Chalcedonian formulation of the two natures of Christ.

> We affirm and believe that glorified human being Jesus Christ with his one, undivided person, according to Holy Scripture, to be the true, almighty God in or with his two united natures.[135]

Nevertheless Marpeck's understanding of the inner/outer "*wesen*" influences his description of the two natures of Christ and gets him into trouble. Jesus Christ, Word of God, has two distinct natures: the one is "Spirit and life" (John 6:63) and the other is "a bodily voice."[136] The bodily nature of Jesus never acted in a person's heart in the absence of his spiritual nature. Within history the Holy Spirit did not come in its fullness before Pentecost. Only then did Jesus first share the Spirit and with all humanity. Before that event, Jesus' words were not "Spirit and life." The disciples only knew the true identity of the Messiah after Pentecost and the reception of

---

[133] Since the *Response* repeatedly cites the *Testamenterleutterung*, the inclusion of citations from this important (but very understudied) text seems legitimate.

[134] *Testamenterleutterung* (TE) CCCCII, Darumb sei Christus wol gestern und von ewig gewesst / als ewiger Gott / aber sein menscheit sei noch nit geboren / ...

[135] Loserth, 507, 38; translated by Rempel, *The Lord's Supper in Anabaptism*, 116.

[136] Loserth, 297, 22.

the Holy Spirit.[137] In other words before the resurrection and Pentecost, the disciples knew Jesus in the flesh but not yet in the Spirit.[138]

> They [the disciples] knew nothing of the action and power of the Holy Spirit (which is the invisible and true reality of God) until Jesus' Ascension. Only there did the man Jesus receive bodily, as man and flesh, the heritage of the Holy Spirit already promised in him. Of all mortal beings he was the first-born of the dead and he was the first to be given a seat in heaven at the right-hand of God, the Father, in the inherited Kingdom. From there he first shared and spread out the promised Spirit, the true token of eternal life.[139]

This apparent confusion between the Holy Spirit and the eternal divine nature of the Logos is open to at least two possible interpretations. Either Jesus Christ has eternally had two natures but received something additional at the Ascension; or Jesus Christ became divine only at the Ascension, after his resurrection. This latter possibility implies that he was only Son of God by adoption and not from all eternity. Marpeck does not appear to note this problem or to choose between the two. Some texts even mention both side by side. On the one hand Marpeck writes that even if Jesus' words were not Spirit and life before Pentecost, they could have been. Yet God still respects what is ordered through and by his Word.[140] But, on the other hand, other passages affirm that Jesus became Son of God with the reception of the Holy Spirit.

> Christ the man was the first to receive the promised Holy Spirit.[141]

> As Christ the man was the first to become Son of God ... he is also the first born of God.[142]

---

[137] Ibid., 301, 2.
[138] Ibid., 302, 34.
[139] Ibid., 302, 36.
[140] Loserth, 302, 14. Marpeck uses the notion of God's order. Jesus' words weren't spirit and life before the ascension simply because God ordered history in such a manner.
[141] TE, LXXIX: "Christus der mensch der erst sei gewesst heüt in empfahung des verhaissenenen hailigen gaists und salbung."
[142] TE, CCXLIII: "Une gleich wie Christus der mensch in heüttiger sünhaid ... der erst sun gottes sei gemacht/gleich also sei er auch der erst oder erstling in dises heüttiger geburt

Already in 1938, John C. Wenger noticed this contradiction in Marpeck's Christology.[143] More recently, John Rempel has clearly stated the problem, describing it as a "novel christological claim."

> Though Christ was always God, it was through the uniting of his bodily character with the word of God that he became fully God. Before his resurrection, Godness was not fully in him, though he was God as spirit and word.[144]

The Presence of Christ in the Lord's Supper

In the final part of the *Response*, Marpeck discusses at length the Lord's Supper and the manner of Christ's presence therein. Often sounding like Luther, Schwenckfeld's position was that the believer is nourished in the Supper by Christ's glorified body, i.e. Christ's human nature is offered to participants. Nevertheless, Schwenckfeld's understanding of Christ's glorified body was quite different from Luther's. Since Jesus, in his human nature, was never a creature and after the ascension this nature was no longer limited by space or by anything else that limits bodiliness as we know it, the believer need not eat the bread or drink the wine in order to participate in this celestial nourishment. Any statement to the contrary would limit Christ's body in space.[145] It was for this reason that Schwenckfeldian circles felt no need to share physical bread and wine.

---

aus gott..."
[143] J.C. Wenger, "The Theology of Pilgram Marpeck," 222. For Wenger, Marpeck's formulations are unfortunate, nevertheless he affirms Marpeck's orthodoxy.
[144] Rempel, *The Lord's Supper in Anabaptism*, 116. Rempel thinks that this awkward formulation was a way of denying any bodily presence of Christ in the Eucharist. What happened during the Incarnation and the Ascension was a new unity of the two natures, which tied Christ's humanity to his presence at the right hand of God. Finger moves in the same direction and makes the interesting suggestion that this language does not imply a "substantial increase in deity," but rather that "this one person, who was divine, was also greatly transformed by resurrection and functioned quite differently thereafter." In other words Marpeck may have meant that "Jesus' body also began participating in deity at that point." Finger, *Contemporary Anabaptist Theology*, 379-380.
[145] See Maier, *Caspar Schwenckfeld on the Person and Work of Christ*, 15-23 for a complete description of Schwenckfeld's position on this matter.

In the *Admonition* Marpeck had not directly addressed the question of Christ's presence in communion but stated that Zwingli and Oecolampadius' positions were the "closest to the truth."[146] In the debate between Marpeck and Schwenckfeld, the Swiss theologians visibly influenced the Anabaptist and the discussion at times eerily recalls the Eucharistic controversy between Zwingli and Luther, with the irony being that the Spiritualist Schwenckfeld sounded most like Luther, with the Anabaptist Marpeck, so vehemently defending the use of outer means, adopted the logic of the Spiritualist Zwingli.

Marpeck began here by emphasizing the fact that during the Supper, the believer eats and drinks the flesh and blood of Jesus Christ for eternal life. But he immediately clarified that it is not a question of eating physically or externally but eating "by" and "in" faith. In this perspective, "to believe" means "to feed spiritually."

> We eat and drink the flesh and blood of Christ for eternal and spiritual life by faith in the word of proclamation and in memory of the Lord's death.[147]

Commenting on John 6, Marpeck agreed that Jesus is the bread of life, come from heaven. The body of the Lord is real food (*recht speiss*) offered for our life and is the guarantee of our resurrection on the last day. Nevertheless this food nourishes the soul and the spirit and not the body and is thus spiritual food. The material bread and wine have a different function; they announce and recall the Lord's death.

> We confess that in like manner the Lord will give food and drink to the soul, to the inward person, with his holy flesh and blood. The food and drink for spirit and soul must be spiritual; natural bread and the wine do not nourish the soul. But they are used in remembrance and proclamation of Jesus Christ's death…[148]

To better demonstrate that this food is spiritual, the *Response* affirms (similarly to Zwingli) that the body of Christ cannot be present in the

---

[146] *WPM*, 288.
[147] Loserth, 465, 2. See also 464, 44.
[148] *LW*, 109.

bread because it is in heaven. For Schwenckfeld, the transformed body and divinized Christ cannot be separated from the divine nature. In contrast Marpeck writes that the glorified body of Christ is in heaven, seated at the right-hand of the Father.[149] In addition for Marpeck, Paul's words in 1 Cor. 11 affirming that we must "proclaim the death of the Lord until he returns" prove that Jesus is not present in the bread.[150]

When Jesus spoke of the flesh and blood offered during the first Supper, he was referring to the mortal body of Christ sacrificed on the cross for the redemption of sins and not the glorified body that ascended to the Father.[151] Marpeck also cited John 6 ("the Spirit gives life, the flesh serves in nothing") to show that the bodily eating of Christ's flesh would be useless. Moreover in this verse Jesus did not distinguish between unglorified flesh and glorified flesh since neither one nor the other could serve the believer in any way.[152]

Marpeck affirms that one of the most important functions of the humanity of Christ is the sending of the Holy Spirit, which gives life to human beings. In such a context, eating the flesh of Christ in the Lord's Supper is useless because it has already served its purpose for our salvation. Marpeck takes a further step in his reasoning. "Believing" means "eating spiritually" and "eating spiritually" means "to have the Holy Spirit in the heart."

> We believe that the body of Christ, his flesh and his blood, was sacrificed and given in propitiation of sins and of God's wrath. Faith renders useful the act of eating the flesh and drinking the blood of Christ (by which we were saved). By this faith and by the Holy Spirit in our hearts, the word that we believe becomes Spirit and life in our hearts.[153]

The Holy Spirit's presence in the Supper makes the bread into a "*wesen*" with the spiritual reality. This is a natural consequence of Marpeck's

---

[149] Loserth, 501, 40.
[150] Ibid., 482, 33.
[151] Ibid., 483, 8.
[152] Ibid., 483, 17.
[153] Ibid., 484, 15.

theology. But this does not imply that the bread changes or that the human nature of Christ is present in the Supper.[154]

Marpeck sought to affirm the presence of Christ in the Supper, but Christ is present in his divine nature. The bread from heaven is "the Lord Christ himself according to his eternal divine nature."[155] Since he claimed that Christ's divine nature is present in the Supper and not His human nature, Marpeck was forced to explain the relation between the two natures in this context. He cites a series of anthropomorphic biblical texts[156] referring to the eyes, ears, hand, and arms of God. Obviously God sees, hears, and can accomplish all things. Since Jesus is God, he possesses these same attributes.[157] This is also true for Christ's humanity, but only after His resurrection and ascension. As was noted in the previous section, the body of the man Jesus was a mortal body like ours, but became divine by resurrection and reception of the Holy Spirit.

> Before Christ's death, resurrection, and transfiguration, the Godhead did not dwell in him in that form, though by Spirit and Word he was God. But after his resurrection and the transfiguring of his body and flesh, the Godhead is in him not only according to Word and Spirit – as Paul says in Col. 2 – but in fullness, i.e., bodily. Through his exaltation Christ's body and flesh entered divine clarity and became fully God.[158]

After observing this divinization of Jesus' body, it is necessary to distinguish between two kinds of action. When Jesus acts according to his divine nature, he is omnipresent; when he acts in his glorified human nature, he can only be in one place at a time. For Marpeck this capacity of being in only one physical location or to be limited in space is an eternal attribute of the humanity of Christ.[159] Jesus Christ is "alles in allem" (divine) and simultaneously limited and unlimited in space (human).[160]

---

[154] Ibid., 458, 31.
[155] Ibid., 485, 7.
[156] Ibid., 493-495.
[157] Ibid., 496, 47.
[158] *LW*, 119. Loserth, 502, 15.
[159] Loserth, 500, 38.
[160] Ibid., 501, 8.

The union of the two natures does not cause the human nature to lose the attribute of limitation in space. Otherwise there would be no difference between the two natures.[161]

As always, the Anabaptist theologian sought to base his perspective on biblical texts. The following texts are cited amongst others[162]: John 16 where Jesus speaks of sending the Holy Spirit (and not the glorified body); Matt. 26:11, "Poor will always be with you but you will not always have me with you"; Matt. 28:19, "and I will be with you always until the end of the age." Regarding these last two texts, Marpeck claims that the first speaks of Christ's human nature whereas the second speaks of his divine nature. A phrase from the Apostles' Creed is also cited that affirms Jesus has "ascended into heaven" which, as with Zwingli, refers to the humanity of Christ. With these explanations Marpeck believes to have demonstrated his Christological orthodoxy.

> In summary we believe the glorified man Jesus Christ in his unified and non-divided person as in Holy Scripture is all powerful true God with his two natures unified. In the past we fought during a couple years for this affirmation against a few spirits who contradicted it.[163]

Nevertheless, in spite of this strong claim to orthodoxy, it is in the context of this discussion of Christ's presence in the Supper that Marpeck clearly identified the divine nature of Christ with the Holy Spirit.[164]

> Paul demonstrates with great clarity that Christ in his glorified body, human nature, flesh and blood, is not present in the Supper to nourish the soul, as Schwenckfeld believes. Rather he is present in his divine nature or Holy Spirit.[165]

---

[161] Ibid., 502, 29.
[162] Ibid., 502-503.
[163] Ibid., 507, 38. This last sentence recalls perhaps the years Marpeck and Scharnschlager spent in Strasbourg when they had contact with Melchior Hoffman. His name and his Christological errors are mentioned a couple times in this section.
[164] J. C. Wenger, "The Theology of Pilgram Marpeck," 215 already noted this identification.
[165] Loserth, 508, 19. See also 508, 45.

Christ's presence in his divine nature and the Holy Spirit exist, not only in the Supper, but wherever the inner/outer union or *"wesen"* is found.[166]

Two observations follow. First of all Marpeck's identification of the divine nature of Christ with the Holy Spirit is rather surprising considering his claims to remain within the traditional, orthodox Christology of the Church. Why is this the case? Perhaps in large part due to Marpeck's lack of formal theological training. Walter Klaassen has argued that certain Anabaptists (including Marpeck) had this tendency because of their dependence on biblical – particularly Pauline – language.[167] George Williams concurred.

> Marpeck, who would purport to ground his ecumenically Anabaptist churchmanship in the Trinity, again worked without the benefit of any firm grasp of the ancient formularies. Indeed his doctrine was built up from Scripture and especially from the Pauline corpus and John.[168]

Second, the two-nature distinction explains why Marpeck felt no need to defend the doctrine of the real presence of Christ in the Lord's Supper. In the second chapter, similarities were noted between Marpeck and Luther regarding the humanity of Christ. Luther developed his argument amidst a debate with the *Schwärmer* and the logic of his position led him to the notion of the real presence.[169] Now the difference between the two men becomes clear.

Luther conceived of a greater unity between the two natures of Christ and thus attributed omnipresence to Christ's human nature. For Marpeck, in the end, the spiritual element is dominant. If the Spirit (or the divine nature of Christ) is present, the material reality participates in

---

[166] Ibid., 511, 40. Cf. Bergsten, *Pilgram Marbeck und seine Auseinandersetzung*, 123, who notes that Marpeck affirms at the same time that Christ's two natures act and dwell in the heart of the believer. The reference he cites is ambiguous (515, 19) and concludes with Christ's human nature remaining in heaven.

[167] See Walter Klaassen, "Some Anabaptist Views on the Doctrine of the Holy Spirit," *MQR* (April 1961), 131.

[168] Williams, *The Radical Reformation*, 3rd edition, 684.

[169] Lienhard, *Luther Témoin*, 227-229.

spiritual reality and becomes "*wesen*." But the material aspect does not change and this participation in divine reality occurs at the level of meaning and not substance. Marpeck does not conceive of a "transubstantiation" of material reality but of a reality that consists of a unity of spiritual and material aspects. The Anabaptist can use Lutheran concepts and logic but his understanding of the relations between Christ's two natures (or between the inner/outer) leads him to a distinctly non-Lutheran conclusion regarding the real presence of Christ in the Lord's Supper.

Christ's Human Nature

The last question in this debate between Schwenckfeld and Marpeck concerned Christ's human nature and whether or not the term "creature" was a fitting description. As noted earlier, Schwenckfeld believed that Christ never was a creature.[170] In the *Response*, Marpeck adopted the same position as the reformers who disputed this point with Schwenckfeld: the man Jesus had a created flesh and according to his human nature was indeed a creature.[171]

To possess a body and a human nature necessarily implied that Jesus was a creature. More importantly, Christ's human nature retained its creaturely status even after the resurrection and ascension. The resurrection effects a significant transformation but the glorified body remains a created body while also being divine and part of the Trinity.

> Now because of Christ's glorification and the fact that his flesh became conformed with God, all differences that previously existed between him and the Father have disappeared ... i.e. mortality, the capacity to suffer, imperfection, as also other attributes related to temporal, earthly, and natural life of a creature that he had before glorification. Thus his human creaturely body is no longer a mortal body ... it is a new body, glorified, spiritual, and completely perfect, in all things equal to God the Word and to divine reality, now and forever

---

[170] Schwenckfeld did not always hold this view but his thought shifted to arrive at this conclusion in 1538. See Maier, *Schwenckfeld on the Person and Work of Christ*, 33-36.
[171] Maier, 39-40.

> ... Nevertheless the origin of his created flesh... will never disappear.[172]

Schwenckfeld could not imagine the worship of a creature, for that would be idolatry. For Marpeck, that was not the case since Christ even as creature is divine. The human nature is transformed into divinity while remaining creaturely.[173]

The debate necessarily focused on the origin of Christ's flesh. If the man Christ was not a creature, the origin of his flesh would not be the same as ours. Schwenckfeld affirmed that Christ did indeed come in the flesh, but that this flesh had a different origin than our own human and creaturely flesh. It was a "celestial" flesh.

Marpeck compared Jesus to Adam to explain how the Incarnation took place. God created the first Adam without sin. God breathed the spirit into him, the same spirit (natural light) given to all persons. In this view Adam's spirit came from God but was not God or divine. Jesus Christ, the second Adam, was given a created flesh like the first. Nevertheless his spirit was not the natural light but the eternal Spirit and Word.[174] A difference subsisted between Christ's flesh and ours. Because of his being conceived through the Holy Spirit and his birth of the virgin Mary, Jesus was not under the condemnation of eternal death as all other persons are. Natural human beings, as children of Adam, can and do sin and therefore inherit eternal death.[175] But Jesus could not have sinned and consequently could not inherit eternal death.

> From birth onward he was free because of his remarkable, supernatural conception and birth. According to the Spirit he was God, yes, life itself. Because of that he had no desire to sin and no need to die eternally.[176]

---

[172] Loserth, 535, 8.
[173] Ibid., 538, 18.
[174] Ibid., 541, 40.
[175] Ibid., 542, 30.
[176] *LW*, 126. Loserth, 542, 34.

Marpeck finally responded here to Schwenckfeld's criticism regarding Christ and his capacity to sin. The man Christ could not have sinned because of his two natures. Thus it was not necessary for him to die, but he had the freedom to do so.[177] Confronted with this choice, he chose to die in order to participate in our mortal flesh and thus take our weaknesses upon himself to vanquish the world and its "princes."[178] The death of Christ and the sending of the Holy Spirit make possible the believers' participation in divine reality and their union with the flesh of Christ.[179] As seen elsewhere, this transformation of the flesh means first of all the transformation of the inner person, which of necessity transforms the bodily way of life.[180] The final transformation will come with the bodily resurrection, when the believer will become completely conformed to Christ.[181]

Intimate connections between Christology and soteriology are present throughout this discussion. For Schwenckfeld, nothing "material" can be saved, and certainly not by a "creature." Salvation produces a spiritual state that no longer has any relation to the body. For Marpeck, we cannot be saved *apart from* our bodies and the transformation of the flesh of Christ becomes the model of salvation for all. Indeed the logic of each system is the same; what happens to Christ happens to the believer. In both theologies Jesus transforms human flesh. For Schwenckfeld the flesh's transformation implies leaving the material realm behind, whereas for Marpeck, remaining in the flesh is integral to salvation.

---

[177] Loserth, 543, 10: "Er muesst nit sterben, er mocht aber sterben...."
[178] Ibid., 543, 11.
[179] Ibid., 552, 23.
[180] Ibid., 557, 33.
[181] Ibid., 558, 8.

REFLECTIONS ON MARPECK'S CHRISTOLOGY IN THE RESPONSE

When coming to the end of Marpeck's Christological developments in the second part of the *Response*, we must attempt to deal with a very difficult, but important question. Are we, at this point, seeing Marpeck come to the limits of his capacity as a lay theologian who borrows constantly from such different sources as the *Theologia Deutsch,* Luther, Schwenckfeld, Rothmann and finally Zwingli? Is it possible to formulate a coherent theology by combining Luther's insistence on outer means (the humanity of Christ) while still wanting to claim with Zwingli that Christ's body is localized in heaven at the "right hand of the Father?"

Along with Torsten Bergsten, John Rempel sees Marpeck "coming to the edge" in his theology of the Supper. For Bergsten, in the second part of the *Response*, Marpeck arrived at a compromise by claiming that "the undivided Christ is present through the Spirit in the breaking of the bread, but his body, flesh and blood remain in heaven." Such a compromise is explained by "borrowing from incompatible sources."[182] Rempel himself found "two teachings on the Lord's Supper, the first based on the humanity of Christ and Trinitarian 'co-witnessing'" and the second "a memorialist view derived from the German-speaking Reformation in Switzerland."[183] The difference between the two is so great that one could be tempted to imagine a different author for later portions of the *Response*, but Rempel comes to the conclusion that "the contradiction at the end of the *Response* can best be explained as an inconsistent response to an intolerable personal accusation."[184]

Nevertheless, it is not totally clear that what Marpeck was doing was inconsistent borrowing or that he was not able to tie together the various elements of his theology. John Rempel seems to put his finger on the problem when he says that

---

[182] Bergsten, cited by Rempel, *The Lord's Supper in Anabaptism*, 118.
[183] Rempel, *The Lord's Supper in Anabaptism*, 127.
[184] Rempel, *The Lord's Supper in Anabaptism*, 142.

Marpeck stood against the spiritualistic tendency of late medieval thought and its appropriation by the Reformation. He rejected an ontological barrier between the worlds of spirit and matter. His theology of the Lord's Supper led him to a belief in the "real presence" of Christ. Yet he found that language unusable because, as it was conventionally employed, it dwelt on the transformation of the elements rather than on the action of the community and its transformation.[185]

It is not necessarily the case that Marpeck's Christology, even in its most "Lutheran" strands, led necessarily to a belief in the "real presence" of Christ and that his usage of Zwinglian arguments in the second part of the *Response* constituted a total contradiction of his earlier thinking.

Marpeck's use of the "humanity of Christ" and of the notion of the Incarnation countered the extreme Spiritualist position (neo-Platonic in nature) that the "spatio-temporal" world cannot mediate "spiritual" reality. But there is little evidence that his tying together of inner and outer was directly dependent on Christ's physical body and a continued presence of that one body throughout history. For Marpeck, the inner and spiritual *wesen* was not exclusively tied to Jesus' body, but to the created world, to outer and physical reality in general. The Incarnation was seen as the one exclusive principle or illustration of how God works in the world, i.e. through a combination of inner and outer. Since the world was ordered by God into historical, physical and material reality, God was "bound" to take that reality into account in the process of revelation. Therefore, when Marpeck used concepts such as the "humanity of Christ" or the "unglorified body of Christ" to refer to the church, to ceremonies or to people, they were used as metaphors to describe what continues to happen in the world when the Spirit of God and faith are present.

The importance of history in Marpeck's thought must not be forgotten. The "material" function of the humanity of Christ was always complemented by its "historical" function. What happened in the Incarnation was not only that the Eternal Logos took on flesh, i.e., the Incarnation, but that because of the New Covenant and the historical

---

[185] Rempel, *The Lord's Supper in Anabaptism*, 145.

working out of the promise, the Holy Spirit now began working within history in a new way. In some senses, Marpeck remained a Spiritualist, but a Trinitarian Spiritualist. The Incarnation made possible the sending of the Spirit into history and prolonged not the "human body" of Jesus, but the principle of inner and spiritual reality transforming the outer and material world in the image of Christ.

Of course Marpeck's lack of formal training and his tendency to borrow got him into trouble. The real problem is his identification of the Holy Spirit with the divine nature of Christ. The classical understanding of the Incarnation is that the eternal Logos, the second person of the Trinity, became flesh. This Logos is the second person of the Trinity and the Spirit is the third. Marpeck's characterisation of the inner/outer *wesen* in the *Admonition* as corresponding to the work of the Trinity is probably a more helpful image than tying it to the two natures of Christ as he did in the *Response*. A consistent use of Trinity would have allowed him to say that as God worked outwardly in the Word became Flesh, so the sending of the Spirit into history allows God's action to continue to be visible and tied to physical and material reality. The Word incarnate demonstrates within history, in a definitive and final manner, the possibility of human and divine reality "coexisting" within time and space. When that continues to happen after the Ascension, it is not a prolongation of the "Incarnation" in the sense of the presence of Christ's glorified body, but in the sense that God, through the sending of the Spirit and the human response of faith, continues to work within the circumscribed limits of created reality.

So the Lord's Supper, baptism, acts of love or service, can still be described as the "humanity of Christ," not because Christ is present in his "transfigured" body, but because God's Spirit is present within history, transforming outward reality to become conformed to the image of the Son in terms of self-giving love and service that overcomes self-will and sin.

Marpeck was Lutheran in that he insisted on the importance of outer means. The Incarnation means that God works with matter and time. Nevertheless he differed from Luther because he tied the continued use of outer means to the presence of the Spirit and not to Christ's human nature. Marpeck was Zwinglian in that he insisted that even the transfigured and divinized body of Christ retains the characteristics of a created body. Nevertheless, he differed from Zwingli because he refused an ontological barrier between Spirit and matter and saw physical reality as capable of being "really" transformed by the Spirit of God. Marpeck, in his sometimes clumsy borrowing, did come to a position that was truly coherent and truly his.

EXCURSUS:

Marpeck and Schwenckfeld's Turn-around

One of the most interesting aspects of Schwenckfeld's criticisms of Marpeck is what he wrote in relation to the faith of the ancients and the relationship between the Old and New Testaments. When in Strasbourg together, Marpeck and Schwenckfeld thought in similar ways about this subject – enough so, as we have seen, that Schwenckfeld appears to have influenced Marpeck's thinking. In the *Judgment* Schwenckfeld made a complete turn-around and adopted the opposite point of view, similar to Bucer's position that Marpeck had confronted in his *Confession of 1532*. In the *Response*, Marpeck reacted quite strongly to Schwenckfeld's reversal by citing an extensive series of Schwenckfeld's writings that demonstrate how the latter changed positions regarding the faith of the ancients.[186]

Schwenckfeld's Christology evolved over the years, for example in the question of the creatureliness of Christ's humanity. Marpeck was greatly disappointed with the evolution of Schwenckfeld's theology, particularly on this point of the faith of the ancients with its implications for the humanity of Christ being the new covenant accomplishment of the old covenant promise. If we assume that Marpeck learned this concept from Schwenckfeld, the change would have been that much harder for him to accept.

Considering the notable similarity between Marpeck and Schwenckfeld's theologies on this point in 1531 and Schwenckfeld's radical change in the 1540's, returning to the conversation between Bergsten and Klassen seems necessary. For Bergsten, it is this dispute in the 1540's that

---

[186] He dedicates 18 pages of the *Response* to this task. Loserth, 409-427.

marks the break between the two men.[187] But for Klassen, who discovered the two 1531 treatises, the separation took place earlier and *A Clear Instruction* was aimed against Schwenckfeld.[188]

First it is noteworthy that the adversaries themselves claimed that their relationship before the dispute was good.[189] Second, if Schwenckfeld's position in 1542 is used as a starting point, discovering traces and roots of the more fully "spiritualist" theology in the Strasbourg writings would certainly be possible. But if that knowledge is lacking as it was for Marpeck in 1531,[190] the similarities between their thinking in 1530 remains striking. They were in accord on more than the topic of the ancients' faith.

Even though Schwenckfeld was not an Anabaptist during his stay in Strasbourg, Klassen's evidence for an earlier break is insufficient, considering their many theological similarities at that time. In addition Klassen's proof based on the presence of the word "*Stillstand*" (literally a "truce") in the *A Clear Instruction*,[191] is weak. Though the *A Clear Instruction* argues against spiritualists who advocate a "*Stillstand*," the suspension of the ceremonies attacked in that text by Marpeck is different than the one found in Schwenckfeld's writings from that period. A more detailed study of the similarities between Marpeck and Schwenckfeld and of the "*Stillstand*" debate will illumine these points.

---

[187] Bergsten, *Pilgram Marbeck und seine Auseinandersetzung*, 46.
[188] *Covenant and Community*, 43. "While it is granted that Sebastian Franck and Bünderlin parted ways with Anabaptism in about 1530, scholars have been reluctant to draw the lines of distinction between Schwenckfeld and the Anabaptists. On the basis of this newly discovered material, however, it is necessary to make the distinction between spiritualism and Anabaptism earlier and sharper."
[189] Marpeck writes to Schwenckfeld in a letter of introduction to the *Response*, Loserth, 57: "weil ir doch vor in glaubenssachen so vil mit mir gehandlet habt." Schwenckfeld responds in 1560 "…Pilgram, der mir viel Jahr gewesen ist, bis er anfieng, vor mir und vor unsere Lehre zu warnen, auch dem Herrn Christo an seiner Ehr' und Glorien Abbruch zu tun." Loserth, 176.
[190] Contra *WPM*, 28, where Klassen affirms that "Marpeck knew that the quietism of Schwenckfeld would ultimately lead to a conventicler type of religion with its emphasis on the cultivation of inner piety."
[191] *WPM*, 69.

In addition to the differentiation between the two testaments, these two theologians were close to each other on a number of other questions during their years together in Strasbourg. Schwenckfeld's spiritualist tendency was already visible, but honest dialogue and friendly relations remained possible and apparently occurred. In Strasbourg the two greatest subjects of dispute between Marpeck and Bucer were divergent understandings of baptism and civil government. Though Schwenckfeld rejected re-baptism, while still in Strasbourg (and even a year and half after Marpeck left the city) he criticized infant baptism as false to Scripture and unfaithful to Christ's baptism. Similarly to Marpeck, he also countered Bucer with the argument that outer baptism serves nothing if it is not preceded by the Spirit's baptism.[192]

Regarding civil government,[193] Schwenckfeld was more flexible than was Marpeck, but the Silesian opposed the "Church/State" union that Bucer advocated in Strasbourg. Schwenckfeld also tended to reject the use of force and violence, another point where he would have been closer to Marpeck than to Bucer.[194] Thus regarding baptism and civil government at least, Schwenckfeld and Marpeck appear closer to each other than either one was in relation to Bucer. Therefore, amidst the polemics in Strasbourg, they could plausibly have seen themselves as allies in a common cause against Martin Bucer.

A more exhaustive study would be needed to determine how close Marpeck and Schwenckfeld truly were on these theological points. Nevertheless the most important question in this discussion is whether Schwenckfeld's spiritualism was already radical enough to be under attack in the *A Clear Instruction*. In 1531 Marpeck was challenging the spiritualists who completely rejected all outer means and rituals. Schwenckfeld had not yet reached that point in Strasbourg but continued to affirm the use and even necessity of outer practices. Like Marpeck, the Silesian affirmed that by means of the visible realm one arrives at the invisible or spiritual

---

[192] *QGT* VIII, 86-87. See also CS 3, 813 ff, *Von dem Kindertauf.*
[193] *CS* 4, 475 (1531).
[194] *CS* 4, 476.

realm.[195] In 1533 he was still proclaiming that God ordered preaching and the sacraments,[196] a far cry from the radical spiritualist positions challenged in the *A Clear Instruction*.

Klassen's perspective that the *A Clear Instruction* was written against Schwenckfeld depends on the concept of "*Stillstand*" used to describe Marpeck's adversaries. Indeed Schwenckfeld had ceased to celebrate the Lord's Supper already on April 21st 1526.[197] But Schwenckfeld's reasoning justifying this suspension and the reasoning criticized in *A Clear Instruction* are not one and the same. In the first two pages of the *A Clear Instruction* Marpeck describes his opponents. They are persons who have placed themselves under the proclamation of John the Baptist, waiting for a new prophet, for signs and miracles that confirm the words of the New Testament. These persons claim that none have the power to practice Christ's rituals and reject in fact all New Testament ceremonies. Due to these "deceitful snakes," many persons have fallen into a dangerous "*Stillstand,*" have stopped celebrating and using the ceremonies.[198]

Schwenckfeld's arguments for his "Stillstand" displayed an utterly distinct reasoning at this point in time. Schwenckfeld refused to break bread because the Church was in a situation of unfaithfulness, without love, without fruits of the Spirit and without discipline. If this situation changed he would be ready to celebrate the Lord's Supper again.[199] In 1532, Schwenckfeld wrote that one of the reasons (amongst others) for refusing the Lord's Supper is that there is neither discipline (bruderliche straff) nor exclusion (bann) in the Church, and that these disciplinary practices

---

[195] *CS* 4, 423.
[196] *QGT* VIII, 82 "Das ewig war wort gottes gehe durch den menschen Jesum Christum; dannoch hat er verordnet zu predigen, sacrament eingesetzt..." and CS 3, 821; Schwenckfeld is writing concerning outer baptism (end June 1530): "Es ist aber der eusserlich tauff auf einen gewissen handel gottes gestellt nemlich auf das bekantnus des glaubens auf den breisss der gnad gottes." Those critiqued in Marpeck's *Clear Instruction* could never have affirmed such things.
[197] Schultz, *Caspar von Schwenckfeld von Ossig*, 111.
[198] *WPM*, 71.
[199] *CS* 3, 384.

are necessary for celebrating the Lord's Supper.[200] In contrast, Marpeck's opponents in *A Clear Instruction* rejected church discipline.[201] It appears that that there were two different concepts of "Stillstand" circulating in Spiritualist circles in Strasbourg and that more proof is needed than simply the presence of the words "Stillstand" and "still zu stehen" to claim that *A Clear Instruction* is taking aim at Schwenckfeld. Moreover *A Clear Instruction* notes from the first page that its opponents were once part of the Anabaptist movement, which never was the case with Schwenckfeld.[202] We must conclude that Bünderlin and Entfelder, but not Schwenckfeld, were Marpeck's intended opponents in 1531.

---

[200] *CS* 4, 634.
[201] *WMP*, 71.
[202] I have developed these arguments in much greater detail in "Pilgram Marpeck and Caspar Schwenckfeld: the Strasbourg Years," in: J. Rott and S. Verheus (eds), *Anabaptistes et dissidents au XVI° siècle* (Baden-Baden, Koerner, 1987), 371-380.

Chapter 6

Salvation and Ethics:
Marpeck, the Reformation and Medieval Theology

As our study has moved forward, we have highlighted the various ways in which Pilgram Marpeck formulated his understanding of salvation in Christ and how it related to justification by faith and to ethics. His earliest writings spoke of "suffering with Christ" while the *Confession of 1532* used the notion of *Fromm-Machung* to join together justification and sanctification, thereby guaranteeing that a new life was one of the fruits of salvation. In the *Admonition* and the *Response*, we observed the concept of the "child of God," where the believer receives a new "nature" and a renewed intentionality via the Holy Spirit and thus participates in the new *wesen* made possible by the humanity of Christ. All these ways of speaking about salvation and justification have one important element in common: they are a conscious critique of an exclusively forensic concept of justification that, in Marpeck's eyes, was in danger of relegating discipleship to a less important level of Christian life.

This chapter will take one final look at Marpeck's soteriology, placing it in the larger context of the sixteenth-century debates between Anabaptists, Reformers and the medieval theology they were all leaving behind. Marpeck shared a common Anabaptist critique of Reformation soteriology and in some ways, a closeness to more medieval understandings of justification. It is to these larger questions that we now turn, with the hope of arriving at a better understanding of what it means to say that Anabaptism is neither Catholic nor Protestant or perhaps, both Catholic and Protestant.

In describing the difference between Anabaptist and Zwinglian theologies, John Yoder underlined the importance of history in the Anabaptist understanding of the redemptive activity of Christ. As was the case for Luther, sin and salvation in Zwingli's thought concerned primarily the inner being, rather than the outer order. According to Yoder, the Zurich reformer formulated his theology particularly in ontological and platonic terms. In contrast, as we have seen consistently with Marpeck, the Swiss Anabaptists conceived of sin and redemption in more concrete and historical terms. Evil is not only invisible or metaphysical; it is embedded in the world and its structures, which means that salvation must also concern the historical and visible aspects of reality.

In the same way, although redemption is indeed an inner and spiritual reality, it equally manifests itself in history in the lives of believers, in the midst of the world. It is more than simply the imputation of forgiveness to the believer. God's redemptive activity in Christ truly changes the course of human history and the everyday lives of men and women. Yoder again points out that, instead of assuming a platonic inner/outer dualism located outside of time, the Anabaptists conceived of life's dualities in historical and eschatological terms. Redemption inaugurates (in part) the age to come, introduces a new life, and incorporates believers into "the perfection of Christ."[1]

Profound divisions marked the sixteenth century and theology was often done in a reactionary mode. A reaction to an exaggerated position often created a newly exaggerated position, more often than not formulated with a strongly polemical intent. For example Luther's theology can be explained as a strong reaction to medieval Catholicism, and his perception

---

[1] John Howard Yoder, *Anabaptism and Reformation in Switzerland*, 174.

of its "salvation by works." Similarly the first generation of Anabaptists often responded in direct reaction to their context. Thus, in its own way, Anabaptism was a strong reaction to what was seen as "cheap grace," i.e., salvation as an invisible transaction, imputed to the sinner, too easily permitting "belief" without a journey of conversion and engagement. One of the objectives of this chapter is to examine these reactionary sixteenth-century positions by placing them in the broader context of the history of theology. Division and exaggerated reactions – often backed with persecution and violence – created a challenging climate in which to theologize and did not always allow the various participants to respect or understand the positions of their adversaries.

Even though Swiss Anabaptism first developed in the context of Zurich and of the Zwinglian Reformation, it was Luther's thought that mostly determined the terms of debate on redemption and the cross. In fact the debates about justification by faith placed the question of salvation at centre stage of the sixteenth-century Reformation movements, continuing and developing the medieval debates surrounding redemption and atonement.

In the middle of these medieval debates we find an important theologian of the eleventh century, Anselm of Canterbury, who produced a precise atonement theory. Jaroslav Pelikan notes that

> ... it would be more accurate to see in Luther's Reformation a further stage in the development of the "old dogmatic Christianity," as the Anselmic doctrine of atonement through the satisfaction wrought by the suffering and death of Christ had represented an earlier stage of the development.[2]

The key recurring questions concerned how to understand and live out the meaning of Christ's death. In the debates between the Reformers and Anabaptists, the role of the cross was essential. Obviously for each and everyone "Jesus died for us," he was "the lamb of God who takes away the sins of the world." In a sense the Anabaptists agreed with Luther when

---

[2] Jaroslav Pelikan, *The Christian Tradition, Reformation of Church and Dogma (1300-1700), Volume 4* (Chicago: The University of Chicago Press, 1984), 156 (henceforth cited as "Pelikan 4").

he emphasized the theology of the cross as the centre of the reforming process: "At the basis of the theology of the cross was the proposition that 'God can be found only in suffering and the cross'…"[3]

Nevertheless a number of differences exist between standard Reformation and Anabaptist theologies of redemption and understandings of Christ's cross. The central issue was the ethical significance of the cross. How does one articulate the two major dimensions of a theology of the cross? On the one hand Christ freely "gave himself" for our salvation. On the other, Christ's death on the cross was perceived as an ethical model or example. Both of these dimensions take their source in Scripture and traverse the history of Christian theology. Once again, the Lutheran and Anabaptist positions were embedded in the medieval traditions that preceded them.[4]

The expression of these two functions of Christ varied throughout the centuries relative to theologians and contexts. For Luther, "Christ as gift" was the pinnacle, but this was the case for medieval theology in general.[5] But the pinnacle was now formulated in a new way, as Luther strongly downplayed any suggestion that the cross of Christ might serve as an ethical example. Thus for Luther, who reacted strongly to medieval "salvation by works," emphasizing Christ's teachings and example – as did the Anabaptists – risked returning to what he was leaving behind. A theology of the cross that insisted on the importance of the ethical life seemed too close to the medieval theology he was rejecting. It was this rejection that became the source of Anabaptist reactions to Luther, raising an important question: to what extent can the importance of the cross as example and ethical norm be highlighted without falling back into a "salvation by works?"

John Yoder formulated quite well the Christological question at the heart of this matter. If Christ is "the Word made flesh," what is the

---

[3] Pelikan 4, 155.
[4] "For, as Luther had learned from Augustine, 'Scripture presents Christ in two ways: first, as a gift…; secondly as an example for us to imitate.'" Pelikan 4, 164.
[5] Ibid. "Like Anselm and Bernard before him, Luther emphasized Christ as gift far more than Christ as example. As example, Christ was "comparable to other saints," therefore this was "the least important aspect of Christ."

normative character of Jesus' humanity? Is he exclusively the saviour who died on the cross, or are his words and teaching also normative? As Yoder suggests, if the death of Christ had no ethical implications for our lives, if this death exclusively concerned an abstract or spiritual salvation, Christ's obedience "unto death" is shorn of its humanity.[6] As will be shown, such questions were not alien to medieval theology.

As with Luther, the Anabaptist position should first of all be understood in relation to the specific contexts and questions in which they were formulated without forgetting the fact that they both grew out of centuries of Christian thought and practice. The historian will of course look for possibilities of comparison. But it is not always easy to find Anabaptist texts that deal systematically with such questions. Anabaptist theologians were few and far between and had neither the leisure nor university teaching positions that allowed for "systematic theology." Their writings were circumstantial, practical and more often intuitive than explicitly theological. Nevertheless, several pages from Pilgram Marpeck's letter "concerning the humility of Christ"[7] offer a well-framed window into how he understood the relationship between salvation and ethics. In these few pages Marpeck recites, from beginning to end, the history of salvation in Christ. He starts with the fall of humanity, touches on the unfulfilled promises of the old covenant, follows with the Incarnation, the death of Christ, descent into hell, the resurrection, and his ascension to the right hand of God.

In these several seemingly obscure pages written in 1547, salvation is conceived of and described in historical and narrative terms. For Marpeck, redemption is clearly located in the midst of human history. This will become evident as the text clearly describes the benefits or concrete consequences of the redemption and the way that the cross ("the humility of Christ") functions as an example for believers.

Our examination of Marpeck's letter, in accumulation with the various other aspects of his soteriology examined in previous chapters, will show

---

[6] Yoder, *Anabaptism and Reformation*, 288.
[7] "Concerning the lowliness of Christ," *WPM* 427-463. We will deal more specifically with pages 429-434.

a certain continuity of Anabaptist thought with medieval understandings of justification, salvation and ethics as well as its particular relation and familiarity with some central affirmations of Reformation theology. Indeed Luther and Marpeck both represent tributaries of medieval theology. Our hope is that uncovering this broader common medieval heritage will help to free the debates from their "reactionary" tendencies and thus to better understand the theological differences in order to reformulate them in a less polemical manner in our own context.

Three important and interlinked questions emerge in this study.
- How did Marpeck understand the death of Christ?
- What is the relationship between Christ as saviour and Christ as example?
- Is the justification procured by the work of Christ an exclusively forensic transaction or does it bring about "real" change within believers?

Aspects of Marpeck's Salvation History

Before approaching Pilgram Marpeck's text, an overview of the major stages of Christian thought on atonement in Christ will illumine the broader historical context.

Atonement in Medieval Theology as a Backdrop to the sixteenth-century

No doctrine of atonement was established in the first centuries of church history with much detail or reflection, as can be seen in the doctrines of the Trinity (Nicea 325 and Constantinople 381) and of the two natures of Christ (Chalcedon, 451).[8] The "official" position, i.e. the symbol of

---

[8] Jaroslav Pelikan, *The Christian Tradition, Reformation of Church and Dogma (1300-1700), Volume 3* (Chicago: The University of Chicago Press, 1984), 108 (henceforth cited as "Pelikan 3"). "The relation between life, death, resurrection [...] had not been formulated definitively in the dogmas of the church councils and creeds, but now Western theologians sought to make explicit what they took to have been implicit in those dogmas."

Nicea-Constantinople may be summarized in a few lines: "For us people, and for our salvation, he came down from heaven."[9]

Prior to Anselm's medieval formulation, the first Christian centuries knew and taught the soteriological concept of *Christus Victor*. In this perspective, based on biblical texts such as Colossians 2:13-15, Christ's death was understood as a concrete liberation from the forces of evil, from Satan, and death.[10] Christ was given as a "ransom" to Satan, who then was tricked by the resurrection. Satan thus vanquished, humans therefore were freed from the powers of evil and death.

But the idea that God owed something to Satan or that Christ himself could be offered to him in ransom was problematic to many theologians. Not until the eleventh century did any theologian re-formulate atonement theory with a widespread impact. Anselm of Canterbury's re-articulation of the atonement and death of Christ, without official conciliar mandate, became nevertheless almost normative for the western Church.[11]

The Anselmian theological formulation was well-prepared by monastic christocentric spirituality, with roots at least as far back as St. Benedict, that is to the sixth century. This fact is a key to seeing that medieval understandings of Christ's work did not exclude ethics.

> In the tenth and eleventh centuries there was being developed and articulated the characteristically Western understanding of Christ, so that "the monastic period from 900 to A.D. 1100" has been identified as "the uncompromisingly christocentric period of Western civilization"; it was christocentric for the very reason that it was monastic. The Rule of Benedict of

---

[9] *Qui propter nos homines et propter nostram salutem descendit de caelis.*

[10] Concerning the atonement theories, see Gustaf Aulén, *Christus Victor: A Historical Study of the Three Main Types of the Idea of the Atonement*, (New York, 1961); John Driver, *Understanding the Atonement for the Mission of the Church*, Scottdale, (Herald Press, 1986); John Howard Yoder, *Preface to Theology, Christology and Theological Method*, (Grand Rapids: Brazos Press, 2002), in particular chapter 12, "Christ as Priest: Atonement."

[11] "To the extent that any formulation could be called 'definitive' for this doctrine in the Latin West, it would be the understanding of the work of Christ set forth by Anselm of Canterbury, ..." Pelikan 4, 23. Abelard's "moral influence" theory of the atonement was contemporary with Anselm, but received no major attention until the advent of liberal Protestant theology in the 19th century.

Nursia had prescribed that one should "put nothing ahead of the love of Christ," and monastic writers vied with one another in extolling Christ as the source of all good.[12]

Formulated largely in the context of medieval understandings of penance, Anselm's thinking became the backdrop for all subsequent debates on the subject.[13]

Why did Christ need to die and how is his death a source of salvation? Human sin offends God's honour. This offense requires "satisfaction" in order to restore the broken relationship. Thus Jaroslav Pelikan summarizes Anselmian thought.

> God did not require satisfaction be a means of appeasing his wrath, for he was impassible and therefore could not be wrathful as men are. Instead of speaking of the "wrath" of God, Anselm spoke of his justice: the justice of God had been violated by the failure of man to render to God what he owed Him; the justice of God also made it impossible for God to forgive this sin by mere fiat, for this would have been a violation of the very order of the universe that God had to uphold to be consistent with himself and with his justice. Any scheme of human salvation, therefore, had to be one that would render "satisfaction" to divine justice and leave the "rightness" and moral order intact.[14]

The Chalcedonian doctrine of the two natures of Christ allowed Anselm to articulate his understanding of satisfaction. No sinful human being would be capable of satisfying divine justice because of the debtor

---

[12] Pelikan 3, 106. "Eventually, scientific theology would catch up with Benedictine piety. In 1098, Anselm, the exiled archbishop of Canterbury, who was a Benedictine, composed his 'remarkable book,' *Why God Became Man,* on the purpose of the incarnation of Christ." For Anselm's text, see "Why God Became Man" in *Oxford World's Classics: Anselm of Canterbury: The Major Works,* Eds. Davies, Brian and Gillian Evans (Oxford: Oxford University Press, 1998), 260-356. (Henceforth cited as 'Anselm').

[13] "The essential point, however is that Anselm considers, presumably on the basis of the established satisfaction-merit model of the penitential system of the contemporary church, that the payment of a satisfaction by the God-man would be regarded by his readers as an acceptable means of satisfying the demands of moral rectitude without violating the moral order of creation." McGrath, *Iustitia Dei,* 81.

[14] Pelikan 3, 140-141.

status. God alone could render justice but was not responsible for the universe's disorder. Only Christ, because of his human and divine natures could bring into effect God's salvation.[15] Christ, as man, freely chose to obey the will of God the Father, but only his divine nature was capable of "satisfying" the debt of humanity.[16] This voluntary death of the incarnate Son re-establishes justice in the universe and provides salvation to humanity. This Anselmian background is an integral part of the sixteenth-century debates that are the focus of this study.

Marpeck's "Letter concerning the humility of Christ" comes from the later period of his life, when he was engaged in his polemic with Schwenckfeld. The few pages examined here are part of a letter written in February 1547 to Swiss and Alsatian Anabaptists.[17] The letter includes a severe critique of the Schmalkaldic War taking place at that time between Protestants and Catholics. Marpeck was a direct witness of these events since the city of Augsburg capitulated a couple of months before this writing, and the final battle won by the Catholics occurred in April 1547, a few months after the letter was written. It is especially important to note that the understanding of salvation portrayed in this text is intimately tied to a theological analysis that rejects violence in the name of Christ. For Marpeck, salvation could be separated neither from the history and real life of the world, nor from the way Christ taught and lived.

---

[15] Pelikan 4, 154. "Working within an Augustinian understanding of sin and grace, Anselm had taken as his starting point the Western reading of the settlement achieved at the Council of Chalcedon: Christ was "the God-man," who was not under the necessity of dying (since he was almighty) nor under the obligation of dying (since he was sinless), but who of his own free will had assumed human nature into the person of the Son of God, so that by his dying he might voluntarily achieve the satisfaction owed by humanity and make it available to his fellowmen (since he did not need it for himself)."

[16] Pelikan 3, 142. "The blood of the suffering God-man possessed infinite worth, far beyond that of any of the bloody sacrifices of the Old Testament. What gave it such worth was the utterly voluntary and spontaneous character of Christ's suffering, which was motivated not by any debt but by the honor of the Father and the plight of mankind. The Father did not force him to undergo such suffering and death, but Christ took it upon himself." And (143) "As the God-man and as the one who died voluntarily, 'he was offered because he himself wanted to be,' which meant that 'he was offered not because he needed to be or because he was subject to the edict of the law, but because he chose to be'."

[17] This same context was the backdrop for a second edition of the *Exposé*.

Christological Presuppositions: The Person of Christ and the Trinity

As was the case in the *Admonition* and the *Response*, Pilgram Marpeck's theology here continues to refer to the classical western Christological tradition. While grounded most directly in Scripture, he also argued at times directly from the doctrines of the Trinity or of the two natures of Christ. These same Christological assumptions pervade this letter as well. For example:

> For no one has seen the Father, much less known Him, except the Son who is in the bosom of the Father. Similarly, no one has known the Son except the Father who sent Him.[18]

> He was born of a virgin from the generation of the fathers. He was born the true Son of God, full of grace and truth and according to the Spirit.[19]

> He ascended and seated himself to the right of the majesty of God the Father and in the glorification of the Father, with that eternal, pre-existent glory which he had with the Father before the foundations of the world were laid.[20]

The Christological heritage that Marpeck embraced was common to medieval theology, to Luther, and to the Reformation in general, including most of its Anabaptist wing.[21] In other words the great sixteenth-century debates on justification and salvation assume a shared Christological background. "The presupposition for the doctrine of redemption in the Reformation period was the orthodox Christological dogma."[22]

---

[18] *WPM*, 429.
[19] Ibid., 431.
[20] Ibid., 434.
[21] Except for Anabaptists like Melchior Hoffman and Menno Simons, who advocated a "celestial flesh" Christology, inconsistent with the Chalcedonian formulation of the two natures of Christ.
[22] Pelikan 3, 116. "But here in this 'uncompromisingly christocentric period' it was the doctrine of the person and work of Jesus Christ, rather than the doctrine of justification or even the doctrine of grace, that became the principal vehicle for affirming the character of salvation as a free and utterly unearned gift of God; and in the period of the Reformation, this medieval understanding of the person and work of Christ was to be a presupposition shared, at least in principle, by both sides in the dispute over justification by faith versus justification by faith and works, with each claiming that its idea of justification was the

Christological assumptions having now been explicitly stated, Marpeck's description of salvation follows.

The Fall of Humanity and the Need for Redemption

Marpeck located the drama of salvation in the narrative context of humanity and the origins of evil. The history of redemption begins with the fall and the origin of sin in the world, i.e., the reality that rendered salvation in Christ necessary.

> He (Christ) was born to liberate man from the power of the devil, sin, death, and hell, that is from the guilt of Adam into which all men have come. [23]

Sinful humankind is trapped in the power of evil, which implies that redemption will be a (concrete and historical) liberation from this power.

The letter also contains a series of classic affirmations on "the wages of sin," from which sinners need redemption.

> [They have come into it] because of the guilt of sin, and because of the pains of hell and death which were laid on men. Men have been given over to the devil, who has the power of death and torment as well as of sin. And it is sin which causes the wrath of God so that, even among men who possess the salvation given by the Son of God, there can be no cessation of sin. Thus the wrath of God delivers to sin, death, hell, pain, and the devil. Because of the one sin of disobedience, man in all eternity is no longer able to know his God, Father, and Creator. Even today, man is utterly under the wrath of God and because of sin, man is outside of Christ, the Lord and Savior.[24]

---

only one consistent with the doctrine of redemption through Christ." It is important to remember that in the medieval period, salvation as a "free gift" of God's grace was never questioned.

[23] *WPM*, 429. This is a clear statement of the "universal guilt" of humanity, something Schwenckfeld saw as lacking in the *Admonition*.

[24] *WPM*, 429-430.

It is clear from this passage that Marpeck shared certain elements of the Anselmic tradition in terms of sin being subject to the wrath of God and standing in need of reparation.

The Death of Christ

In a primarily biblical vocabulary, Marpeck reproduces a great part of the traditional medieval discourse on salvation and atonement. Isolated from the larger context of his writings and thought, many sentences would appear completely Anselmian or Lutheran, since Marpeck emphasized strongly that Christ's death plays a fundamental role in the redemption of humanity.

> …because of our sin, the Father did not spare the Son. He has given him for the sake of man, and delivered him into the suffering and pain of death, even unto condemnation, as a salvation for men.[25]

> But because of sin, suffering and death came upon Christ … [but] Christ is without guilt.[26]

> … the Lord Jesus Christ, has liberated his people from their eternal burden; he has put it on His own shoulders and has fastened it to the cross.[27]

> Thus the Father did not spare the Son, but gave him up so that all who believe in Him may have eternal life.[28]

At no point does Marpeck offer a self-conscious critique of these "Anselmian" presuppositions as being contradictory to an ethic of discipleship. In fact the notion of "payment" or "satisfaction" for sin is reinforced by his understanding of Christ's descent into hell.

---

[25] *WPM*, 430.
[26] Ibid.
[27] Ibid., 431.
[28] Ibid., 432.

Descent into Hell

Following the narrative pattern of the Apostles' Creed, Marpeck next refers to the descent into hell. The suffering and humiliation of Christ extend to the very depths of hell to ransom lost humanity. The descent into hell is the prolongation of his death and humiliation and is understood within a historical framework, since it occurs "chronologically" between Christ's death and resurrection.

For Marpeck this descent means, first of all, that Christ had to pay the full price for human sin by descending into hell and suffering the consequences of Adam's disobedience. The cross represents the encounter between the redeemer Christ and evil in all its power.

> Because of the guilt of the first Adam, death and hell had seized, and held captive Him who had brought and accomplished salvation on earth, and who had also brought salvation to the prisoners of death and hell. Then all faith and hope disappeared from the earth and from the dead in the Pit... Even as Jonah was swallowed by the actual leviathan in the real depth of the sea, so, too, was the Lord, together with the rest of the dead, swallowed and made captive by the spiritual leviathan... And just as Jonah was in the whale only a short while, Christ remained in death and hell until He had completely paid, for our sake, the guilt of sin.[29]

Second, Christ descended into hell to liberate, concretely and historically, those waiting from the old covenant.

> In the depth of death and in the abyss of hell, the Lord of both life and death proclaimed the Word to the dead. Here the soul of Christ preached the gospel. On earth, Christ's physical suffering and death proclaimed the word to men living in the body.[30]

Once again at this point Marpeck is simply the heir of medieval thought.[31]

---

[29] *WPM*, 432.
[30] Ibid.
[31] McGrath, *Iustitia Dei*, 58. Cf. the following citation from Pelikan 3, 154: "Standing in close relation to the resurrection and the ascension was the descent into hell, which was part of the text of the Apostles' Creed and therefore had to be dealt with by Western

The descent into hell helps to maintain the narrative understanding of salvation. Redemption is indeed accomplished in time and history, since the ancients needed to wait for Christ's coming. There is a before and an after, a concrete work within history.

Resurrection and Ascension

Next Marpeck emphasizes the importance of the resurrection (and ascension) of Christ in salvation history in a manner reminiscent of the *Christus Victor* theology of the first centuries of the Church.[32] It is especially here that Marpeck differs from a purely Lutheran or Anselmian perspective. By his victory over death, Christ defeated the powers that imprisoned human beings.

> The whale could not hold Jonah, nor could the Pit hold Him there. Life broke through in its power, which the Lord had had in Himself against all the power of hell. By means of the glory, dominion and power of life He took life back again out of the midst of death, together with all who have hoped for the Lord and his Salvation.[33]

The death of Christ alone does not suffice for human salvation. The resurrection is an integral part, because by this means the power of evil was vanquished.

> Thus death has been swallowed up in victory, and Christ has emerged from death to life with all His chosen ones. To do so He had both to descend and ascend, for His soul did not remain in hell. Death could not possibly keep the life of all life imprisoned, and darkness could not put out or comprehend the light, even though the light had come into the darkness

---

theologians as a part of the plan of salvation. Because it stood in the creed between the burial of Christ and the resurrection, they ascribed it to the soul of Christ, since his body was in the grave and his deity was in heaven. Its purpose was 'to open a way of return to heaven for those who were being detained [in hell] for other reasons than punishment,' that is, for the patriarchs of the Old Testament who had been awaiting the coming of Christ to be set free." See also Williams, *The Radical Reformation*, 3rd edition, 1271-1273.

[32] See Thomas Finger, "Pilgram Marpeck and the Christus Victor Motif," *Mennonite Quarterly Review*, (January 2004), 53-78.

[33] *WPM*, 433.

> of hell. ... But the Lord, as the true light, has broken out of the darkness of the devil, death, sin, and hell, through the brilliance of his light and clarity and returned alive from death. In His own power He took life back.[34]

As the death of Christ precedes his resurrection, likewise the historical movement continues with the ascension. Once again Marpeck is close to medieval theology, for which "...it was characteristic ... that the resurrection of Christ was inseparable from his ascension into heaven."[35]

> He ascended, and seated Himself to the right of the majesty of God the Father and in the glorification of the Father with that eternal, preexistent glory which he had with the Father before the foundations of the world were laid.[36]

In these texts the resurrection and the ascension are described in terms of concrete victory over the forces of evil. The implications are that the "effects" of redemption will also be understood in terms of a concrete liberation, i.e. a salvation that takes places in the midst of history and not only in the inner person or in an eschatological future. Thus the particularity of Marpeck's theology is visible in the historical consequences of the saviour and redeemer's atonement.

Effects of Redemption

Our analysis of Marpeck's narrative of salvation began with the fall. This does not mean that creation is not a part of the story. If nothing else, the notion of God's order reminds us of the importance of the created realm in the drama of salvation. One of the ways that Marpeck spoke of salvation in this letter was as a return to the original intention of creation.

> Thus, Christ's sufferings enable men to regain their original purity and innocence in which they were created and to be prepared for their God, Father, Creator, and Maker. The Holy Spirit, who cannot be where sin is, can again find a place and gain a dwelling in men and then [transfer them] from

---

[34] Ibid., 433.
[35] Pelikan 3, 153.
[36] *WPM*, 434.

> the earthly to the heavenly. Thus man is created an earthly creature but, through the Incarnation of Christ, the earthly may become heavenly. .... Grace and the justification which leads to true devotion and which proceeds from faith, transfers man from the earthly to the eternal, heavenly state.[37]

To be transferred from earthly reality to heavenly reality does not mean that the believer leaves this world. The text clearly states that it is as "an earthly creature" that one becomes "heavenly." "Heavenly" refers to the gift of the Spirit who comes to dwell in "justified" believers so that they may be restored to the original intention of creation and do the will of God, i.e. live according to the teachings of Christ. This spiritual transformation, appropriated through faith, is the concrete manifestation of salvation. It is what allows discipleship to become a visible reality within human history.

Using a creative reading of 1 Samuel 4-6 and Ephesians 4, the letter moves next to the topic of "treasures" and "gifts" poured through the death of Christ and shared as a consequence of redemption.

> That same Lord, King, and true God has given Himself with all His treasures and gifts, and He will be the acceptable new year [Lk. 4:19]. These treasures were hidden and locked in the trunk of His body, the ark of the covenant. This ark He destroyed on the cross, and then He pried it open, which was the finishing of His work. The child fulfilled the Father's promise to us. The suffering and death on the cross completed His work on earth. Then He made the descent into hell, and dwelt with the condemned, with those imprisoned in perdition, and with those held by death.[38]

The treasures and gifts are freed and shared because of Christ's work on the cross.

> Therefore the precious gems, pearls, and sacred things are to be given to all who are washed, cleansed, and redeemed through

---

[37] *WPM*, 430. This text speaks of redemption as being a restoration to the state of creation. This is an important point, as it allows us to see that the salvation narrative does not begin with the "Fall," but in the creative intentions of God from the very beginning.
[38] Ibid., 431-432.

the blood of the lamb. They are children of and fellow-heirs to all the treasures of Christ's grace.[39]

These treasures and gifts are both fruit and consequences of redemption, permitting believers to do God's will. Thus empowered they partake in building a new communal reality, the Church, which is the temple of the Holy Spirit. The creation of this new social reality is thus one of the fruits of salvation in Christ. In this new community each and everyone receives a gift for the upbuilding of Christ's body.[40] This same body is called to resemble the head, Christ. He is described both as high priest and as example. He is the source of salvation, but also the one to whom believers are oriented as the example for life.[41]

This is where the intimate relationship becomes visible between the cross as "means of salvation" and the cross as "way of life" and "example." Nonviolence is held up as one of the concrete implications of this way of life. To follow the example of Christ, in the context of this letter, means the opposite behaviour of those engaged in the Schmalkaldic War. Following Christ is described as "patience," i.e. the refusal to defend the Gospel with the sword. Marpeck compares the Church, the temple of the Holy Spirit, to the Ark of the Covenant stolen by the Philistines (1 Samuel 4-6). The treasure of the Gospel cannot be taken or defended by violent means.[42] In a Church redeemed by Christ, Reformation can only be brought about with patience, thus by nonviolent means. The Catholics and Protestants that are fighting are compared to the Philistines who stole the ark during a military strike.[43]

---

[39] Ibid., 443.

[40] Ibid., 442

[41] Ibid., 444.

[42] "The ark of the New Testament is not compatible with the Philistines, I mean with the world. The impatience of the Philistines opposes the true patience of Christ." *WPM*, 448.

[43] "If, indeed, it is the ark of the New Testament, and it is truly called patience, tribulation always accompanies the ark. And when tribulation comes, they impatiently send it away again. Ignorant and unbridled animals, soldiers armed with weapons, accomplish for them what patience cannot." *WPM*, 448.

To follow Christ is to live like Christ, in the context of the new community, in light of his words, of his example, and of the example of the cross that is the source of salvation. Furthermore this redemption is Trinitarian. The Father sends the Son who humbles Himself and fulfills the high priest's role that brings about salvation. Once salvation has occurred, the Holy Spirit transforms the believer's life in the image of Christ.[44]

The Humility of Christ and our Humility

An ever-present and fundamental connection between redemption through the cross (Christ's death and resurrection) and the ethical importance of the cross as a model for living is indeed a key characteristic of Marpeck's theology. Against the Spiritualists (like Schwenckfeld) who emphasized the glory of the heavenly Christ rather than the importance of the Incarnation and its implied lowliness, Marpeck insists that there can be no victory over evil without living out the model of the cross. "To do so, he had to descend and ascend."[45] The humiliation of the Incarnation and death is the only means to victory over evil.

> The Son conquered the sin of many precisely by this descent into the depths, this greatest humility with which he humbled himself before the Father, and by which the Father afflicted and humbled the Son.[46]

As in Philippians 2, Christ's descent, the source of redemption, becomes the model for the believer's behavior. First and foremost, Christ's lowliness is a source of redemption.

> All the saints of God must learn the depths of Christ, these same depths of humility and damnation, into which the leaven of our sin brought Christ. They must learn the consequences of sin. Provided the devil completes sin's work in man, sin brings man into death.[47]

---

[44] *WPM*, 451.
[45] *WPM*, 433.
[46] Ibid., 434.
[47] Ibid., 434.

But this lowliness is also a model. Redeemed believers follow the same "downward" path.

> Here only the deep humility of Christ brings any possibility of salvation. Whoever does not grasp that he must be condemned with and in Christ in the depths can never understand nor achieve the height of Christ.[48]

It becomes clear at this point just how much Marpeck's writings are part of the framework of medieval theology. For Bernard of Clairvaux, for example, the humility of Christ is considered both as the source of salvation and as an ethical example. But, contrary to what a "Protestant" interpretation of medieval theology may assume, he did not prioritize the ethical over the soteriological.

> Example though he was, also and especially in his suffering, Christ was always more than an example – especially in his suffering.[49]

In general, medieval theology saw three meanings in the Incarnation: the proof of God's love, the mystery of salvation and the example of humility. This humility of Christ is a sign of the humiliation of God in the Incarnation and an example for Christian living.[50] Marpeck's letter picks up this theme and continues in its trajectory.

---

[48] Ibid., 434. For Marpeck, Christ's death was an integral part of the Incarnation and the means and model in relation to how God deals with evil. Thus his death was an integral part of his mission. The only way the forces of evil can be defeated is not to enter into the downward spiral of their logic, which in Jesus' case, meant death. Denny Weaver tends to downplay the integral significance of Christ's death. "Since Jesus mission was not to die but to make visible the reign of God, it is quite explicit that neither God nor the reign of God need Jesus' death in the way that his death is irreducibly needed in satisfaction atonement." J. Denny Weaver, *The Nonviolent Atonement* (Grand Rapids: Eerdmans, 2001), 72. Even within the Christus Victor model (to which Marpeck obviously holds), the significance and even the necessity of Jesus' death cannot be avoided. Only the refusal to retaliate to the evil of murder can break the power of death.

[49] Pelikan 3, 150.

[50] Ibid. "The humility of Christ came along through 'the condescension of God to men, proceeding completely from the fountain of divine goodness,' so that it was more appropriately called 'humiliation' than merely 'humility.'"

The preceding observations raise the question of the relationships between Marpeck, medieval thought, and Reformation theology. In some regards, he appears close to medieval positions on salvation in Christ. Integrating salvation and ethics seems to locate his thought on the "catholic" side. In other places where Marpeck accentuates justification by faith and denies the sacraments as "means of salvation" he appears on the protestant side. On this precise question (cross as source of salvation and cross as ethical example) is Marpeck's view "Catholic" or "Protestant?" Or is it neither Catholic nor Protestant? Or is there yet another way to pose the question? The final section turns to these questions.

Redemption and ethics in medieval theology

Up until 1300

It was already noted that the period from 900 to 1100 could be described as that of an "absolute christocentrism," due mainly to monastic life and theology. During this same period the monk Anselm (1033-1109) wrote his significant treatise on atonement (*Cur deus homo*). Most strikingly, at that time, the concept of a contradiction between the cross as source of redemption and the cross as ethical example was unknown. Thus during those centuries the incarnate Christ who died on a cross was not conceived of as a Christ "parachuted" into history only at this moment to atone for sin without any relationship to the kind of life he lived on earth. To speak of Christ was to speak of his death and resurrection but also to speak of his life and teachings.[51] The monastic tradition of this period – which was essentially Benedictine – conceived of Christian life as a life of discipleship.[52] The issue truly was one of the "discipline of Jesus" that

---

[51] Pelikan 3, 118-119. "The plan of salvation as defined and refined in this period, did not restrict itself to the theory of redemption in the narrow sense of that word. The 'picture of Christ' underlying it included not only the narrative of his suffering, death, and resurrection, but the entire account of his life and work, his miracles and parables as well as his crucifixion."

[52] Ibid. 119. "'Man did not need only to be redeemed,' according to this understanding of Christ's coming in search of the lost, 'but also to be instructed about how he ought

included the total span of human experience as this was to be brought into conformity with the divine will that had been revealed through the Incarnation of the Son of God in a fully human life.[53]

Anselm's thought was no different in this respect.[54]

At the same time, and contrary to some protestant readings of the Middle Ages, ethical life did not take priority over the necessity of salvation by grace. The theologians of that time were conscious of the need to connect redemption and ethics, the cross as gift and the cross as example.

> Christ as teacher and pattern, even Christ crucified as example, needed to be related to the larger definition of Christ as Redeemer. He who provided the example of virtue must also provide the assistance of grace. 'It would,' according to Anselm, 'be useless for men to be imitators of him if they were not participants in his merit.'"[55]

In other words, for Anselm, the death of Christ for our salvation (grace) and the cross as example (works) were not mutually exclusive. Redemption was primary but established simultaneously the possibility of a life of discipleship in the footsteps of the master. Anselm writes:

> For who may explain how necessary and wise a thing it was for it to come about that he who was to redeem the human race and bring it back from the way of death and destruction to the way of life and eternal happiness, should live in the company of human beings and, while he was teaching them verbally how they ought to live, should, through this very behaviour, present himself as an example? Furthermore, how was he to

---

to live after redemption.' Acceptance of such instruction was the hallmark of true discipleship."

[53] Ibid. Odon of Cluny quoted by Pelikan.

[54] Ibid. "But now the very one 'who was to redeem men and to lead them back from the way of death and perdition to the way of life and eternal blessedness' would at the same time be the one who lived as a man among men and who, 'in this association with them, as he was teaching them by word how they ought to live, would provide himself as an example for them.' The discipline of Jesus gave instruction to his followers 'by teaching and by example.'" (Anselm quoted here by Pelikan.)

[55] Pelikan 3, 129.

present himself to weak and mortal humans as an example of the fact that they should not depart from righteousness on account of injustices, insults, pain or death, if they were not aware that he himself had experience of all these things?[56]

When Christ endured with kindly patience the sufferings – injuries and insults and death on the cross along with robbers – which were inflicted on him because of the righteousness which, as we have said earlier, he was obediently maintaining, he set an example to mankind, the purpose of which was that people should not turn aside, without the provocation of any perceptible discomforts, from the righteousness which they owe to God. He would certainly not have been setting this example if he had taken advantage of his power and turned aside from the death which, for such a reason, was being inflicted on him. Do you not understand this?[57]

Medieval theology did not conceive of a separation between redemption and ethics.[58] Benedictine thought and practice remained fundamentally that of "imitatio Christi." For Odon of Cluny, Jesus

had become a man so that human beings could imitate his human life and could not dismiss his virtues as something beyond the realm of possibility; "that was why he did not give them an archangel, but himself as model."[59]

As it was also for sixteenth-century Anabaptism, the supreme example of *Nachfolge Christi* for medieval monasticism was the cross.

To obey and follow Christ implied that one hearken to his word and imitate his actions, but above all it meant that one "follow in the footsteps of his passion."[60]

---

[56] Anselm, *Why God became Man*, 331.
[57] Ibid. 349.
[58] Some of Denny Weaver's statements about medieval atonement theology and ethics are not totally accurate from an historical point of view. "Another way to talk about the absence of the specifics of Jesus in Anselmian atonement is to say that it separates salvation from ethics." Weaver, *The Nonviolent Atonement*, 90. "The theology of Anselm is a theology specific to a church that has separated ethics from salvation and from the saving work of Jesus." Ibid., 91. Weaver's statements are truer of Protestant interpretations of Anselm than they are accurate readings of Anselm.
[59] Pelikan 3, 125.
[60] Pelikan 3, 127.

The same thing is visible in the work of Bernard of Clairvaux (1090-1153), for whom the Sermon on the Mount was Christ's teaching par excellence.

> Christ set himself forth to others as the example of humility and as the model of gentleness, so that by following him they might find "the way that leads to truth." The discipline of following Christ consisted in taking one's cross.[61]

If important similarities on this one issue between monastic theology and Anabaptist theology can be pointed to during this period, a significant difference must nevertheless be mentioned. In the Middle Ages, the call to follow Christ applied only to the clergy and members of religious communities and not to all Christians. In affirming the priesthood of all believers, Anabaptism followed Luther and the Reformation in its rejection of an "ontological separation" between clergy and laity. Marpeck's ethics address all believers and not solely a specific and limited category of Christians.

The Centuries Immediately Preceding the Reformation (14th and 15th centuries)

In a fundamental way, the close link between the cross as "source of salvation" and the cross as "ethical model" remained present in the centuries preceding the Reformation. The birth of the mendicant orders led to monastic theology's moving beyond the more rural Benedictine context into the new urban centres and the recently-founded universities. The close link that was seen in the previous section is still present in the thought of the Dominican theologian Thomas Aquinas (13th century), as the following extended text demonstrates.

> But what need was there that the Son of God should suffer for us? There was a great need; and indeed it can be assigned to two reasons. The first is that it was a remedy against sin, and the second is for an example of what we ought to do. …

---

[61] Pelikan 3, 150.

From all this then is seen the effect of the passion of Christ as a remedy for sin. But no less does it profit us as an example. St. Augustine says that the passion of Christ can bring about a complete reformation of our lives. Whoever wishes to live perfectly need do nothing other than despise what Christ despised on the cross, and desire what Christ desired. There is no virtue that did not have its example on the Cross.

So if you seek an example of charity, then, "greater love than his no man hath, that a man lay down his life for his friends." And this Christ did upon the Cross. If, therefore, He gave His life for us, we ought to endure any and all evils for Him: "What shall I render to the Lord for all the things that He hath rendered to me?"

If you seek an example of patience, you will find it in its highest degree upon the Cross. Great patience is exemplified in two ways: either when one suffers intensely in all patience, or when one suffers that which he could avoid if he so wished. Christ suffered greatly upon the Cross: "O all ye that pass by the way, attend, and see if there be any sorrow like to My sorrow." And with all patience, because, "when He suffered, He threatened not." And again: "He shall be led as a sheep to the slaughter and shall be dumb before His shearer, and shall not open His mouth. He could have avoided this suffering, but He did not: "Thinkest thou that I cannot ask My Father, and He will give Me presently more than twelve legions of Angels?" The patience of Christ upon the cross, therefore, was of the highest degree: "Let us run by patience to the fight proposed to us; looking on Jesus, the author and finisher of faith, who, having joy set before Him endured the cross, despising the shame."

If you seek an example of humility, look upon Him who is crucified; although He was God, He chose to be judged by Pontius Pilate and to be put to death: "Thy cause has been judged as that of the wicked."[20] Truly "that of the wicked," because: "Let us condemn Him to a most shameful death." The Lord chose to die for His servant; the Life of the Angels suffered death for man: "He humbled Himself, becoming obedient unto death, even to the death of the cross."

If you seek an example of obedience, imitate Him who was obedient to the Father unto death: "For by the disobedience of one man, many were made sinners; so also by the obedience of one, many shall be made just."

If you seek an example of contempt for earthly things, imitate Him who is the King of kings, the Lord of rulers, in whom are all the treasures of wisdom; but on the Cross He was stripped naked, ridiculed, spat upon, bruised, crowned with thorns, given to drink of vinegar and gall, and finally put to death. How falsely, therefore, is one attached to riches and raiment, for: "They parted My garments amongst them; and upon My vesture they cast lots."[24] How falsely to honors, since "I was covered with lashes and insults;" how falsely to positions of power, because "taking a crown of thorns, they placed it upon My brow;" how falsely to delicacies of the table, for "in My thirst they gave Me to drink of vinegar." Thus, St. Augustine, in commenting on these words, "Who, having joy set before Him, endured the Cross despising the shame," says: "The man Christ despised all earthly things in order to teach us to despise them."[62]

The christocentrism of the Franciscan order also contributed to the emphasis on Jesus as model to follow.[63] Like the Dominicans, the Franciscans played a central role in the theological developments of this period. The growing urbanization and the Franciscan and Dominican presence in the cities led to new "lay" movements that sought to live their faith in the world, without having to join religious orders.[64] Probably these lay movements served to popularize and make comprehensible the medieval theology that later influenced Anabaptism. For example, these lay groups were, in the 15th century, the locus and source of foment for

---

[62] Thomas Aquinas, *Collationes super Credo in Deum*, Collins, Joseph B., trans. In *The Catechetical Instructions of St. Thomas*, 3-66 (New York: Wagner, 1939; reprint, Ft. Collins, CO: Roman Catholic Books, 2000); e-text, www.ewtn.com/library/SOURCES/TA-CAT-1.TXT; e-text with word lists.

[63] Pelikan 4, 36. "During the fourteenth and fifteenth centuries, however, the devotion to Christ as man and the imitation of his example became more intense, partly through the devotion to Francis of Assisi…"

[64] The Waldensians were one of these "lay" movements, but there were many others, including Third Order Franciscans who remained within the Church.

the most popular devotional book in Europe: *The Imitation of Christ* by Thomas a Kempis. Anabaptism is rooted in these spiritual movements that began slowly to "laicize" the church as did the *Devotio moderna*.[65]

Nevertheless during the centuries preceding the Reformation, the questions of predestination and the sovereignty of God entered in a new way into the debates surrounding redemption.[66] Towards the end of the Middle Ages some theologians began to strongly emphasize the sovereignty of God. Duns Scotus was one example of this movement. "The statement of Augustine, that 'the will of God is the first and the highest cause of all bodily appearances and motions,' was treated as axiomatic..."[67]

This current of thought, named *schola Augustiniana moderna*, was a reaction against another school designated as the *via moderna*.[68] One of their differences concerned the doctrine of salvation, and in particular the justification effected by the death of Christ. A brief review of this debate will help us set the stage for the Reformation, particularly as Martin Luther's thought illustrates much of this problematic.

For the *via moderna*, (represented by theologians such as William of Ockham and Gabriel Biel), God promises to justify humans because of the work of Christ. But humans must "deserve" this justification by

---

[65] The *Devotio moderna* was another of these lay movements connected to monasticism at this time. *The Imitation of Christ* and Erasmus were probably the best known elements of this phenomenon and probably provided indirect channels into Anabaptism. Cf. C. Arnold Snyder, *Following in the Footsteps of Christ. The Anabaptist Tradition*, (Maryknoll NY: Orbis Books, 2004), 44.

[66] Jean Delumeau reminds us of how important it is to situate doctrinal discussions within their historical contexts and demonstrates that this strong emphasis on the sovereignty of God, the sinfulness of humanity and predestination was the fruit of centuries of medieval thought in conjunction with the very difficult circumstances of 14th and 15th century Europe, i.e; the Hundred Year's War, the Bubonic plague, the papal schism, the advance of the Turks. Jean Delumeau, *Le péche et la peur. La culpabilisation en Occident XIIIe-XVIIIe siècles*, (Paris : Fayard, 1983). He also sees Anabaptist "rejection of the world" as an exacerbation of these same tendencies, cf. 41. Contemporary Mennonite debaters on the atonement would do well to read Delumeau.

[67] Pelikan 4, 25.

[68] Cf. McGrath, *Iustitia Dei*, 171-175.

"doing what they can."[69] According to the covenant God concluded with humanity, those who "do what they have within themselves" will be justified.

Other theologians, influenced by their reading of Augustine, reacted against this tendency. The "modern Augustinian school," represented amongst others by Thomas Bradwardine and Gregory de Rimini, affirmed that God alone is the cause of all that creatures do. In other words, humans do not participate in the process of justification by faith. God's justice is simply given. No gesture or action merits it. Jaroslav Pelikan claims that such a concept already transforms Anselm's theory.[70] Human acts and thoughts have no origin in mankind, but exclusively in God.[71] From this point of view history no longer is the theater where the salvation drama is played.

> The mercy of God was also an expression of that immutable will and completely subordinate to it: "God does not begin loving someone or hating someone at a certain point.... Neither prayers nor any merits, whether good or bad, can turn or change the divine will in the least, either this way or that; but whatever is to be saved or damned, rewarded or punished, in whatever degree, this he willed from eternity to be saved or damned."[72]

Luther followed this school of thought. Marpeck and Anabaptism in general did not, at least in its full implications. The debate between

---

[69] "*facere quod in se est*" is what God requires of us if we desire to receive grace. We must desire to be justified and turn toward God. Marpeck's *erbgnad*, seen in the previous chapter plays this kind of role in his anthropology.

[70] Pelikan 4, 25. "As in the Reformation period, so already in the late medieval period with which we are dealing here, the Anselmic metaphor of Christ's death as an act of satisfaction coexisted, often in the same theologians, with other ideas that contrasted with it or even contradicted it or that at the very least gave it a special coloration. The most important such idea in the fourteenth and fifteenth centuries was the widespread emphasis on the sovereign will of God." Moreover (26) "[n]ot only justice and mercy, however, but the central Anselmic doctrine of satisfaction itself was 'relativized' under the impact of this primary stress on the divine will."

[71] "Hence a human act was intrinsically good not in and of itself, but only by virtue of its having been defined as good by the free and sovereign will of God." Pelikan 4, 26.

[72] Pelikan 4, 26.

Anabaptists and Luther was not between the "Reformation" and "medieval theologies," but between different medieval schools picked up and "protestantized" by Luther, Calvin, and the Anabaptists.[73] This question was not settled in the medieval period, or during the Reformation, except insofar as Luther (and Calvin's) positions heavily influenced the "Protestant" tradition.

Nevertheless even in the decades before the Reformation and in contrast to Luther, the emphasis on God's sovereignty did not minimize the importance of the life of discipleship and the exemplary character of Christ's cross in the plan of salvation.

> Although among scholastic theologians these issues of predestination, contingency, and grace may have occupied a prominent, perhaps a dominant, place in the presentation of the doctrine of salvation, even a predestinarian theologian like Wycliffe was obliged to acknowledge that the "primary" component of salvation lay elsewhere, namely, in "coming to Christ through imitation," which was to be followed by the hearing of the words of Christ and by obedience to hearing of the words of Christ and by obedience to them in deeds.[74]

> The imitation of Christ was the true rule of life, which would bring salvation to all who followed it (meaning of course the predestined). The example of Christ was the most familiar and the most reliable of all, and "every action of Christ is an instruction to us." What Christ had done in his deeds, he also taught in his words.[75]

Anabaptist particularity

in relation to justification and salvation

One could be tempted to claim that Anabaptist notions of salvation and justification, as seen for example in Marpeck's work, were much closer to medieval theology than to that of the Reformation. The following

---

[73] "In its radical anti-Pelagianism, the Reformation, in its first phase, demonstrated a remarkable degree of continuity with well-established currents in late medieval thought." McGrath, *Iustitia Dei*, 214.

[74] Pelikan 4, 35-36.

[75] Ibid., 36.

final observations will seek to demonstrate how Anabaptist theology differentiates itself from the medieval period by adopting certain Reformation perspectives, yet also distinguishes itself from the Protestant Reformation by certain continuity with medieval theology.

First of all, if Anabaptism remained close to medieval theology in regards to a Christ-centreed ethic, it followed the Reformation in rejecting many of the sacramental developments of the Middle Ages.

> To no area of Christian doctrine had the medieval development added more than it did to the communication of grace through the saints (especially through – and to – the Virgin Mary) and through the sacraments (especially through the Eucharist).[76]

In rejecting the sacramental mediation of grace (*ex opera operato*) and in adopting the "protestant" theses of justification by faith and of *sola scriptura*, Anabaptism left behind the institutional and theological framework of the medieval Church.[77] But at the same time, nothing in the sixteenth-century reined in the diverging theologies amongst those who left the Catholic Church. In sum, in light of these above-noted tendencies, one could say that Luther represents a "protestantization" of the *schola Augustiniana moderna*, while Anabaptism is a protestant version of other medieval schools of thought. But the difference is not strictly that of Luther's Augustinianism versus Marpeck's anti-Augustinianism. Both build on aspects of Augustine's legacy, each one in its particular way.[78]

As already said, Luther formulated his doctrine of justification by faith in terms adopted from medieval currents influenced by Augustinian thought concerning the sovereignty of God.

> The presupposition for the doctrine of justification was a vigorous reassertion of Augustinian anthropology. Joining himself to the criticism leveled by late medieval Augustinianism

---

[76] Pelikan 4, 38.

[77] This analysis in confirmed by C. Arnold Snyder: "The inherent connection in late medieval Catholicism between the reception of the sacraments and growth in holiness was severed by the Anabaptists, following as they did the initial Protestant (and more specifically, Zwinglian) lead in these questions." *Anabaptist History and Theology*, 300.

[78] "There are…serious difficulties attending *any* attempt to characterize the theology of any later medieval thinker 'Augustinian'…" McGrath, *Iustitia Dei*, 203.

against "the new Pelagians," Luther identified Pelagianism as the one perennial heresy of Christian history, which had never been fully exterminated and which, under the patronage of the church of Rome, had now become dominant.[79]

But surprisingly enough, in relation to the doctrine of justification by faith, Marpeck (and Anabaptism in general) was much closer to Augustine than Luther ever was. As noted above, Marpeck proclaimed loud and clear that justification creates a change in the believer.

> Thus, Christ's sufferings enable men to regain their original purity and innocence in which they were created and to be prepared for their God, Father, Creator, and Maker. The Holy Spirit, who cannot be where sin is, can again find a place and gain a dwelling in men and then [transfer them] from the earthly to the heavenly. Thus man is created an earthly creature but, through the Incarnation of Christ, the earthly may become heavenly. …. Grace and the justification which leads to true devotion and which proceeds from faith, transfers man from the earthly to the eternal, heavenly state.[80]

Through the Holy Spirit, justification transforms the human being giving him or her the power to accomplish (imperfectly) what is pleasing to God. This corresponds to how Augustine understood justification. For "the doctor of grace," God's justice is not only something that is declared but an event that transforms the believer.[81] For Marpeck and Augustine, the gift of the Holy Spirit during the process of justification has precisely this goal of transformation and empowerment.[82]

---

[79] Pelikan 4, 139.
[80] *WPM*, 430.
[81] "The righteousness which God bestows upon humanity in justification, is regarded by Augustine as inherent rather than imputed, to use the vocabulary of the sixteenth century." "The righteousness which they thus receive, although originating from God, is nevertheless located within humans, and can be said to be theirs, part of his being and intrinsic to their persons." McGrath, *Iustitia Dei*, 48.
[82] "It is certainly true that Augustine speaks of the real interior renewal of the sinner by the action of the Holy Spirit, which he later expressed in terms of participation in the divine substance itself." Ibid.

For Augustine and for Anabaptism, the believer is declared righteous, but is also made righteous in his being. Augustine (as also Marpeck) believed that justification was the beginning of God's work in the believer. By this event God affirms the righteousness of the Christian. But this same process involves God's continual work of transforming the Christian's life.[83]

Augustine's writings did not, in all likelihood, directly influence Marpeck. It was simply the case that all medieval theology – and not just mysticism – agreed on this specific point. Justification was simultaneously an initial act and a continual process. The Christian is declared righteous in light of the work of Christ and is made righteous to live a new and different life.[84]

To the extent to which the Anabaptists were indebted to Erasmus and to humanism and also to Augustinian and medieval understandings of justification, Luther could not countenance them. Jaroslav Pelikan notes that

> Luther accused Erasmus of reviving the Pelagian heresy, in fact of going even beyond it, in his willingness to ascribe freedom to the fallen will of man…[85]

What Luther fought most fiercely was the idea that a person played any role in his or her salvation. For him, justification meant that God does everything and Christians do nothing. Marpeck was in complete agreement with that statement. For Anabaptists, no one can please God, no one can merit salvation and the only access to the grace of and in Christ's work passes through faith.

---

[83] "Augustine's understanding of adoptive filiation is such that the believer does not merely receive the *status* of sonhood, but *becomes* a child of God. Justification entails a real change in a person's *being*, and not merely in his or her *status*, so that this person *becomes* righteous and a child of God, and is not merely *treated as if he or she was* righteous and a child of God." McGrath, *Iustitia Dei*, 48. "Justification, according to Augustine, is fundamentally concerned with 'being made righteous'." Ibid., 49.

[84] "…The medieval theological tradition was unanimous in its understanding of justification as both an act and a process, by which both the status of humans *coram Deo* and their essential nature underwent alteration." McGrath, *Iustitia Dei*, 213.

[85] Pelikan 4, 140.

In his struggle against "salvation by works," Luther refused the possibility of that which medieval theology called "infused" grace. Such infused grace is also given by God and contributes to a real change of the Christian, permitting "cooperation" with God in the process of salvation.[86]

The Anabaptist insistence on a transforming redemption and justification certainly resembled, in Luther's eyes, a theology of infused grace, even if for Marpeck (as for Augustine) all came from God.[87] For Luther, "infused grace" equaled "salvation by works." Thus he distanced himself from a concept of justification that was both "event" (declaration of justice) and "process" (grace that transforms). For him justification was uniquely a declaration of justice coming from God, totally alien to the believer. In this way Luther moved away from Saint Augustine.[88]

Thus on the specific point of considering justification strictly a declaration, Luther was the one to innovate and move away from the western theological tradition. All throughout the medieval period justification was understood as a process by which a person becomes righteous (and/or just). Justification and sanctification were unified; *justificare* also meant *justum facere*. It was Luther who created a "new" theology.[89]

---

[86] Pelikan 4, 152-153.

[87] Such a position can also be found in Aquinas' theology. "God does not justify us without ourselves, because whilst we are being justified we consent to God's justification by a movement of our free-will. Nevertheless this movement is not the cause of grace, but the effect; hence the whole operation pertains to grace." *Summa Theologica*, (Pt. I-II, Q. 111, Art. 3), Volume 1 (New York: Benziger Brothers, 1947), 1137.

[88] "However, it will be clear that the medieval period was astonishingly faithful to the teaching of Augustine on the question of the nature of justification, where the Reformers departed from it." McGrath, *Iustitia Dei*, 216.

[89] "The significance of the Protestant distinction between *iustificatio* and *regeneratio* is that a fundamental discontinuity has been introduced into the western theological tradition where none had existed before." McGrath, *Iustitia Dei*, 184. Contra Finger, who at many points in his *Contemporary Anabaptist Theology* suggests parallels between an Anabaptist understanding of justification and Orthodox "divinization," it makes more sense historically to see Anabaptism's resemblance with the medieval understanding of justification as being literally "made righteous."

Thus in official protestant territories, soteriology was formulated in terms of justification by faith following Luther's – and particularly his successor Melanchthon's – understanding of Augustine as seen through the *schola Augustiniana moderna*. This formulation dominated the protestant side, even if more by political imposition than rhetorical persuasion.[90]

The "official" Reformation made therefore a distinction between "justification" and "sanctification," whereas Anabaptism held them together in one and the same movement of salvation. In the sixteenth-century the difference loomed large from Luther's perspective, particularly in a polemically charged context. With further developments in the protestant world (Calvinism, pietism, Wesley, and Pentecostalism), Anabaptism appears less unique today than in the century of its birth.

It is rather Anabaptist non-violence, based on the cross as an example, which distinguishes Marpeck's soteriology from other protestant positions. Christ the Saviour and Christ the example, bearing his cross until death, excludes the recourse to violence. Marpeck's severe critique of the churches that were at war is a significant aspect of his understanding of salvation. Once again, his thought was closer to the medieval monastic tradition. The priest and the monk were not permitted (at least in theory) to wage war nor use violence. An ethical dualism separating clergy and laity characterized the universal medieval church but for Anabaptism the split was between the Church and the "world."

In a radicalized Augustinian theology as with Luther, salvation depends on God's decrees before the foundation of the world. Such salvation is conceived as spiritual and inner and does not effect a "real" change. Justice (and righteousness) are pronounced, i.e. forensic, but never "transmitted." In Marpeck's theology, salvation depends on God, on his initiative, on his beneficent grace. Nevertheless this salvation occurs in history and in time and calls forth a concrete response from believers, who

---

[90] "Thus Luther's 'forensic' doctrine of imputation, as made precise by Melancthon, gained dominance in the confessional interpretations of justification (whether Lutheran, Calvinist, or Arminian) over other ways of speaking that could also find a legitimate place within the full range of Reformation thought." Pelikan 4, 152.

enter a new social reality that is "sent into the world" to live following the footsteps of the one who redeemed them.

If Marpeck's soteriology was indeed close to the medieval conception of infused grace, he appears to have arrived at such a conclusion by a different theological path, in at least two ways. First of all, in medieval theology, infused grace was transmitted basically through the sacraments. Marpeck's path was another. He adopted the Reformation notion of "justification by faith," thus placing the response of the believer in the place of a more sacramental mediation of grace. Secondly, his move towards a "Christus victor" understanding of the atonement led him away from the more predominantly Anselmian interpretation of the work of Christ, even though he did not consciously reject its logic or vocabulary. While underlining the importance of the death of Christ, Marpeck also insisted on the fundamental significance of the resurrection in relation to the defeat of sin and evil. The gift of the Holy Spirit, made possible by Christ's victory, became the source of ethical transformation of Christians and replaced the medieval notion of infused grace transmitted through the sacraments.

Marpeck's understanding of salvation brings us back to John Yoder's analysis of Anabaptism in the context of the Reformation. Over against a platonic and ontological dualism which allows salvation to be conceived in strictly inner or juridical terms, Marpeck presented a theology of redemption grounded firmly in history and every day life, a theology which took into account the cross of Christ as the unique source of salvation while at the same time being held up as the supreme example of nonviolent discipleship. The victory of resurrection over the forces of evil and the subsequent sending of the Holy Spirit, allowed Marpeck to understand the process of justification as one which brings forgiveness and reconciliation while at the same time empowering believers to follow Christ, to be transformed collectively in his image in the context of the new community, Temple of the Spirit and Body of Christ. Salvation is individual and collective. Just as Christ walked upon the earth in a visible and tangible manner to reveal God's intention for humanity, the "unglorified" body of Christ is "sent" into the world to take on the same form as Jesus of Nazareth, the form of self-giving and nonviolent love.

The historical nature of salvation – over against an ontological and static understanding – can be reinforced theologically by thinking of it in eschatological terms, something which Marpeck already did in his own writings.[91] Salvation is historically anchored in the work of Christ, but also in the future reality of his return, which means that present manifestations of salvation within the church and the world can only be incomplete

Thomas Finger has made a quite helpful suggestion by underlining the importance of eschatology for conceptualizing justification and ethics in contemporary discussions of the question: "When the new creation's call awakens us, and we respond in faith to God's faithfulness in Jesus, we already begin participating in the new creation's dynamic righteousness. It already transforms us. Nevertheless, we are far from fully righteous."[92]

Concluding remarks

Marpeck's emphasis on discipleship, non-violence and the importance of the church clearly places him within the Anabaptist tradition. At the same time it should be said that he was quite aware of the danger and the reality of "works righteousness" and of the legalism that so quickly became a part of ecclesiastically structured Anabaptism already in his time in the sixteenth century.[93]

Already in literary exchanges with some of the Swiss Brethren groups, Marpeck underlined the dangers of legalism that accompanied the strong ethical component of Anabaptist theology.[94] Against the Swiss Anabaptists, Marpeck often sounds like Luther, using the distinction between law and

---

[91] Cf. Blough, "Eschatologie, christologie et éthique: la fin justifie les moyens," in N. Blough (ed), *Eschatologie et vie quotidienne* (Cléon d'Andran : Excelsis, 2001), 13-37.

[92] Finger, *Contemporary Anabaptist Theology*, 144.

[93] "This legalistic, Christocentric reading of Scripture and definition of community boundaries became the norm for all surviving Anabaptist groups, whose descendants (not coincidentally) have had a long history of schism and division." Snyder, *Anabaptist History and Theology*, 380.

[94] Cf. *Christologie anabaptiste*, 203-214 and N. Blough, "Pilgram Marpeck et les frères suisses vers 1540," in *...Lebenn Nach der Ler Jhesu... Das sind aber wir!: Berner Täufer und Prädikanten im Gespräch* (Bern: Schweizerischen Verein fur Täufergeschichte, 1989), 147-164.

Gospel to insist on freedom over against legalistic regulation of ethical questions in the church.[95]

Marpeck's Trinitarian theology was also important in his fight against legalism. The lives of Christians are to be incorporated into the "humanity of Christ," their outward lives are to correspond to the earthly Christ in the way that he lived (and died). The Incarnation was a model for earthly life. But the Incarnation was also the source of salvation and of the pouring out of the Spirit. Marpeck insisted over and over again that it was only through the power of the Spirit that such a life was possible. Following Jesus was the result of a gift and not of human capacity. One last quotation from the letter we have been using in this chapter makes this quite clear.

> Without the artistry and teaching of the Holy Spirit, who pours out the love, which is God, into the hearts of the faithful, and which surpasses all reason and understanding, everything is in vain. The Holy Spirit proceeds from the Father and Son, and He witnesses to the Father and Son in the hearts of all the faithful; He copies and repeats the perfect law of the liberty of Christ. The faithful look into this law of liberty in order that they may fervently do what Christ spoke and commanded.[96]

In such a Trinitarian perspective, ethics becomes an extension of spiritual life rather than the requirement of "having to accomplish" something or "having to be like Jesus."[97] Salvation as a gift, as something done for us, retains priority over the Incarnation as example. Without this

---

[95] "It was Pilgram Marpeck who insisted on the importance of the distinction between law and Gospel as one that provided a crucial counter balance for those who tended to emphasize literal obedience to the commands of Scripture... Marpeck emphasized, from a thoroughly Anabaptist perspective, human dependence on God's love and grace; recognition of our dependence on grace, he maintained, acts as a hedge against human presumption." Snyder, *Anabaptist History and Theology*, 385.

[96] *WPM*, 458.

[97] "Discipleship, then, is not fundamentally an issue of obedience to the law, but rather it depends upon God's grace and regeneration; true discipleship grows from the heart, and not as a result of an external legal code or the threat of punishment." Snyder, *Anabaptist History and Theology*, 386.

priority, "discipleship" becomes a legalistic cage from which we cannot escape.[98]

---

[98] "Mennonites have never allowed themselves to separate ethics from ecclesiology in their theology. The greater risk has always been to overestimate the possibilities that humans can bring about the kingdom of God and to underestimate the evil within human nature." Fernando Enns, "Space for Theological Reflection on Being (Peace) Church," in Enns, Holland & Riggs, *Seeking Cultures of Peace*, 35.

Chapter 7

Christ In Our midst:
Incarnation, Church and Discipleship Then and Now

Chapter by chapter, step by step, the various contexts and building-blocks of Pilgram Marpeck's theology have become apparent. In his earliest writings in Strasbourg in conversation with Spiritualists and Reformers, Marpeck already laid the foundation of a theology firmly grounded in the Incarnation (*die menscheit Christi*). Finding help in the writings of Luther, a Reformer, and of Schwenckfeld, a Spiritualist, Marpeck insisted on the foundational significance of God's having become flesh in Christ. Against the Spiritualists, Marpeck argued that since God was fully present in Jesus of Nazareth, a human being sharing our own flesh and blood, the visible and material realms of our existence (water, bread, wine, words, books, human relationships) cannot be dismissed, despised or relativised as means for knowing God or for making God known. Against Martin Bucer, Marpeck used another line of reasoning: since Christ's humanity was circumscribed within time and understood as the fulfilment of earlier promises, and also since Christ has promised to come again, history becomes the necessary theatre where the drama of salvation is played out.

With the passage of time, Marpeck developed and reinforced his theology. In the *Admonition of 1542*, once again relying on Luther and Schwenckfeld, he gave new coherence to two formerly more or less independent ways of depicting Christ's humanity. At the same time, this apparent attempt to rally the non violent German-speaking Anabaptist communities after the catastrophe of Münster laid bare deep rifts between former friends. Schwenckfeld reacted strongly to what he perceived as a personal attack which, in turn, provoked the *Response*, one of the Marpeck-circle's profoundest writings. An even more penetrating description of a sacramental community following Jesus in the power of the Spirit is observable, as well as some of the awkwardness occasioned by an untrained lay theologian's eclectic borrowing from sometimes contradictory sources.

It must not be forgotten that Marpeck's Christology is profoundly Trinitarian and reflects a dynamic of *sentness*. With the Incarnation, the Word was *sent* into the world. At Pentecost, the Spirit was *sent*, a Spirit which then indwells the community which in turn is *sent* into the world to image the same life as the "Word made flesh." Thus, within history and in a visible manner, Christ's humanity is prolonged within the believing community in the power of the Spirit of Pentecost. Discipleship, i.e., individuals in community following Jesus in the power of the Spirit, becomes the primary sacrament of God's presence in the world. Preaching, baptism, sharing bread, wine and possessions, forgiveness, reconciliation, feeding the hungry, service, confrontation of false theological, political or ethical options (the *Exposé*), love of neighbour and love of enemy all become ways in which "Christ's humanity" continues to act in the midst of history by becoming the "body of Christ." There is no way to separate Incarnation, church and discipleship in Marpeck's writings. Although Christology is primary, because it is Trinitarian, it necessarily flows via the Spirit into the ethical life of the gathered community of believers. For this very reason, Christ remains "in our midst" for as long as human history will go on.

The preceding chapters have been an exercise in historical theology, an attempt to discover and demonstrate the categories and coherence in

Marpeck's thinking as well as situating his theology within the context of his own life and time. This explains the serious consideration of chronology and development, of context, of the debates at hand, and of possible sources of influence, both direct and indirect. As an historical study, the book could legitimately end at this point, offered as a modest contribution to the history of Christian thought in general and of sixteenth-century Anabaptism in particular. This effort could be called "Marpeck then." But what about "Marpeck now"?

It so happens that the author of these chapters cares deeply about theology and the church in today's world and has benefited both personally and theologically from numerous years of studying Pilgram Marpeck's life and theology. Since Marpeck's writings are more widely discussed than ever and are considered relevant to contemporary Anabaptist theology,[1] it seems appropriate to enter into some of the debates about the relationship between history and theology as well as demonstrating how some of Marpeck's key ideas are being used in contemporary theology, both inside and outside of Anabaptist-Mennonite circles.

Methodology and Historical Theology:
Classical Theological Categories or Anabaptist Specificity?

The main focus of the following sections will underline the importance of Marpeck's use of classical theological categories such as the Incarnation and the Trinity. This will initially lead us into a debate as to how such categories relate to doing theology from an Anabaptist perspective and secondly demonstrate the importance of an Incarnational and Trinitarian theology to any contemporary formulation of Anabaptist theology.

---

[1] References to the importance of Marpeck in North American discussions of Anabaptism are quite numerous and need no documentation. Marpeck's importance was recognized in France before my initial research. According to the "dean" of Anabaptist studies in France, Jean Séguy, Marpeck was the "most profound theologian of the peaceful Anabaptists." Jean Séguy, *Les assemblées anabaptistes de France*, (Paris-La Haye: Mouton, 1977), 94. Much more recently, Marpeck is referred to frequently in Frédéric de Coninck's *Agir, travailler, militer. Une théologie de l'action* (Cléon d'Andran : Excelsis, 2006), 156-182.

Of course, drawing attention to Marpeck's use of such categories is nothing new and has only been reinforced by recent studies.[2] The question arises as to what this means when these categories are identified as part of his theology, or for that matter of our theology today? One of the current ongoing debates today concerns how to situate Anabaptism in relation to classical theological categories such as the Incarnation, Trinity or the two natures of Christ.[3] One possible approach is that of J. Denny Weaver, who begins with and unremittingly emphasizes Anabaptist particularity over against "classical theology."

> One does not discover the character of Anabaptism by simply identifying roots in some prior medieval or Protestant tradition, or by locating some middle point between two groups. Anabaptism is a comprehensive perspective in its own right.[4]

Weaver asks skeptically: "does one know more about Anabaptism through seeking points of commonality with other traditions?"[5] His main concern is that such an approach does little if anything to enhance the originality of Anabaptist theology and therefore relegates Anabaptist

---

[2] "More than any other Anabaptist, Marpeck sought to express Christology in classical terms." Finger, *Contemporary Anabaptist Theology*, 376. "The conclusion of this study is simply that Marpeck understood and identified with the doctrines of the Trinity and the two natures of Christ as the creed and councils had defined them. He shared their conviction that these two doctrines were the indispensable guardians of the deposit of faith." Rempel, *The Lord's Supper in Anabaptism*, 143.

[3] "One approach is characterized by A. James Reimer, who is well-known for his argument that Anabaptist theology should accept standard Nicene orthodoxy as a foundation, and then build on it with Anabaptist distinctives. Variation on this same format might include Ron Sider's suggestion that a full-orbed theology would combine the orthodoxy of Evangelical Anabaptism with Anabaptist social concerns, and C. Arnold Snyder's claim that sixteenth-century Anabaptist theology has the classic creeds of Christendom at its core." J. Denny Weaver, "Parsing Anabaptist Theology: A Review Essay of Thomas N. Finger's *A Contemporary Anabaptist Theology*," *Direction*, Volume 32, N° 2 (Fall 2005), 241-263. The quote is from page 3 of the electronic version: http://www.directionjournal.org/article/?1403.

[4] J. Denny Weaver, *Becoming Anabaptist, The Origin and Significance of Sixteenth-Century Anabaptism*, Second Edition (Scottdale: Herald Press, 2005), 222.

[5] Weaver, "Parsing Anabaptist Theology," 20, electronic version.

insights to a secondary or negligible status.⁶ This leads either to supporting the status quo as opposed to challenging it,⁷ or relegates Anabaptism to being little more than "a barely visible rivulet."⁸

Instead of situating Anabaptism within the history of doctrine or seeking "points of agreement" with what he labels "standard theology," Weaver argues that historians and theologians should begin with the particularity of Anabaptist theological emphases in order to see how they can be used to formulate a coherent and comprehensive theological perspective.⁹ He does of course recognize that sixteenth-century Anabaptists did use classical theological categories and the "standard" creeds. Nevertheless, "they did not simply repeat these formulations. They continually *added* to these formulas and confessions, demonstrating the Anabaptists' sense of the inadequacy of the standard formulas and creeds."¹⁰ These categories were inadequate because what the Anabaptists added "was actually more important than the received formulations."¹¹

Citing an earlier French draft of the previous chapter of this study, Weaver highlights Marpeck's use of "classical theology" as an example of Anabaptist originality.

---

[6] "Anabaptist theologizing is left to appear as pale, less informed versions of the older, standard story for questions of Christology, atonement, and Trinity." Weaver, "Parsing Anabaptist Theology," 10. "Stated another way, defining Anabaptism in terms of core theological statements shared with Catholicism and Protestantism implies that Anabaptists were theologically unoriginal. In fact, it means that their theological validity depends on agreement with the received formulas and innovation is problematic." Weaver, *Becoming Anabaptist*, 226.

[7] "Although (C. Arnold) Snyder's work has much that is commendable, at the same time I believe that the theological orientation of his project supports rather than rejects Christian identification with the surrounding social order, thereby contradicting a plain theological-ethical commitment of Anabaptist dissent." Weaver, *Becoming Anabaptist*, 225.

[8] Weaver, "Parsing Anabaptist Theology," 18, electronic version.

[9] "I do not present Anabaptism as a combination of Catholic and Protestant elements, or as a middle way between these Catholic and Reformation perspectives. Anabaptism appears as its own kind of movement, with the potential to develop a comprehensive perspective on the world." Weaver, *Becoming Anabaptist*, 223.

[10] Weaver, *Becoming Anabaptist*, 215.

[11] Ibid.

Marpeck charted a new theological path. That new theological path and the uniqueness of Marpeck's Anabaptist theology are not visible if one chooses to stress his agreement with the received views of Trinitarian theology, the humanity and deity of Jesus, and atonement images as these are found in both medieval theology and in Martin Luther.[12]

So argues Weaver. In response it can be said that Weaver's formulation of the options seemingly forces an unnecessary choice, as if we were obliged to choose between "classical theology" and "Anabaptist originality." Such a methodology suggests that there is a timeless classical theology necessarily tied to Christendom assumptions and practices of violence on the one hand, and Anabaptist originality that rejects violence on the other.

From their very beginning, doctrines such as the Incarnation or the Trinity have had histories of interpretation and meaning. They were formulated in the heat of intense conflicts, and were an attempt to gather together the most important insights of differing positions. They are in a sense "limit-statements," i.e., boundaries which, while claiming fundamental truth necessary to any faithful understanding of the Gospel,[13] have accorded latitude for discussion and debate.

One helpful analogy might be the formation of the canon of Christian Scripture. Among the many Gospels circulating in the early centuries of church history, four of them were recognized as legitimate ways to tell the story of Jesus. There was not only one way, but several. This does, however, signify that there are also illegitimate ways of telling the story. The canon establishes boundaries, within which there has also been much room for discussion and theologizing.[14]

Just as the fixing of the canon has never totally settled hermeneutical debates about the meaning of Scripture, dogmatic formulations are meant

---

[12] *Becoming Anabaptist*, 211.
[13] Jon Sobrino, *Christology at the Crossroads. A Latin American Approach*, (London: SCM Press, 1978), 317.
[14] "The real function of the notion of canon then is that it enables a norming process within diversity, rather than assuming (with modernism) that pluralism is the end of all norms, or (with 'orthodoxy') that norms are the end of pluralism." John Howard Yoder, *To Hear the Word* (Eugene OR: Wipf and Stock Publishers, 2001), 106.

to be limits or perhaps "grammar rules" for helping the church interpret the meaning of the foundational events to which Scripture refers.[15] They are boundary statements, but also leave sizable degrees of maneuvering space for interpretation and debate. As Jon Sobrino helpfully says:

> Dogma is not the source of what is positive in the faith; generally speaking, we can say it is a formulation designed to defend the faith against error…. Dogma is an explanation of Scripture, not vice-versa…[16]

This implies that there have always been different interpretations of "dogma" between the Eastern and Western churches, between the classical and medieval periods, between Catholics and Protestants, between Lutherans and Reformed. To say that Anabaptists have their own original insights on the Trinity or the Incarnation is true. Nevertheless, the same could be said of Luther and Calvin, of Augustine and Aquinas.

Mennonites need to recognize that violence is not the only issue that theology addresses or that has caused serious debates. That there is an original Anabaptist interpretation of theology on the one hand, and a classical (unified and unchanging) understanding of theology on the other hand, is not the most cogent way of framing the question of Anabaptist originality or coherence. That Anabaptists had their distinctive reading of classical doctrines is true. That they owed nothing to the past or that they thought they were *adding* something to what those doctrines had "originally" meant or were "supposed" to have meant is not the case.

---

[15] By saying that dogma functions as grammar rules or boundary statements, I am not calling into question the ontological reality that lays behind those formulations. But following Marpeck's logic, I would argue that we only arrive at the "invisible" by means of the "visible." Human language and conceptualization are part of the "outer means" that we have at our disposal in this world. Language allows us to formulate ultimate convictions about reality that in a sense cannot be proven. They can only be pointed to by "witness" and "testimony," i.e. by language and argumentation, but perhaps in a more important way by the reality those convictions help to shape within history. The most real Word became flesh and dwelt among us.

[16] Sobrino, *Christology at the Crossroads*, 318-317. Cf. also Stanley Hauerwas: "Doctrines, therefore, are not the upshot of the stories, they are not the meaning or heart of the stories. Rather they are tools … meant to help us tell the story better." Stanley Hauerwas, *The Peaceable Kingdom*, 26.

Christian theology is a continual process of interpretation and reinterpretation, i.e., an ongoing debate over the meaning of what Weaver calls the "Jesus narrative." As stated previously, it seems to me that the choices he is urging us to make are formulated in unnecessary opposition. Weaver writes,

> The credibility of Anabaptism as a movement thus depends on references to the story of Jesus rather than its agreement with the traditions of Christendom, even though Anabaptism emerged in conversation with these traditions of Christendom.[17]

I have yet to meet or read a Christian theologian regardless of tradition who would not say that the credibility of his or her theology depends on an ultimate reference to the story of Jesus. The real debate centres on: what does the Jesus story mean? What is the truest and most adequate reading of that story? What are the implications for how we live? How is today's meaning faithful to and in continuity with the original meaning? Obviously these questions have evoked differing answers, spawning ongoing disagreements and debates.

Weaver asserts that the narrative of Jesus – and not later tradition – is the final authority.[18] Once again, I am unaware of any serious Christian theologian who would contest that statement as it stands, at least on a methodological level. Evangelicals who insist on the authority of Scripture also argue in favour of a (different) Christocentric reading of Scripture. Liberal Protestants would claim that the true meaning of the Jesus narrative came to fruition in the Enlightenment. Catholics or Orthodox who affirm the authority of tradition, also make it clear that tradition is the reformulation and transmission of the original meaning of the Jesus narrative in new contexts. "Tradition" is essentially "reinterpretation" and is not intended to be something that changes the meaning of the original story.[19] Of course, those who disagree with a given reinterpretation will claim that it does in fact change the meaning of the original intention.

---

[17] *Becoming Anabaptist*, 230.
[18] Ibid.
[19] Cf. *Dei Verbum* (*Dogmatic Constitution on Divine Revelation*), in Marianne Lorraine Trouvé, FSP (general editor), *The Sixteen Documents of Vatican II*, (Boston: Pauline Books & Media, 1999), 403-431.

The question which surfaces lies not in whether the final authority is Scripture, tradition or the "Jesus narrative." The question is whether or not Scripture and/or tradition are being interpreted in a way faithful to the original meaning(s) of the Jesus narrative. Nevertheless, without Scripture, we have no Jesus narrative. Without dogmatic formulations, we have no "grammar rules" for reading Scripture. It is true that throughout much of Christian history, Scripture and classical theology have been used to justify violence. The story of Jesus has been told in ways that allow people to kill each other in good conscience. Scripture has been interpreted to justify warfare in the name of God. Medieval tradition reinterpreted the Jesus narrative so that "taking up one's cross" could mean participating in a Crusade. All claimed to be faithful to the original meaning of Jesus.

Nevertheless, sixteenth century Anabaptists did not think they were standing outside Christian tradition, or *adding* anything to Scripture or to the "classical doctrines." To the contrary, they claimed to be reformulating the true, i.e., original and apostolic meaning of Scripture and doctrine. In his *Exposé*, Marpeck claims that he is returning to a pre-constantinian reading of Jesus, Scripture and theology. In his perspective, the alliance between empire and church compromised the true understanding of the "Jesus narrative." It was not that "classical theology" was untrue, but that it was being used inaccurately to underwrite the betrayal of the very Gospel it claimed to represent. Marpeck's theology insisted that "social location" made a serious difference in interpreting the message of salvation. A church that had tied herself intimately to political power was no longer capable of truly comprehending the message of Jesus and could too easily formulate its theology – however "orthodox" it might have been – in a way that contradicted the claims of Jesus.

From an historical point of view, identifying theological and conceptual similarities and differences between Anabaptists and their contemporaries as well as their predecessors, is not an attempt to betray their own particular understanding of the Gospel. It is the simple recognition that ideas don't "fall from heaven" and that theology is always done in context. Anabaptist theologians, pastors and martyrs did not invent their theology in a vacuum. Posing the question as to the source of their ideas and calling attention to their similarities with other theologies in no way disparages the insights particular to sixteenth-century Anabaptists. To the contrary, attentiveness to specific historical contexts and social location helps to interpret the "particularity" of Anabaptism's reading of the Christian theological tradition of which it was a part.

In contemporary Western Europe, "Christendom" is dead and most people including theologians are applauding its disappearance. Churches and theological traditions grounded in Christendom's assumptions or in classical theology have been compelled to take serious stock of their theology and their role in the world. This is the context in which I have lived for over thirty years. In the United States experience, on the other hand, and especially in areas where Mennonite educational institutions are found, the Evangelical world all too often uses "classical doctrine" to continually justify violence. As in the sixteenth-century, social location makes a difference today, which is one reason a "French" or "European" perspective added to the discussion can perhaps be of some benefit.

The council of Nicea (325) transpired before Christendom was a political, theological and cultural reality. It reflected generations of preceding theological debates, i.e. from the period when Christians had been severely persecuted by pagan emperors. At the beginning of the 4th century, Christianity was at a major turning point in "social location" that would strongly influence its theology and ethics throughout the medieval period. While some would claim that the purport of Trinitarian formulations of Nicea and Constantinople inherently supported or led to later Christendom justifications of violence, my years of studying and teaching church history have encouraged me to consider more nuanced conclusions that will hopefully become clearer in the following pages. It might be added that if such a case could be made against the classical doctrines, an even stronger case could be made against the very Scripture those doctrines attempt to explicate. Throughout most of church history, the medieval period included, Scripture always played a much stronger role in the justification of violence than have the classical doctrines.

With methodological preferences firmly stated, let us now proceed to the final three sections and with the help of other contemporary theologians, undertake the task of demonstrating how Marpeck's use of "classical categories" such as the Incarnation and the Trinity can actually enhance a better conceptualization and sharing of the "Jesus narrative" in today's world, and why forsaking them would weaken our case in the arena of theological discourse with other Christians and the wider world. Stanley Hauerwas captures this correctly when he suggests that

> the Mennonite understanding of the church's position to the world is possible only if such a church is sustained by the kind of theology found in the church fathers, and in that confession we call the Nicene Creed.[20]

Incarnation and Trinity:
Maintaining a Peace Theology Anchored in Jesus

One of the common critiques of creedal language which speaks of "consubstantiality" between the Father, Son and Spirit as used at Nicea (325) and Constantinople (381) maintains that it freezes dynamic and historical descriptions of Jesus into the ontological categories of Greek philosophy. That this could and did happen throughout the medieval period will not be denied. That it was the original intent of fourth century theologians is less obvious.

As stated in the previous section, one of the primary functions of Christian theology is the ongoing task of restating and reinterpreting the original message of the Jesus event in continuously changing contexts. This process – described and theorized in John Yoder's article "But We Do See Jesus" – already began in the New Testament.[21] Yoder does a parallel study of five different New Testament Christological texts to show how

---

[20] Stanley Hauerwas, *A Better Hope: Resources for a Church Confronting Capitalism, Democracy and Postmodernity* (Grand Rapids MI: Brazos Press, 2000), 169.
[21] "…The New Testament is the document of a transition made by a message-bearing community from one world to another." John Howard Yoder, "'But We Do See Jesus': The Particularity of the incarnation and the Universality of Truth," in *The Priestly Kingdom. Social Ethics as Gospel*, (The University of Notre Dame Press, 1984), 49.

various apostolic authors learned the cultural and philosophical language of their addressees in order to restate the meaning of the "Jesus narrative" for that particular context. Yoder's conclusion is that "a high Christology is the natural cultural ricochet of a missionary ecclesiology when it collides as it must with whatever cosmology explains and governs the world it invades."[22]

According to the Jesuit theologian Bernard Sesboüé, when moving into a new context, theology must fulfil two tasks. It must faithfully transmit the original meaning and message of the Gospel while simultaneously speaking creatively to the new situation which will be asking new questions and using concepts not necessarily found in Scripture.[23] As the church moved out of the apostolic period into Greek culture, the task was not easy. How do you tell and embody the Jesus story to people steeped in Greek concepts of "substance" and "being"?

One of the first challenges was to maintain the true humanity of Jesus in the face of Gnostic and Greek claims that invisible and spiritual reality cannot be seen or known in visible and material ways. Yes, Jesus was a true human being argued theologians such as Irenaeus and Tertullian. But this response evoked a new quandary. If Jesus is truly human, then he cannot be truly God. According to what we know of Arius, the solution was to be found somewhere in between: Jesus was more than a human, less than God. In other words, Jesus was neither truly human neither truly God.

In Sesboüé's reading, the character of Arius' solution would have hellenized the Gospel. "Being" defined exclusively as spiritual and invisible signified that God could not be fully present in human form. Hence, Arius gave priority to the philosophical concepts of his context. At the very moment when the church was becoming at ease in the Greek world of thought, what Nicea achieved was not a reformulation of the Gospel into Greek categories, but rather the use of Greek concepts to assert what

---

[22] Yoder, "But We Do See Jesus," 54.
[23] Bernard Sesboüé, *Jésus-Christ dans la tradition de l'Eglise* (Paris : Descléé, 1982), 52.

Greek philosophy found unacceptable, i.e., when you see Jesus, you see God.[24]

These words of John Milbank emphasize the importance of what transpired in this process.

> Disconcerting as it may appear, one has to recognize in the doctrinal affirmation of the Incarnation a radically inventive moment, which asserts the 'finality' of God's appearance in a life involving suffering and violent death, and claims also that in a certain sense God 'has to' be like this, and has not just 'incidentally' chosen this path.[25]

What is important in today's context is perhaps not so much to use the vocabulary and concepts of Nicea as it is to restate and reinterpret the conclusions the Trinitarian doctrine reached: 1) in Jesus, God was fully and definitively present within time and space, 2) in the Spirit, God continues to work within the world and history, and 3) that the "Jesus-project" of a non-violent reconciliation of the universe is at the very heart of God's being and essence.

I would claim that this is what Marpeck was doing in the sixteenth-century. His comprehension of non-violence was clearly rooted in his understanding of the Incarnation and the Trinity. When we see Jesus and listen to Jesus, we see and listen to God, which means that Jesus's teachings and example are definitive. When the Spirit works in the life of the church, it will produce non-violent practices and behaviour that "look like" Jesus. For Marpeck in the sixteenth-century, just as for John Yoder in the 20th century, peace theology was grounded in a "high Christology."[26]

---

[24] Sesboüé, 102. I agree with Craig Carter's reading that John Howard Yoder agreed with such a perspective. "Yoder says that the Nicene solution ... was a verbal formality that met a real need because 'it safeguards the New Testament content ... in a different thought world'." Cf. Craig A. Carter, *The Politics of the Cross. The Theology and Social Ethics of John Howard Yoder*, (Grand Rapids MI: Brazos Press, 2001), 115. This does not of course mean that at various points in church history, especially during the period of Christendom, that Greek categories never had negative influence on Christian theology.

[25] John Milbank, *Theology and Social Theory. Beyond Secular Reason* (Oxford: Blackwell Publishers, 1993), 384.

[26] "It is therefore in the person and work of Jesus, in His teachings and His passion, that this kind of pacifism finds its rootage, and in His resurrection that it finds it enablement."

Some may continue to object that such "speculative" concepts move us away from the historical Jesus and from the real world where discipleship transpires. Should not priority be given to the "real world," to narrative and the historical? This is of course a valid concern and it is important that any Anabaptist formulation of Christology begin with narrative and history and affirm the foundational importance of the historical and truly human Jesus. True Christology starts "from below," i.e. from the life and narrative of Jesus but necessarily arrives at the fundamental importance of New Testament claims about the identity of Jesus. As John Sobrino, the Latin American liberation theologian, has written:

> The proper logical order of Christology is the chronological order. We are justified in starting our Christology with the historical Jesus because that is the only way in which our dogmatic formulas can have any real meaningfulness.[27]

Marpeck continually worked from Scripture, much more so than he did from the theological categories we have been discussing. He was ultimately more of a biblical theologian than he was a dogmatic theologian. His main concerns focused on the historical Jesus, his teachings, and how the presence of the Spirit makes a difference in the everyday life of Christians in the everyday world. This did not, however, cause him to shy away from "theological" questions that had to do with how history and the world are to be understood and to be conceptualized. His Christology "from below" flowed into a high Christology, in much the same way as does the Christology of Sobrino, the praxis-oriented liberation theologian.[28]

John Howard Yoder, *Nevertheless. The Varieties of Religious Pacifism* (Scottdale: Herald Press, 1971), 123. "What becomes of the meaning of incarnation if Jesus is not normative man? If he is a man but not normative, is this not the ancient ebionitic heresy? If he be somehow authoritative but not in his humanness, is this not a new Gnosticism?" Yoder, *The Politics of Jesus*, 10. "The convictions argued here do not admit to being categorized as a sectarian oddity or a prophetic exception. Their appeal is to classical catholic Christian convictions properly understood." Yoder, *The Priestly Kingdom*, 11.

[27] Jon Sobrino, *Christology at the Crossroads*, 334

[28] "An authentically orthodox Christology must end up with the ontological affirmation of the Incarnation. Epistemologically, however, it must work in the opposite direction." Sobrino, *Christology at the Crossroads*, 339.

Nevertheless, once the importance of narrative and history as the starting point in the elaboration of Christology has been affirmed, the role of "ontology," or conceptual claims about "how the world is" must still be made. Narrative and history are necessary and remain the epistemological starting point, but they are not sufficient for the task of theology. As Milbank claims, narrative "anticipates the speculative task of ontology and theology."[29] Human experience within history, the source of narrative, always leads to claims about "what the world is really like" and "how we should live on the basis of what the world is really like." Narratives are full of implicit assumptions about life and the world that need to be explicated. At any given point in history, the church is living in a world with many different stories and ways of understanding the world. The "ontological" or "theological" claims of the Incarnation and the Trinity mean that Christians "treat Christ as 'measuring' all reality, in the same way that God's generated wisdom, his word, is taken to do."[30]

Since theology is an ongoing task of reinterpretation and contextualisation, it is important to be at home in the cultural and conceptual worlds in which we live in order to reinterpret and restate the claims of Christ's lordship. Through narrative, we tell the story of Jesus and stay anchored in history and everyday life. Through theology, we claim the ultimate meaning of that narrative in relation to the world in which we live.[31] The Incarnation is that point from which we "read" the rest of human history and offer a lived-out critique and alternative in the life of the Christian community.

The temptation at any point in history is for the church to allow other stories to read and re-define the "Jesus story." Surrendering a "high Christology," i.e., the claims of the Incarnation and the Trinity, severely weakens our ability to critique other narratives and can allow the implicit and explicit historicism of Western secularism and the reductionist

---

[29] Milbank, *Theology and Social Theory*, 385.
[30] Ibid., 383.
[31] "One then must face up to the real implication of a narrative that is at one and the same time a recounting of 'real history' and yet has also an interpretative, regulative function in respect to all other history." Milbank, *Theology and Social Theory*, 387.

presuppositions of the social sciences to govern our discourse.³² In a Western world governed by the assumptions of the autonomous individual, the sovereignty of the free market and of the relativity of any claim to truth (other than the two previous claims), there is little hope of finding the basis of a praxis that will refuse violence and economic exploitation.

Anabaptist peace theology needs to be derived from a Trinitarian Christology and not from the basic presuppositions and methodologies of Western (or any other) culture. Given the continuing prevalence of violence justified in the name of God, whether by Christians or Muslims, the elaboration of a theology and practice of peace is one of the most important tasks to which the church is called to in today's world.³³ It must be acknowledged, however, that there are different notions, understandings and practices of peace. In spite of the urgency and importance of the task, the question still needs to be asked: when theologizing about peace, "do we still see Jesus?" In the same fashion that early theologians were tempted to interpret Jesus in terms of Greek concepts of "being," certain theologians today may be tempted to constitute a peace theology by redefining Jesus or God in terms of how our culture defines peace. As Chris Huebner suggests, it is possible for "the category of peace (to be) abstracted from its larger theological home, idealized, and turned into a criterion for adjudication of all subsequent reflection, theological or otherwise."³⁴ It is Jesus who defines peace and not peace that defines Jesus.

---

[32] "In this fashion, a gigantic claim to be able to read, criticize, say what is going on in other human societies, is absolutely integral to the Christian Church, which itself claims to exhibit the exemplary form of human community. For theology to surrender this claim, to allow that other discourses – the 'social sciences' – carry out yet more fundamental readings, would therefore amount to a denial of theological truth." Ibid.

[33] It is interesting to note that Mennonite theologians in Europe do not hesitate to use Trinitarian theology when formulating their ideas about peace, ecclesiology or forgiveness. Cf. Fernando Enns (all the works cited in this chapter), Antonio Gonzalez (*The Gospel of Faith and Justice*, Maryknoll NY: Orbis Books, 2005) and Linda Oyer, "Le pardon, une anticipation eschatologique," in N. Blough, *Eschatologie et vie quotidienne*, 83-94.

[34] Chris K. Huebner, "What Should Mennonites and Milbank Learn from Each Other?" *The Conrad Grebel Review* (Spring 2005), 10.

Mennonites and Other Christians: The Importance of Ecumenical Relationships and Catholicity as Peacemaking

It is important to remember that Pilgram Marpeck penned his writings in the context of an extremely violent disruption of Western Christendom. He wrote about the "humanity of Christ" at the same time the visible "body of Christ" was tearing itself apart. While Marpeck never hesitated to critique positions that he considered false and his theology contained a biting critique of the violence of sixteenth century religious wars, he was still apparently able to learn from Martin Luther, Caspar Schwenckfeld, Martin Bucer and probably many others. Pilgram Marpeck's theology was forged in dialogue with others and the necessity to explain his position to those with whom he disagreed.

We are still strongly under the influence of that disruption (usually called the "Reformation"). It has determined the shape of Western and much of world Christianity. The body of Christ continues to be broken and all too often, we do our theology in a way that takes this brokenness for granted, without even seeing it as a fundamental problem for the very being of the church. As Miroslav Volf has pointed out: "it has ... become quite self-evident that *all* of us are poor Christians if we live divided, and that no ecclesiology can proceed in self-satisfied isolation."[35]

Mennonites tend to revel in the thought that their critique of medieval constantinianism points to one of the major failures of the church. I share that thought and point to its importance in ecumenical dialogue.[36] Unfortunately that critique can on occasion be made in such a way that somehow excludes us from history or puts us above it in a specially privileged position that allows us to deliver glib judgments on the thousand years of church history that preceded the sixteenth-century.

---

[35] Miroslav Volf, *After Our Likeness, The Church as the Image of the Trinity* (Grand Rapids: Eerdmans, 1998), 19.

[36] "The particular contribution that the theology of Radical Protestantism can make to any ecumenical discussion of the fourth century resides in its suspicion of all forms of 'Constantinianism'; that is, in its critique of all political theology in which theology and politics are fused, or worse, where theology functions as an instrument of political ideology." A. James Reimer, *Mennonites and Classical Theology*, 269.

Like all theologies elaborated in the context of a divided church, Mennonite theology is only a partial theology, a partiality that reflects the brokenness of Christ's body. As we move into the world, intent on being part of a reconciling community working for peace and justice, we can no long theologize in a vacuum, presuming that the theology and practice of other Christians is totally bankrupt, as if our tradition has nothing to learn from other members of Christ's body.[37] We can no longer do theology without taking into consideration some of the difficult questions that other traditions have often answered differently than we. Sometimes, although certainly not always, what Anabaptism has considered as "unfaithfulness" refers to times and places where Christians found themselves in very complex situations that necessitated the making of decisions Mennonites have never had to make, or when they did, made them very much in the same way.

Recognition of this fact clearly demonstrates that it is no longer possible or expedient to continue doing theology in a way that separates us from the history of other Christians and the rest of the world. We are also active participants in the church's failure to live and communicate the Gospel. The history of the medieval church is also our history. Doing theology in ecclesiological isolation without really engaging those people or traditions with whom we disagree allows our own convictions to go unchallenged. Historians such as Jean Delumeau or Brad Gregory, who have studied specific questions across confessional boundaries and over longer periods of time, help us to see that common convictions were often shared by those who thought they were fundamentally different from one another. If this be the case, insisting exclusively on our differences or on the particularity of our own position as the non-negotiable starting point of

---

[37] Miroslav Volf's citation of Karl Barth on this subject is quite apt. "If a man can acquiesce in divisions, if he can even take pleasure in them, if he can be complacent in relation to the obvious faults and errors of others and therefore his own responsibility for them, then that man may be a good and loyal confessor in the sense of his own particular denomination, he may be a good Roman Catholic or Reformed or Orthodox or Baptist, but he must not imagine that he is a good Christian." *After Our Likeness*, 19.

our theological identities can blind us to how much we share with others.[38] Once there has been a conflict that results in separation, theologizing is all too often a justification of why the separation happened, and why "our" side is right and the "other" side is wrong.

Ever since their beginnings in the sixteenth-century, Anabaptists and Mennonites have consistently underlined the visibility of the church and its function as a sign. If the church is a sign, we must remember that signs can be ambiguous or even communicate something contrary to the original intention.[39] Except for the impossible case that that our own history has been a flawless and spotless example for other Christians and all of humanity, an important part of being a sign is also to articulate the church's failures and to ask for forgiveness. If the peace of the Gospel is the answer we propose to others, we and our history are also a part of the problem. The Anabaptist tradition must learn to incorporate its own weaknesses and failures (as well as human weakness and sinfulness in general) into its theology of the visibility of the church.

A contemporary Anabaptist reconsideration of the notion of "catholicity" could be of great help in this regard.[40] One aspect of this catholicity entails recognizing that Mennonite theology is not *sui generis*,

---

[38] For example, J. Denny Weaver argues that "...Anabaptists were not martyred because they had an outlook that made them look as much like Catholicism or Protestantism as possible." *Becoming Anabaptist*, 229. This is of course true in an important sense, but Brad Gregory's work implies that one of the real tragedies of sixteenth-century martyrdom was how much all those concerned shared in common. "In the sixteenth and seventeenth centuries, the most basic Christian convictions were shared among Roman Catholics, Anabaptists, and Protestants.... Catholics as well as varieties of Protestants and Anabaptists concurred that scripture was the word of God, that it was true, that it was every bit as relevant in the sixteenth century as it had been in ancient times, and that correct faith was necessary for eternal salvation. The embrace of these fundamental convictions grounded the martyrs' experience in all three traditions." *Salvation at Stake: Christian Martyrdom in Early Modern Europe* (Harvard University Press, 1999), 106.

[39] Yves Congar, *Un peuple messianique: l'Eglise, sacrement du salut. Salut et libération* (Paris: Editions du Cerf, 1975), 84.

[40] "...The challenge for an Anabaptist ecclesiology has always been to look beyond the absolute locality of the church and include its visible catholicity." Fernardo Enns, "Space for Theological Reflexion," 38.

and that we are part of the universal church in both time and in space. Only a catholicity which takes each local context seriously, but is at the same time international, intercultural and transhistorical can save the church from the blindness of nationalism and the tendency to consider as universal the particular and arbitrary goals of the nations in which we find ourselves. Only an internationally embodied Gospel can combat the disparities of wealth and privilege. Only a catholic church can embody the fullness of our historical, cultural and theological differences in the context of a larger unity, which means that we need to more consciously position ourselves in relation to other traditions and theologies and also be willing to learn from them. It is in this respect that Marpeck's use of traditional theological categories of Incarnation and Trinity reminds us that it is possible to both claim the specific treasures of our own tradition and affirm the common language of the larger body of Christ of which we are a part.[41]

It is a strange paradox to note that Mennonite "peace theology" has all too often neglected the importance of making peace between divided Christians and churches. Some have simply refused to even speak with "unfaithful" Christians, while others fear that our own particular insights will simply disappear into a generic Christianity, be it evangelical or ecumenical. Far from diluting denominational identity, discussion and dialogue with other Christians often reinforces particular identities. This has also been the case for Mennonites.[42] The most coherent and influential Mennonite formulation of peace theology in the 20th century (i.e. John Howard Yoder) was done in the context of ecumenical contacts

---

[41] At the March 2006 meeting of the General Council of the Mennonite World Conference, the world-wide Anabaptist-Mennonite family adopted a statement of "common convictions" which includes an explicit reference to the Trinity. "God is known to us as Father, Son and Holy Spirit, the Creator who seeks to restore fallen humanity by calling a people to be faithful in fellowship, worship, service and witness." (http://www.mwc-cmm.org/MWC/Councils/2006SharedConvictionsENG.pdf) This statement of common convictions underlines Anabaptist particularity while at the same time affirming commonality with the larger body of Christ.

[42] "Through ecumenical encounter and dialogue our genuine denominational identity and profile has not been relativized but sharpened." Enns, "The Peace Church," 9.

and discussions about peace in post WWII Europe and Cold War North America.[43] Long term contacts, dialogue and teaching within Evangelical or Catholic contexts have strongly reinforced my own theological identity. But at the same time, I can no longer do theology as a Mennonite without the help of Catholic or Evangelical friends and colleagues, without taking into account their objections and insights, without remembering what I have learned from them. Making peace among Christians must be a priority if the church of Jesus Christ is to preach peace to the rest of the world. Serious dialogue and engagement with others is a step on the road to peace that we cannot afford to miss taking.

In a period of time when European Mennonites have helped the World Council of Churches adopt a decade for "Overcoming Violence," when Catholics and Mennonites are discovering that they are "Called Together to be Peacemakers," what would happen if instead of despising Evangelicals for their militarism, North American Anabaptist theologians would make a concerted effort to communicate peace theology to those who claim such a strong allegiance to Christ? What would happen if Anabaptist peace theology could make inroads into a vastly expanding global and largely Pentecostal Christianity in Latin American, Africa and Asia? Are these not relevant tasks to be pursued by those deeply concerned about peace?

Marpeck and Missiology: The Church as Sacrament

One widely accepted result of contemporary research leads us to the knowledge that Pilgram Marpeck's Trinitarian Christology points to an understanding of the church as "sacrament," i.e. a visible manifestation of an invisible reality. The concrete visibility of the Christian community within history becomes the primary place for the action and presence of

---

[43] "My guess is that Yoder wouldn't have developed his representative theology from a Mennonite perspective without these early years in ecumenical formation." Enns, "The Peace Church," 13. For a more detailed look at Yoder and ecumenism, see Mark Thiessen Nation, *John Howard Yoder. Mennonite Patience, Evangelical Witness, Catholic Convictions* (Grand Rapids MI: Eerdman's, 2006), especially ch.3, "Faithful Ecumenism: A Call to Unity in Disciplined Discipleship."

God's Spirit.[44] Such visibility is both a means for God's self-revelation and for God's "being present" within the world.[45]

Pilgram Marpeck's logic – which he probably learned from Luther – parallels that of the Gospel of John. What God did as the Word become flesh in Jesus is prolonged throughout history in the concrete life of the believing community through the power of the Holy Spirit. "Peace be with you. As the Father has sent me, so I send you... Receive the Holy Spirit." (John 20: 21-22).[46] Throughout much of Mennonite history, Anabaptist particularity has taken shape in the lives of communities who saw themselves as "separate" from the world. Marpeck's ecclesiology has the opposite thrust: instead of "pulling out," it "sends" the church into the world.[47] In terms of their mission history, Mennonites have often times accepted the common Western dichotomies of "evangelism" over against "social action" and have all too often taken sides, making unnecessary choices that have led either to claiming evangelism as the only worthy task or considering social action, and especially peace-witness, as the exclusive means of Christian presence in the world.

---

[44] "For Marpeck the church as the Body of Christ was a sacramental offer of God's grace, mercy, and salvation to all. As in the Incarnation, God's grace continues to be offered through the physical Body of Christ to individuals and to the world by means of external and visible testimonies, ceremonies and acts of love." Snyder, *Anabaptist History and Theology*, 362.

[45] "The church is the primal sacrament. It is the paradigm for all other embodiments of the gospel. The ceremonies, as Marpeck explains them, become manifestations of the humanity of Christ in *both* ways that concept is used. The ceremonies reveal Christ as he took on flesh historically *and* as he indwells his people by means of the Spirit." Rempel, *The Lord's Supper in Anabaptism*, 148.

[46] For a recent study of the missiological import of the Gospel of John from an Anabaptist perspective, see Linda Oyer, *Interpreting the New in Light of the Old: A Comparative Study of the Post-Resurrection Commissioning Stories in Matthew and John*, doctoral dissertation presented at the Institut Catholique de Paris, Faculté de Théologie et de Sciences Religieuses, June 1997.

[47] I have attempted to lift out the missiological import of Marpeck's theology more fully in "Messianic Mission and Ethics: Discipleship and the Good News," in Wilbert R. Shenk, *The Transfiguration of Mission: Biblical, Theological and Historical Foundations* (Scottdale, Herald Press, 1993), 178-198.

In the following quotes, Marpeck vividly demonstrates to what measure a Trinitarian theology framed the basis of a "missional" ecclesiology.

> Without the artistry and teaching of the *Holy Spirit*, who pours out the love, which is God, into the hearts of the faithful, and which surpasses all reason and understanding, everything is in vain. The *Holy Spirit* proceeds from the *Father* and *Son*, and He witnesses to the *Father* and *Son* in the hearts of all the faithful; He copies and repeats the perfect law of the liberty of *Christ*. The faithful look into this law of liberty in order that they may fervently do what *Christ* spoke and commanded.[48]

The love poured out from God in Christ is embodied in the lives of the community and becomes the basis for "mission." All that Christ spoke and commanded is an integral part of the mission, part and parcel of the reason for being present in the world. Love of neighbour, love of enemy, practices of reconciliation and peace-making become sacramental, congruent to mission, as much as preaching and teaching the Jesus meta-narrative. Marpeck writes,

> (Christ's) untransfigured body (understand his church) … is his outward work: teaching, baptism, Lord's Supper, admonition, ban, discipline, evidence of love and service for the common good, a handclasp, improving and retaining Christ's commands and teachings… This outward work is brought about in and through the church by the reigning, glorified *Christ* with his and the *Father's Holy Spirit*.[49]

In terms of "Marpeck now," it is interesting to note that his Trinitarian theology bears certain similarities to the Catholic notion of the "church as sacrament," formulated during the second Vatican Council.[50] At the same time, it also anticipates and resembles the positions of other contemporary theologians' conceptions of a relationship between the Trinity and the

---

[48] *WPM*, 458.
[49] *Response*, LW, 85.
[50] How this is both similar to and different from contemporary Catholic theology is discussed in "The Church as Sign or Sacrament? Trinitarian Ecclesiology, Pilgram Marpeck, Vatican II and John Milbank," *MQR*, (January 2004), 29-52. I have freely adapted parts of this article in several sections of this chapter.

church's presence in the world.⁵¹ John Milbank has argued that the modern concept of a secular realm which is autonomous effectively "squeezes" the presence of God out of history. In response, Milbank insists on the importance of a Trinitarian understanding of the Christian God as that which allows God to be present and active within history.⁵² Such presence becomes evident in the communal and concrete existence of a church transformed into the image of Jesus by the Spirit.⁵³ Visible relationships within the community of faith make the reality of God visible. "Without mutual forgiveness and social peace ... no-one will be able to see God,"⁵⁴ Milbank writes. The Spirit's transforming work within the body of Christ mirrors the "shape" of Jesus.⁵⁵

The Spanish Mennonite theologian, Antonio Gonzalez, also underlines the important link between a Trinitarian understanding of God and the presence and action of God within history.

> More than a model, the Trinity is the concrete form in which our God brings about a community that is not our community, but God's own community, the community between the Father

---

⁵¹ One could argue that such an anticipation is less dependent on the originality of Marpeck than on the implicit meanings of the doctrines of the Trinity and of the Incarnation themselves. That there is convergence in today's world is a reflection of the "non-constantinian" social location of theologies that are being cited, as well as the Anabaptist-Mennonite identity of several of these authors, i.e. Fernando Enns and Antonio Gonzalez.

⁵² "Salvation is available to us after Christ, because we can be incorporated into the community which he founded, and the response of this community to Christ is made possible by the response of the divine Spirit to the divine Son, from whom it receives the love that flows between Son and Father." Milbank, *Theology and Social Theory,* 387.

⁵³ "The association of the Church with the response of the Spirit which arises 'after' the Son, and yet is fully divine, shows that the new community belongs from the beginning within the new narrative manifestation of God. Hence the metanarrative is *not* just the story of Jesus, it is the continuing story of the Church, already realized in a finally exemplary way by Christ, yet still to be realized universally, in harmony with Christ, and yet *differently,* by all generations of Christians." Ibid., 387.

⁵⁴ Ibid., 409.

⁵⁵ "...The attribution of 'a final perfection'.... must be meant to call our attention to, and to reinforce, a discovery of the 'shape' of Jesus's life and death, of the type of an exemplary practice which we can imitate and which can form the context for our lives together, so that we can call ourselves 'the body of Christ'." Ibid., 396.

and the Son by work of the Spirit. The Spirit, by including us through faith in the relationship between the Son and the Father ... incorporates us into the very life of the Trinity, thus radically transforming human history, from this moment and from below.[56]

For Gonzalez, such transformation of history is intrinsically linked to the Trinity through our own human experience of God's reigning action within history.[57] The reign of God is made known through concrete experiences of liberation that take on a specific shape, experiences of "pardon, reconciliation, bodily and spiritual health, or the beginnings of a renewed life in community."[58] As with Marpeck, Gonzalez' Trinitarian theology is inseparable from the existence of a people and by necessity is closely linked to the cross of Jesus.[59] At the same time, the existence of "a people who has experienced the liberation of God's Spirit linked to the cross of Jesus" has a specific role or mission to play within history.

The mystery of God's plan for history requires the existence of a people over whom God's reign becomes explicit, so that it can be proclaimed clearly to all humanity what actually happens when God reigns.[60]

A Trinitarian and sacramental theology conceives of the church as being sent into the world and is therefore missiological. It also claims that the primary locus of God's action within the world is wherever gathered communities allow themselves to be "christomorphically" transformed through faith by the Spirit. God's reign is displayed through social visibility. As Milbank writes,

The *logic* of Christianity involves the claim that the 'interruption' of history by Christ and his bride, the Church, is

---

[56] Gonzalez, *The Gospel of Faith and Justice*, 158.

[57] "The reign of God is indissolubly united to the Trinity, not because the Trinity is a model, but because the Trinity expresses our experience of God who in fact reigns in history, as true as it may be that the reign has not yet reached its culmination." Ibid., , 150.

[58] Ibid., 151.

[59] "There is no reign if there is no people to reign over." Ibid., 152. "This experience of the Spirit is a valid Christian experience only when enthusiasm in the Spirit does not lead to forgetting the cross of the Son..." Ibid., 151.

[60] Ibid.,152.

the most fundamental of events, interpreting all other events. And it is *most especially* a social event, able to interpret other social formations, because it compares them with its own new social practice.[61]

One common objection which emerges asserts that such an approach is sectarian and allows the church to presume that she possesses truth for the entire world. A Trinitarian approach can help to mitigate such a temptation. First of all, "social visibility" is a gift of God through the Spirit and is not something that culminates in self satisfaction or exclusivism. Rather, it comes to be a "particular" expression of God's reconciliation project for all. As all are in Adam and in Christ, as all families are to be blessed through Abraham and Sarah, so the particular visibility of the "body of Christ" within the world exists for others. It is an "open" particularity, directed toward others and not toward self.

> Obviously, this experience of the Spirit is a valid Christian experience only when ... newness of an unexpected fraternity with other believers does not degenerate into separatist isolation. The perfect community is one that, like the Father himself, remains universally open to the just and to sinners.[62]

As is the case with all ideas and convictions, Christian convictions take on a particular shape and become visible within history.[63] The reality of the Incarnation implies as much. The logic of the Gospel cannot escape the claim that there are privileged places within history where God is at work so that the Gospel may become visible to all. Be that as it may, "visibility"

---

[61] Milbank, *Theology and Social Theory*, 388.
[62] Gonzalez, *The Gospel of Faith and Justice*, 151. Fernando Enns also argues that a Trinitarian foundation for ecclesiology is more adequate than a strictly Christological one: "Mennonites have tended to ground their ecclesiology in Christology, which at times has led to Christomonism... In the Trinitarian model of community, by contrast, the understanding of church as subject is overcome, and a model to relate to others who are different is envisioned." Enns, "Space," 39.
[63] "Any community and politic is known and should be judged by the kind of people it develops." Stanley Hauerwas, *A Community of Character: toward a constructive christian social ethic* (University of Notre Dame Press, 1981), 2.

does not, however, mean "identification" between the Kingdom and the church nor "exclusive possession" of the truth. Gonzales writes,

> The reign is already present there where Jesus reigns, in the community of his disciples. This community, however, is not the reign of God. The reign of God is the dynamic exercise of God's sovereignty in creation and in history, exercised by the Son through the Spirit. This Spirit, although it blows where it will, becomes explicitly present there where believers can call God "Father" without fear, forming fraternal communities of brothers and sisters.[64]

In suggesting that the Spirit is "explicitly present" in the community, Gonzalez leaves space for the presence of the Spirit elsewhere. Since the church opts for unfaithfulness all too often, and since God is sovereign, we have no rightful authority to contend that the Spirit is not at work outside of the church. The reality of church history painfully demonstrates that a strict identification between the Church and the Reign of God cannot be made. As Fernando Enns aptly says: "The Holy Spirit inhabits the church and stays beyond it at the same time."[65] On the other hand, wherever the Spirit is at work, it will "look like" Jesus, i.e. it will take on the form of self-giving, forgiving and reconciling love.

Another possible objection to the missiological claim that the Christian community is a privileged vector of God's action within history is that it reeks of epistemological imperialism. In today's world, is it in the domain of possibility for anyone to claim to have a truth valid for all of history? Or in other words, metanarratives are either arrogant or implicit attempts to grab power. Alas, the latter has been the case in Christian history and such an objection must seriously be taken into consideration. Here again, a high Christology allows us to claim that truth cannot be imposed, and that the truth of the Gospel does not stem from the desire to manipulate people. Only a visible non-violent and non-coercive presence can respond to the accusation of "imperialism." If the Gospel claim of a "true reading" of history appears to be arrogant, it must be said at the same

---

[64] Gonzalez, *The Gospel of Faith and Justice*, 157.
[65] Enns, "Space," 39.

time that the "truth" which lies at the very heart of this claim cannot be imposed, and that peace, forgiveness and reconciliation are fundamental components of the "truth" that is being communicated. Christian truth claims can only be made in ways consistent with the claims themselves.[66] Contemporary theologians such as John Milbank and Stanley Hauerwas argue that the only means for claiming Christian truth is the "lived out" and "non-violent" visibility of the Gospel.[67]

Once again we retrace our steps to the narrative claims of the Gospel and their relation to a more theological formulation of the Jesus story. Grounding peace and reconciliation in the narrative of Jesus of Nazareth makes an explicit claim as to the nature of God and the world. The life, death and resurrection of Jesus Christ and the sending of the Holy Spirit to create community mean that we are involved in a divine project of reconciliation that is "with the grain of the universe."[68] A "Marpeckian"

---

[66] Stephen Boyd emphasizes how much the refusal to impose truth was an integral part of Marpeck's Trinitarian project. "The task of the transformed community and the transformed individual within it is the extension of Christ's humanity and thereby Christ's justice in the world. As we have consistently observed in Marpeck, that justice involves the reordering of social relationships, as well as of the life of the individual. The reordering Holy Spirit, willingly poured out by Christ in his cross, constitutes and is mediated by the new community, which patiently offers that Spirit to others *without coercion.*" Boyd, *Pilgram Marpeck*, 157.

[67] "*Testimony* is here offered to the Good, in a witnessing that also participates in it. This commitment to a rhetorical ... path to the Good opens out the following implication: only persuasion of the truth can be non-violent, but truth is only available through persuasion. Therefore truth, and non-violence have to be recognized simultaneously in that by which we are persuaded. Without attachment to a particular persuasion – which we can never *prove* to be either true, or non-violent – we would have no real means to discriminate peace and truth from their opposites." Milbank, *Theology and Social Theory*, 398.

[68] Cf. Stanley Hauerwas, *With the Grain of the Universe: The Church's Witness and Natural Theology* (Grand Rapids Michigan: Brazos Press, 2001). In much the same way that Milbank speaks of persuasion and rhetoric, Hauerwas pleads for lived out "witness" of the Gospel as the best way of doing theology. While probably neither of them see their

Trinitarian theology claims that God's non-violent love and reconciliation is the "truest reality" of human history. When this non-violent love and reconciliation can be seen in the flesh and offered to others in the power of the Spirit, Truth becomes visible and the mission of the church is being fulfilled. That the truth of the Gospel cannot be imposed is at the very heart of who God is.[69] This God took on flesh in the life, death and resurrection of Christ, and continues to be present by means of the Spirit in the midst of history.

---

work as missiology, what they have written is of utmost importance for any theology of mission in today's world.

[69] "The real issue is not whether Jesus can make sense in a world far from Galilee, but whether — when he meets us in our world, as he does in fact — we want to follow him. We don't have to, as they didn't then. That we don't have to is the profoundest proof of his condescension, and thereby of his glory." Yoder, "But we do see Jesus," 62.

Index

Names and Places

A

Abelard, 193n
Abraham, 51, 53, 70n, 116, 121, 137, 154, 250
Anselm of Canterbury, 189, 190n, 192-195, 199, 201, 206-208n
Aquinas, Thomas, 209-211, 218n, 231
Aristotle, 13
Arius, 236
Armour, R.S., 49n, 65n, 113
Atkinson, J., 113n
Augustine, 19, 59, 114, 144, 190n, 210-220, 231
Augsburg, 10, 16, 52, 71, 82- 83, 85n, 101, 104n, 134, 135, 138, 195

B

Baecher, Claude, 106n
Barth, Karl, 242n
Beachy, Alvin, 126n, 163n
Bernard of Clairvaux, 190n, 205, 209
Biel, Gabriel, 212
Bender, Harold S., 10n
Bergsten, Torsten, 53, 70n, 88n, 110n, 124n, 133n, 134n, 135n, 139n, 140n, 146n, 157n, 174n, 178, 181
Blaichner, Martin, 142
Blaurer, Ambrosius, 139

Bohemia, 26
Bosch, Sigmund, 142
Bradwardine, Thomas, 213
Boyd, Stephen, 8, 11n, 27n, 31, 32n, 47n, 58n, 67, 68n, 82n, 97n, 101n, 107n, 133n, 146n, 162n, 163n, 164, 252n
Bucer, Martin, 8, 16, 21, 22, 23, 46, 47- 49, 52- 54, 55- 56, 58, 62, 69, 71-80, 83-84, 86, 91, 94, 98, 115-116, 139, 181, 183, 225, 241
Bünderlin, Hans, 26, 27, 34, 35n, 44, 46, 182n, 185

C

Capito, Wolfgang, 54n, 77
Castenbaur, Stephan (Agricola), 25
Carter, Craig, 237n
Charles V, 14, 15, 82, 84, 89
Congar, Yves, 243n
Coninck, Frédéric de, 227n
Constantine, 96

D

Delumeau, Jean, 212n, 242
Denck, Hans, 31, 35n, 122, 125
Derksen, John D., 47n
Dipple, Geoffrey, 58n

E

Enns, Fernando, 223n, 240n, 243n, 244n, 245n, 248n, 250n, 251

Entfelder, Christian, 26, 34, 44, 46, 57, 86, 185
Erasmus, 13, 14, 17, 18, 20, 21, 97n, 149n, 212n, 217

F

Fast, Heinold, 30n, 57, 58n, 62n, 106n
Ferdinand I of Austria, 15, 16, 25
Franck, Sebastian, 58n, 96, 182n
François I, 15
Finger, Thomas, 8, 31n, 59n, 105n, 131n, 132n, 147, 148, 159n, 162n, 163n, 165n, 169n, 200n, 218n, 221, 228n
Freyberg, Helena von, 135, 139
Frecht, Martin, 139
Friedmann, Robert, 68, 69, 71, 72

G

Goertz, Hans-Jürgen, 10n, 61, 62, 74, 79, 113, 120n, 163n
Gonzalez, Antonio, 240n, 248-251
Gregory, Brad, 242, 243
Greschat, Martin, 48n
Grimm, Harold J., 83, 84n

H

Harrison, R.L., 139n
Hauerwas, Stanley, 231n, 235, 250n, 252, 253n
Hoffmann, Melchior, 16, 26, 52, 88n, 124n, 125-126, 173n, 196n
Hubmaier, Balthasar, 14, 16, 19, 22, 61, 69-70, 88n, 163

Huebert Hecht, Linda A., 110n, 134n
Huebner, Chris K., 240
Huss, John, 12
Husser, Daniel, 53, 57n, 134n
Hut, Hans, 30-32, 61
Hutterites, 17, 101, 106n

I

Ickelsamer, Valentin, 135
Irenaeus, 236

J

Jakob, Hans, 143
Jecker, Hanspeter, 8, 106

K

Karlstadt, Andreas, 40-41, 52
Klaassen, Walter, 8, 10n, 81, 83n, 84n, 85, 87n, 113, 174
Klassen, William, 8n, 10, 34, 49n, 52, 57, 63, 79, 103, 110n. 113n, 115, 124n, 125n, 181-184
Kiwiet, Jan, 104n, 110n, 122, 123n, 125, 132, 134n
Krahn, Cornelius, 126n

L

Liechtenstein, Leonard von, 54
Lienhard, Marc, 40n, 41n, 42-43, 114, 115n, 174n
Luther, Martin, 8, 12-15, 17-23, 27, 31-34, 40-46, 51, 56, 57, 58, 61-64, 65, 68-69, 71-72, 75, 79, 82-99, 108, 113-115, 132, 146, 149, 158, 169-170, 174-175, 178,

180, 188-192, 196, 198, 200, 209, 212-222, 225-226, 230, 231, 241, 246

M

MacCulloch, Diarmaid, 12n, 22n
Maier, Paul, 126n, 139n, 140n, 141n, 151, 154n, 170n, 175n
Marschalk von Pappenheim, Magdalena, 110n, 134
McGrath, Alistair, 45, 75n, 194n, 199n, 212n, 214n, 215n, 216n, 217n, 218n
Milbank, John, 237, 239, 240n, 247n, 248, 250, 252, 253n
Moeller, Bernd, 13n, 77
Moravia, 16, 26, 46, 72, 101, 106, 134
Müler, Annthoni, 142
Münster, 16-17, 57, 102-104, 226
Müntzer, Thomas, 14, 31-32, 40-41, 120n

N

Nation, Mark Thiessen, 245n
Nilsson, K.O., 41n

O

Oberman, Heiko, 87n, 99
Odon of Cluny, 207n, 208
Oyer, Linda, 240n, 246n
Ozment, Steven, 13n, 69, 120n, 158n, 165n

P

Packull, Werner O., 8, 30n, 31, 45-46, 58n, 69, 81n, 82n, 84n, 85n, 88n, 93n
Pelikan, Jaroslov, 189, 190n, 192n, 193n, 194, 195n, 196n, 199n, 201n, 205n, 206n, 207n, 208n, 209n, 211n, 212n, 213, 214n, 215n, 216n, 217, 218n, 219n
Prenter, Regin, 41n, 43n, 114

R

Rattenberg, 10, 15-16, 25-26, 31
Reimer, A. James, 228n, 240n
Rempel, John, 8, 10, 58n, 81n, 133n, 134n, 147, 167n, 169, 178, 179n, 228n, 246n
Reublin, Wilhelm, 16
Rimini, Gregory de, 213
Rothkegel, Martin, 8, 106
Rothmann, Bernhard, 16, 56-57, 103, 108n, 109n, 112n, 115, 124n, 125n, 126, 127, 132, 178

S

Sattler, Michael, 14, 16, 77
Scharnschlager, Leupold, 8, 53, 142, 173n
Schlaffer, Hans, 25, 31-32
Schleitheim, 16, 23, 75n
Schiemer, Leonhard, 25-26, 31-32
Schmalkaldic League, 83, 85n, 91, 98, 139
Schmalkaldic War, 195, 203
Schoeps, H.J., 126n, 154n

Schwärmer, 33, 40, 45, 68n, 174
Schwenckfeld, Caspar, 16, 19, 23, 34, 51, 52-58, 80, 94, 102, 104n, 110n, 115, 122-126, 131, 132, 133-185, 195, 197n, 204, 225-226, 241
Scotus, Duns, 212
Servetus, Michael, 16, 56n-57n
Séguy, Jean, 227n
Sesboüé, Bernard, 236, 237n
Shenk, Wilbert R., 246n
Sider, Ron, 228
Simons, Menno, 104, 125, 196n
Sobrino, John, 230n, 231, 238
Snyder, C. Arnold, 8, 10, 35n, 106, 110n, 134n, 135n, 142n, 212n, 215n, 221n, 222n, 228n, 229n, 246n
Stauffer, Richard, 71n
Strasbourg, 8, 10, 16, 23, 26, 27, 28n, 29, 31, 34, 41, 43, 46, 47, 48n, 52-57, 58n, 62, 71-74, 75n, 76-77, 79, 80, 81-86, 88n, 92n, 98, 101, 104, 116, 120-121, 122-123, 126, 132, 134, 156, 173n, 181-183, 185, 225
Streicher, Helena, 110-113, 114n, 134, 139, 144
Swiss Brethren, 8, 17, 19, 26, 45, 101, 106, 221

T

Tauler, 68, 69n, 163
Tertullian, 236

U

Ulm, 110n, 134, 139

V

Vadian, 139
Volf, Miroslav, 241, 242n

W

Waldshut, 16, 70
Weaver, J. Denny, 8, 205n, 208n, 228-232, 243n
Wenger, John C., 169, 173n
Werner, Valtin, 142
Williams, George R., 56n, 58n, 60, 63n, 68-72, 105n, 110n, 126n, 133n, 139, 140n, 147, 155-156, 174, 200
William of Ockham, 212
Wray, Frank J., 103, 126n
Wyclif, John, 12

Y

Yoder, John Howard (J.H., John), 19n, 49n, 61n, 70n, 76n, 77n, 78, 188, 190-191, 193n, 220, 230n, 235-237, 238n, 244, 245n, 253n

Z

Ziegler, D.E., 47n
Ziegler, Clement, 126
Zurich, 16, 49n, 70, 76, 106, 108, 188, 189
Zurich Bible, 63, 70, 72, 108n
Zwingli, Ulrich, 12, 14, 18-19, 21, 22, 27, 40, 44n, 60, 70, 74, 76-78, 95, 106, 115, 170-171, 173, 178, 180, 188

Ideas and Concepts

A

Anthropology
  Erbgnad, 160, 163, 213n
  Fall, 49, 60, 126, 128, 156, 157, 160, 161, 191, 197-198, 201, 202n
  Free will, 20, 194n, 218n
  Light of nature predestination, 159-162
  Original sin, 20, 48, 50, 58, 59-60, 67, 75n, 107, 114, 127n, 128-129, 135, 137-138, 154, 155-159, 162, 163-164, 176, 180, 197, 199, 206, 210, 216, 220
  Pelagianism (Pelagian heresy), 156, 158, 159, 214n, 216, 217,
  Synergism, 163
Antichrist, 27-28, 90, 96-97, 129
Augsburg Confession, 71, 82-83

B

Baptism, 19, 20, 21, 43, 103-105, 109, 111, 113, 114
  Baptism in the Spirit, 64-67, 108, 114, 183
  Circumcision, 48, 64, 65-66, 67, 74, 114, 115
  Infant baptism, 18, 59, 73, 48, 74, 88, 115-116, 128n, 129, 157, 159, 183
  Inner baptism, 40, 65-67, 107-109, 111, 113, 117, 137-138, 142, 145
  Outer baptism, 26, 27, 67, 107-109, 111, 113, 117, 137-138, 142, 145, 183, 184n
  Water baptism, 29, 37, 65-67, 107-108, 119, 146-148, 166

C

Catholicity, 13, 18, 20, 45, 82, 89, 91n, 119, 158, 159, 188-189, 206, 215n, 229n, 232, 241-245, 247
Christology
  Ascension, 50, 51, 53, 73, 141, 143, 150, 153, 168, 169, 172, 175, 180, 191, 199n, 200-201
  Celestial flesh, 125-127, 141, 152, 154, 176, 196n,
  Conception of Jesus (Mary), 126, 154-155, 176
  Death of Christ, 32, 50-51, 58-60, 67, 74, 95, 116, 118, 127-129, 153, 159, 170-172, 176, 189-192, 193-195, 198-202, 204, 205n, 207- 208, 210-211, 212, 213n, 219-220, 248n, 252-253
  Descent into hell, 23, 50-51, 55, 191, 198-201, 202
  Humanity of Christ (menscheit Christi), 22, 26, 33-46, 48-60, 73, 78-80, 107-127, 130-132, 136-137, 139, 141, 143, 144, 149-155, 164, 165, 167- 175, 178- 181, 187, 191, 207-208, 222, 225-226, 230, 236-238

Humility of Christ, 16, 153, 191, 195, 204-206, 209, 210

Resurrection, 50-51, 58, 67, 116, 118-119, 130, 153, 168-170, 172, 175, 191, 193, 199, 200-201, 204, 206, 220, 237n, 252-253

Two-natures of Christ, 23, 43, 111-112, 113, 115, 126, 130-131, 137, 144, 148-149, 154-155, 164, 166-168, 169n, 171-177, 180, 192, 194-195, 196, 228

Unglorified Christ, 144, 149-153, 171, 179, 220

Christendom, 230-234, 241

Civil government, 21, 23, 66, 89, 90n, 93-94, 97-98, 183

Confessionalization, 82-87, 96, 99

D

Devotio Moderna, 12, 212

Discipleship, 20, 37040, 66-68, 71, 75-76, 78, 80, 89, 130-131, 151-153, 188, 190-191, 203, 204-214, 219-223, 226

Discipline, 33, 37, 96, 113, 150, 184, 185, 247

Divinization, 69, 130, 141, 144, 172, 218n

Dominicans, 209, 211

E

Ecclesiology, church, 38, 43, 149-151, 223n, 241, 243 245-253

Ecumenical relationships, 241-245

Empire, 14, 15, 82, 91, 99, 102, 233

Enlightenment, 21, 232

Eucharist, 18, 21, 27, 41, 43, 89, 169n, 215

Communion, 39, 89, 104, 135, 137, 138, 143, 147, 170

Lord's Supper, 20, 26, 28, 37, 39, 43, 103-105, 107, 109, 114-115, 148, 150, 155, 166, 167, 169-175, 178-180, 184

Real presence, 18, 40, 43, 88, 115, 169-175, 179

F

Franciscans, 12, 211

G

Gelassenheit, 153

Gospel of All Creatures, 30-33, 35, 36, 121

H

Hermeneutics, 18, 79, 205, 231-232, 239

Holy Spirit, (see Spirit)

Humanism, 13, 14, 217

J

Justification, 19, 23, 30, 32, 45n, 68-72, 75, 93, 127, 129-132, 187-188, 192, 196, 202, 212, 214-221, 234, 243

Forensic justification, 64, 68-69, 129, 131, 165, 187, 192, 219

Justification by faith, 19, 20-21, 27, 32-33, 39, 42, 45, 58, 61-64, 70, 73, 97-98, 151n, 165, 187,

189, 196n, 206, 213, 215-216, 218-220

M

Medieval theology, 12, 18-19, 20, 59, 60n, 120, 129, 158, 163, 179, 187-197, 199, 201, 205-220, 230, 233, 234, 235, 242

Mennonite World Conference, 244n

Mission, missiology, 23, 163, 245-253

Mysticism, 21, 30, 45n, 60, 68-69, 217

N

Nonviolence, peacemaking, 23, 92n, 97, 203, 219, 221, 237, 240-248, 252-253

O

Order of God (Ordnung Gottes), 33, 117, 119- 121-125

Orthodoxy, 155, 173, 228n
  Apostles' Creed, 173, 199
  Constantinople, 192-193, 234, 235
  Dogma, 12, 77n, 189, 196, 230-235, 238
  Nicea, 192-193, 234-237

Outer means, 21, 33, 35, 36, 40-41, 42, 50, 58, 65, 78, 79, 132, 146, 170, 178, 180, 183, 231n

P

Patristics (patristic theology), 13, 19
Peasants' War, 15, 22, 89, 91
Potentia Dei absoluta, 120, 121
Potentia Dei ordinata, 120
Priesthood of all believers, 13, 209

R

Reformation, 12-21, 22-23, 27-28, 31, 46, 47-81, 84-85, 87-88, 91n, 92n, 94-96, 98-99, 189-190, 214-215, 219, 241

Renaissance, 13, 14, 18

S

Sacrament(s), 20, 27, 37, 39, 43, 45, 79, 104, 220, 226, 245
  Ceremonies, 37, 43, 44, 60n, 62, 78, 103, 104, 129,
  Ex opere operato, 23, 148, 215
  Inner-outer union, 28-30, 35, 50, 107-109, 111-112, 113, 137, 142, 143-148, 166, 175
  Reality (wesen), 107-109, 110-113, 114, 116-121, 124-125, 130, 132, 137, 140-149, 152, 162-164, 166, 167, 172, 174-175, 179-180, 187

Salvation, 21, 32, 37, 48, 50, 58, 61, 67, 68, 69, 71, 73, 78, 92n, 122, 127-133
  Atonement, 50, 58-59, 159n, 192-197, 198, 205n, 208n, 220, 230

Child of God, 66-67, 94n, 130-132, 135, 155, 164-166, 187, 217n
Christus Victor, 193, 200, 205n, 220
Fromm-Machung, 61-72, 74, 76, 130, 131, 132, 161n, 187
Infused grace, 20, 218, 220
Redemption, 50, 51, 55, 58-59, 60, 63, 67, 74, 79, 127, 171, 188-189, 190, 191, 196, 197-198, 200, 201-204, 206-214, 218, 220
Satisfaction, 60n, 189, 194-195, 198, 205n, 213n
Soteriology, 45, 58-60, 75, 132, 141, 164, 177, 187-188, 191, 218-220
Scripture
Bible, 17-18, 70-71, 79, 85
Relation between Old & New Testaments, 48-50, 51, 55, 66-67, 73-76, 78, 80, 94, 116, 117, 119-120, 125n
Sola scriptura, 18, 215
Zurich (Froschauer) Bible, 63, 70-72, 108
Schola Augustiniana moderna, 212-214, 215-219
Simul Justus et peccator, 45, 69
Spirit, 20, 22, 23, 28-30, 32-33, 34-35, 36, 38, 39-40, 42, 44, 51, 53, 55, 64-67, 75n, 76, 79, 90n, 94, 95n, 107-114, 116, 117-119, 126, 130-132, 137, 140, 145-147, 150, 152-153, 154-155, 158, 162, 164, 166, 167-168, 171-181, 183, 184, 187, 196, 201-204, 216, 220, 222, 226, 235, 237-238, 244n, 246-253
Spiritualists, Spiritualism, 21-22, 26-31, 33-37, 39-41, 44-46, 50, 57, 58, 79, 86, 98, 119, 125, 134, 137, 139, 150, 151, 170, 178-180, 182-185, 204, 225
Stillstand, 182, 184-185

T

Theologia Deutsch, 30, 60, 68, 157-158, 163, 164n, 178
Trinity, 19, 51, 108, 110-111, 113-114, 142, 147n, 174, 175, 180, 192, 196-197, 227-228, 230-231, 235-240, 244, 247- 249

V

Vatican II (Second Vatican Council), 246
Via moderna, 212

W

Waldensians, 12, 211n

Bibliography

Primary Sources (original and translated)

Anselm. "Why God Became Man" in Davies, Brian and Evans, Gillian eds. *Oxford World's Classics: Anselm of Canterbury: The Major Works,* Oxford: Oxford University Press, 1998, 260-356

Aquinas. *Summa Theologica,* vol. 1, New York: Benziger Brothers 1947.

Bergsten T. and Westin G., eds., *Balthasar Hubmaier Schriften,* Gütersloh: Gerd Mohn, 1962.

Fast, Heinold, *Der linke Flügel der Reformation,* Bremen: C. Schünemann Verlag, 1962.

Hartranft, Chester David. (editor), *Corpus Schwencfeldianorum,* vol. 4, Leipzig: Breitkopf & Härtel, 1914.

Hoover, Amos. *Die gantze Bibel...* (1536 Froschauer Bibel), Denver PA and Cayley Alberta: Amos Hoover and die Hutterischen Brüder, 1975.

Klaassen, Walter, Packull, Werner O. & Rempel, John, trans. and eds. *The Exposé, a Dialogue and Marpeck's Response to Caspar Schwenckfeld*, Kitchener: Pandora Press, 1999.

Klaassen, Walter & Klassen, William (translators & editors). *The Writings of Pilgram Marpeck*, Classics of the Radical Reformation 2, Kitchener & Scottdale: Herald Press, 1978. (*WPM*)

Krebs M, and Rott H.G., eds. *Quellen zur Geschichte der Täufer,* VII Band, Elsass I Teil, Stadt Strassburg, Gütersloh: Gerd Mohn, 1959 (*QGT VII*)

Pipkin, H. Wayne and Yoder, John H. trans. and eds. *Balthasar Hubmaier, Theologian of Anabaptism*, Scottdale, Herald Press, 1989.

Luthers Werke, Kritische Gesamtausgabe, Weimar : Böhlaus, 1883ff

Maler, J., *Das Kunstbuch*, 1561, (contains many of Marpeck's letters translated in *WPM*).

Marpeck, Pilgram. *Clare verantwurtung ettlicher Artickel / so jetz durch jrrige geyster schrifftlich vnnd mündtlich aussschweben / von wegen der ceremönien dess newen Testaments / als Predigen Tauffen Abendtmal / Schrifft. Etc. zu trost vnd sterck warhaffter Christen / newlich aussgangen. Auch betreffent Christi befelch / sein jüngern gethan. Und die aussgiessung dess heyligen Geystes. Gegründt in heyliger schrifft.* (Strasbourg: Jacob Cammerlander, 1531). (*WPM* 43-68)

Marpeck, Pilgram. *Ain klarer / vast nützlicher unterricht / wider ettliche Trück / vnd schleichendt Geyster / so jetzt in verborgener weiss aussgeen / dadurch viel frommer hertzen verirrt vnd verfürt werden/ kürtzlich / getrewer warnungweiss herfür gebracht.* (Strasbourg: Jacob Cammerlander, 1531) (*WPM*, 69-106).

Marpeck, Pilgram. *Confession of Faith*. January 1-10, 1532, in Krebs M, and Rott H.G., eds. *Quellen zur Geschichte der Täufer,* VII Band, Elsass I Teil, Stadt Strassburg, Gütersloh: Gerd Mohn, 1959, 416-518. (*WPM*, 107-158).

Marpeck, Pilgram. *Aufdeckung der Babylonischen hürn / und Antichrists alten unnd newen geheymnuss unnd grewel / Auch vom sieg / fried und herschung warhaffter Christen / unnd wie sie der Obergkait gehorsamen das creutz on auffrür und gegenwär / mit Christo in gedult und lieb tragen / zum preiss*

Gottes / und Gotsuchenden zu dienst / sterck und besserung / an tag gebracht. (Strasbourg: Jacob Cammerlander, c. 1532). A copy of the later Augsburg edition is found in Hans Hillerbrand, "An Early Anabaptist Treatise on the Christian and the State," *Mennonite Quarterly Review,* 32, 1958, 29-47.

Marpeck, Pilgram. *Vermanung / auch gantz klarer / gründtlicher vnd unwidersprechlicher bericht / zu warer Christlicher / ewigbestendiger pundtssvereyningung / aller waren glaubigen frummen / und gutthertzigen menschen zu hilff und trost / mit grund heyliger schrift / durch bewerung warer Tauff und Abentmals Christi / sampt mitlauffung und erklärung jrer gegensachen und Argumenten wider alle vermeynte Christliche Pünndnus / so sich bissher und noch / under dem nammen Christi zutragend.* edited by Christian Hege in: *Gedenkschrift zum 400 Jahrigen Jubilaum der Mennoniten oder Taufgesinnten,* Ludwigshafen, 1925, 185-282.

Marpeck, Pilgram, *Verantwurtung über Casparn Schwenckfelds Judicium.* 1542 ff. Published by Johann Loserth, *Quellen und Forschungen zur Geschichte der oberdeutschen Taufgesinnten im 16. Jahrhundert, Pilgram Marbecks Antwort auf Kaspar Schwenckfelds Beurteilung des Buches des Bundesbezeugung von 1542,* Wien & Leipzig, 1929.

Marpeck, Pilgram (anonymous work attributed to him and the Marpeck-circle) *Testamenterleütterung. Erleütterung durch ausszug / aus Heiliger Biblischer schrifft, tail und / gegentail sampt ains tails angehangen beireden / zu dienst und fürderung ains klaren urtails / von wegen underschaid Alts und News Testaments / und irer beder sündtvergebung / Opfer / Erlösung / Gerechtigkeit / Gnad / Glauben / Gaist / Folck und anderem / so grundtlich / lauter und nutzlich zue ersehen / genant Testamentserleüterung.* Published sometime in the 1540's.

Stupperich, Robert. *Martin Bucers Deutsche Schriften,* Band 3, Gütersloh-Paris: Gerd Mohn-Presses Universitaires de France, 1969.

Secondary Sources

Armour, Rollin Stely. *Anabaptist Baptism: A Representative Study*, Scottdale: Herald Press, 1966.

Atkinson, J. "Luthers Einschätzung des Johannesevangeliums," in V. Vajta, ed., *Lutherforschung Heute*, Berlin: Lutherisches Verlagshaus, 1958, 49-56.

Aulén, Gustaf. *Christus Victor: A Historical Study of the Three Main Types of the Idea of the Atonement*, New York, 1961.

Baecher, Claude. *Les eschatologies anabaptistes de la haute vallée rhénane en débat avec les réformateurs (1524-1535)*, Villeneuve d'Ascq: Presses Universitaires du Septentrion, 1996.

Baecher, Claude. "Le jugement eschatologique des puissants chez les anabaptistes de la mouvance 'Frères Suisses' au XVIe et XVIIe siècles," in Blough N. (ed). *Eschatologie et vie quotidienne*, Cléon d'Andran: Editions Excelsis, 2001, 38-65.

Band, H. *Luthers Lehre von verborgenen Gott*, Berlin, 1957.

Beachy, Alvin. *Grace in the Radical Reformation*, Nieuwkoop: B. de Graaf, 1977.

Bender, Harold S. "Pilgram Marpeck, Anabaptist Theologian and Civil Engineer," *Mennonite Quarterly Review*, July 1964, 231-265.

Bergsten, Torsten. "Pilgram Marbeck und seine Auseinandersetzung mit Caspar Schwenckfeld," *Kyrkohistorik Arsskrift*, 1957-1958, 39-135.

Blough, Neal. *Christologie anabaptiste: Pilgram Marpeck et l'humanité du Christ*, Geneva, Labor et Fides, 1984

Blough, Neal. "Pilgram Marpeck and Caspar Schwenckfeld: the Strasbourg Years," in: J. Rott and S. Verheus (editors), *Anabaptistes et dissidents au XVI° siècle*, (Bibliotheca Dissidentium, scripta et studia n° 3), Baden-Baden, Koerner, 1987, 371-380

Blough, Neal. "Pilgram Marpeck, Martin Luther and the Humanity of Christ," *Mennonite Quarterly Review*, April 1987, 203-212.

Blough, Neal. "Pilgram Marpeck et les frères suisses vers 1540," in ...*Lebenn Nach der Ler Jhesu... Das sind aber wir!: Berner Täufer und Prädikanten im Gespräch,* Bern: Schweizerischen Verein für Täufergeschichte, 1989, 147-164.

Blough, Neal. "Le Christ glorifié et le Christ humilié: le débat christologique entre Pilgram Marpeck et Caspar Schwenckfeld," in Blough N. (ed.), *Jésus-Christ aux marges de la Réforme*, Paris: Desclée, 1992, 141-162.

Blough, Neal. "Messianic Mission and Ethics: Discipleship and the Good News," in Wilbert R. Shenk, *The Transfiguration of Mission: Biblical, Theological and Historical Foundations,* Scottdale: Herald Press, 1993, 178-198.

Blough, Neal. "*The Uncovering of the Babylonian Whore*: Confessionalization and Politics Seen from the Underside," *Mennonite Quarterly Review*, January 2001, 37-56.

Blough, Neal. "Eschatologie, christologie et éthique: la fin justifie les moyens," in *Eschatologie et vie quotidienne*, Cléon d'Andran: Excelsis, 2001, 13-37.

Blough, Neal. "The Church as Sign or Sacrament? Trinitarian Ecclesiology, Pilgram Marpeck, Vatican II and John Milbank," *Mennonite Quarterly Review*, January 2004, 29-52.

Boyd, Stephen. "Marpeck, Pilgram," in *The Mennonite Encyclopedia*, vol. V, Scottdale: Herald Press, 1990, 538-539

Boyd, Stephen. *Pilgram Marpeck. His Life and Social Theology*, Durham, NC: Duke University Press, 1992.

Congar, Yves. *Un peuple messianique: l'Eglise, sacrement du salut. Salut et libération*, Paris: Editions du Cerf, 1975.

Coninck, Frédéric de. *Agir, travailler, militer. Une théologie de l'action*, Cléon d'Andran: Excelsis, 2006.

Davis, Kenneth. *Anabaptism and Asceticism*, Scottdale: Herald Press, 1974.

Delumeau, Jean. *Le péche et la peur. La culpabilisation en Occident XIIIe--XVIIIe siècles*, Paris: Fayard, 1983.

Deppermann, Klaus. *Melchior Hoffman*, Göttigen: Vandenhoeck & Ruprecht, 1979. (*Melchior Hoffman. Social Unrest and Apocalyptic Vision in the Age of Reformation*, Edinburgh: T&T Clark, 1987).

Derksen, John D. *From Radicals to Survivors : Strasbourg's religious nonconformists over two generations, 1525-1570.* 't Goy-Houton : HES & DE GRAAF Publishers, 2002.

Dipple, Geoffrey. "Sebastian Franck in Strasbourg," *Mennonite Quarterly Review*, October 1999, 783-802.

Driver, John. *Understanding the Atonement for the Mission of the Church*, Scottdale: Herald Press, 1986.

Fast, Heinold. "Pilgram Marbeck und das oberdeutsche Täufertum: Ein neuer Handschriftenfund," *Archiv für Reformationsgeschichte*, 47, 1956, 212-242.

Fast, Heinold. *Heinrich Bullinger und die Täufer.* Weierhof: Mennonitischen Geschichtsverein, 1959.

Fast, Heinold, "'Nicht was sonder das' Marpeckhs Motto wider den Spiritualismus," in: *Evangelischer Glaube und Geschichte. Grete Mecenseffy zum 85. Gerurtstag,* Ed. A. Raddatz and K. Lüthi, Wien 1984, 66-74.

Enns, Fernardo, Holland, Scott and Riggs, Ann. *Seeking Cultures of Peace: A Peace Church Conversation,* Telford PA & Geneva: Cascadia Publishing House and World Council of Churches Publications, 2004

Enns, Fernando. "Space for Theological Reflection on Being (Peace-) Church," in Enns, Holland & Riggs, *Seeking Cultures of Peace*, 2004, 29-41.

Enns, Fernando. "The Peace Church: Dialogue and Diversity in the Ecumenical Movement," *The Conrad Grebel Review*, Fall 2005, 4-18.

Enns, Fernando, "Vaincre la violence: un défi pour l'Eglise et pour la théologie," in Arnold, Matthieu & Prieur, Jean-Marc. *Dieu est-il violent ? La violence dans les représentations de Dieu*, Strasbourg: Presses Universitaires de Strasbourg, 2005, 89-102.

Finger, Thomas N. "Pilgram Marpeck and the Christus Victor Motif," *Mennonite Quarterly Review*, January 2004, 53-78.

Finger, Thomas N. *A Contemporary Anabaptist Theology*, Downers Grove: InterVarsity Press, 2004.

Friedmann, Robert. *The Theology of Anabaptism*, Scottdale: Herald Press, 1973.

Furcha, E.J. *Schwenckfeld's Concept of the New Man*, Pennsburg: Board of Publications of the Schwenckfelder Church, 1970.

Goertz, Hans-Jürgen. *Die Täufer. Geschichte und Deutung*, Munich: C.H. Beck, 1980.

Goertz, Hans-Jürgen. *Innere und äußere Ordnung in der Theologie Thomas Muntzers*. Leiden: Brill, 1967.

Gonzalez, Antonio. *The Gospel of Faith and Justice*, Maryknoll, NY: Orbis Books, 2005.

Gregory, Brad S. *Salvation at Stake: Christian Martyrdom in Early Modern Europe*, Harvard University Press, 1999.

Greschat, Martin. *Martin Bucer, A Reformer and his Times*, trans, by Stephen E. Buckwalter, Louisville: Westminster John Knox Press, 2004.

Grimm, Harold J. *The Reformation Era*, London: MacMillan, 1965.

Harrison, R.L. "Schwenckfeld and the Tübingen Colloquy," *Mennonite Quarterly Review*, July 1978, 237-247.

Hauerwas, Stanley. *A Community of Character*, University of Notre Dame Press, 1981.

Hauerwas, Stanley. *The Peaceable Kingdom*, University of Notre Dame Press, 1983.

Hauerwas, Stanley. *A Better Hope: Resources for a Church Confronting Capitalism, Democracy and Postmodernity*, Grand Rapids: Brazos Press, 2000.

Hauerwas, Stanley. *With the Grain of the Universe: The Church's Witness and Natural Theology*, Grand Rapids: Brazos Press, 2001

Hege, Christian. "Pilgram Marbeck und die oberdeutschen Taufgesinnten," *Archiv für Reformationsgeschichte*, 37, 1940, 249-257.

Hillerbrand, Hans. "An Early Anabaptist Treatise on the Christian and the State," *Mennonite Quarterly Review*, January 1958, 28-48.

Huebner, Chris K. "What Should Mennonites and Milbank Learn from Each Other?" *The Conrad Grebel Review*, Spring, 2005.

Husser, Daniel. "Caspar Schwenckfeld et ses adeptes entre l'Eglise et les sectes à Strasbourg," in: G. Livet and F. Rapp (eds), *Strasbourg au coeur religieux du XVIe siècle*, Strasbourg: Istra, 1977, 511-535.

Jecker, Hanspeter. *Ketzer-Rebellen-Heilige. Das Basler Täufertum von 1580-1700*, Verlag des Kantons Basel Landschaft, 1998.

Kiwiet, Jan. *Pilgram Marbeck. Ein Führer der Täuferbewegung im süddeutschen Raum*. Kassel: Oncken, 1957.

Klaassen, Walter. "Some Anabaptist Views on the Doctrine of the Holy Spirit," *Mennonite Quarterly Review*, April 1961, 130-139.

Klaassen, Walter. "Church Discipline and the Spirit in Pilgram Marpeck," in Horst, Irvin *et al.*, *De Geest in het Geding*, Willink: H.D. Tjeenk, 1978, 169-180.

Klaassen, Walter. *Living at the End of the Ages: Apocalyptic Expectation in the Radical Reformation* Lanham, MD: University Press of America, 1992.

Klaassen, Walter. "Investigation into the Authorship and the Historical Background of the Anabaptist Tract *Aufdeckung der babylonischen Hurn*, *Mennonite Quarterly Reveiw*, July 1987, 251-261.

Klassen, William. "Pilgram Marpeck in Recent Research," *Mennonite Quarterly Review*, July 1958, 211-229.

Klassen, William. "Pilgram Marpeck's Two Books of 1531," *Mennonite Quarterly Review*, January 1959, 18-30.

Klassen, William. "The Relation of the Old and New Covenants in Pilgram Marpeck's Theology," *Mennonite Quarterly Review*, April 1966, 97-111.

Klassen, William. *Covenant and Community. The Life, Writings and Hermeneutics of Pilgram Marpeck*. Grand Rapids: Eerdmans, 1968.

Klassen, William. "Pilgram Marpeck. Liberty without Coercion," in *Profiles of Radical Reformers*. H.J. Goertz (ed). Scottdale: Herald Press, 1982, 168-177.

Klassen, William, "The Limits of Political Authority as Seen by Pilgram Marpeck," *Mennonite Quarterly Review*, October 1982, 342-364.

Klassen, William. "The Legacy of the Marpeck Community in Anabaptist Scholarship," *Mennonite Quarterly Review*, January 2004, 7-28.

Krahn, Cornelius. "Incarnation of Christ," *The Mennonite Encyclopedia*, vol. III, 18-20.

Lienhard, Marc. "La doctrine du Saint-Esprit chez Luther," *Verbum Caro*, I, XXVI, (1965), 11-38.

Lienhard, Marc. *Luther témoin de Jésus-Christ*, Paris: Le Cerf, 1973.

Loserth, Johann "Studien zur Pilgram Marbeck," in *Gedenkschrift zum 400-jährigen Jubiläum der Mennoniten oder Taufgesinnten*, Ludwigshafen, 1925, 134-177.

Loserth, Johann. "Recent Research in the History of the Tyrol-Moravian Anabaptists," *Mennonite Quarterly Review*, January 1928, 5-15.

Loserth, Johann. "Pilgram Marpeck," *The Mennonite Encyclopedia*, vol. III, 491-500.

MacCulloch, Diramaid. *The Reformation. A History*, New York: Viking, 2003.

Maier, Paul. *Caspar Schwenckfeld on the Person and Work of Christ*, Assen: Royal Van Gorcum, 1959.

McGrath, Alister E. *Reformation Thought, An Introduction*, 3rd ed., Blackwell Publishers, 1999.

McGrath, Alister E. *Iustitia Dei. A History of the Christian Doctrine of Justification,* 3rd ed., Cambridge University Press, 2005.

Milbank, John. *Theology and Social Theory. Beyond Secular Reason*, Oxford: Blackwell Publishers, 1993.

Moeller, Berndt. *Villes d'empires et Réformation*, Geneva: Librairie Droz, 1966.

Moeller, Berndt. "Piety in Germany around 1500" in S.E. Ozment (ed); *The Reformation in Medieval Perspective*, Chicago: Quadrangle Books, 1971, 50-75.

Nation, Mark Thiessen. *John Howard Yoder. Mennonite Patience, Evangelical Witness, Catholic Convictions*, Grand Rapids: Eerdman's, 2006.

Nilsson, K.O. *Simul: Das Miteinander von Göttlichem und Menschlichem in Luthers Theologie*, Göttingen: Vandenhoeck & Ruprecht, 1966.

Oberman, Heiko A. *The Reformation, Roots & Ramifications*, Grand Rapids: Eerdmans, 1994.

Oyer, Linda. *Interpreting the New in Light of the Old: A Comparative Study of the Post-Resurrection Commissioning Stories in Matthew and John*, doctoral dissertation presented at the Institut Catholique de Paris, Faculté de Théologie et de Sciences Religieuses, June 1997.

Oyer, Linda. "Le pardon: une anticipation eschatologique," in *Eschatologie et vie quotidienne*, Cléon d'Andran : Excelsis, 2001, 83-94.

Ozment, Steven. *Homo spiritualis. A comparative Study of the Anthropology of Johannes Tauler, Jean Gerson and Martin Luther (1509-16) in the context of their Theological Thought*, Leiden: Brill, 1969.

Ozment, Steven. *Mysticism and Dissent*, New Haven & London: Yale University Press, 1973.

Ozment, Steven. *The Age of Reform, 1250-1550*, New Haven and London: Yale University Press, 1980.

Packull, Werner O., *Mysticism and the Early South German-Austrian Anabaptist Movement 1525-1531*, Scottdale: Herald Press, 1977.

Packull, Werner O. "Pilgram Marpeck: *Uncovering of the Babylonian Whore* and Other Anonymous Anabaptist Tracts," *Mennonite Quarterly Review*, July 1993, 351-55.

Packull, Werner O. *Hutterite Beginnings: Communitarian Experiments During the Reformation*, John Hopkins University Press, 1995.

Pelikan, Jaroslav. *The Christian Tradition: A History of the Development of Doctrine, Volume 3: The Growth of Medieval Theology (600-1300) (The Christian Tradition: A History of the Development of Christian Doctrine)*, Chicago: The University of Chicago Press, 1984.

Pelikan, Jaroslav. *The Christian Tradition, A History of the Development of Doctrine*, Volume 4: *Reformation of Church and Dogma (1300-1700)*. Chicago: The University of Chicago Press, 1984.

Prenter, Regin. *Spiritus Creator*, Munich, 1954.

Quiring, Horst. "The Anthropology of Pilgram Marbeck," *Mennonite Quarterly Review*, October 1935, 155-164.

Reimer, A. James. *Mennonites and Classical Theology: Dogmatic Foundations for Christian Ethics*, Kitchener: Pandora Press, 2001.

Rempel, John. *The Lord's Supper in Anabaptism*, Scottdale: Herald Press, 1993.

Rothkegel, Martin. "Benes Optat, 'On Baptism and the Lord's Supper': An Utraquist Reformer's Opinion of Pilgram Marpeck's *Vermahnung*," *MQR*, July 2005, 359-381.

Schoeps, H.J. *Vom Himmlischen Fleisch Christi*, Mohr, 1951.

Schultz, Selina. *Caspar von Schwenckfeld von Ossig (1489-1561)*, Pennsburg: Board of Publications of the Schwenckfelder Church, 1977

Sciegienny (Séguenny), André. *Homme Charnel, Homme Spirituel.* Etude sur la Christologie de Caspar Schwenckfeld (1489-1561). Wiesbaden: Franz Steiner Verlag, 1975.

Sesboüé, Bernard. *Jésus-Christ dans la tradition de l'Eglise*, Paris: Desclée, 1982.

Séguy, Jean. *Les assemblées anabaptistes de France*, Paris-La Haye: Mouton, 1977.

Shenk, Wilbert R. *The Transfiguration of Mission: Biblical, Theological and Historical Foundations*, Scottdale: Herald Press, 1993.

Snyder, C. Arnold. *Anabaptist History and Theology: An Introduction*, Kitchener: Pandora Press, 1995.

Snyder, C. Arnold & Hecht, Linda A. Huebert, eds. *Profiles of Anabaptist Women. Sixteenth-Century Reforming Pioneers*, Waterloo: Wilfred Laurier University Press, 1996.

Snyder, C. Arnold. "The (Not-So) 'Simple Confession' of the Later Swiss Brethren. Part I: Manuscripts and Marpeckites in an Age of Print," *Mennonite Quarterly Review*, October 1999, 677-722.

Snyder, C. Arnold. "The (Not-So) 'Simple Confession' of the Later Swiss Brethren. Part II: The Evolution of Separatist Anabaptism" *Mennonite Quarterly Review*, January 2000, 87-122.

Snyder, C. Arnold. *Following in the Footsteps of Christ. The Anabaptist Tradition*, Mary Knoll NY: Orbis Books, 2004.

Sobrino, Jon. *Christology at the Crossroads. A Latin American Approach* London: SCM Press, 1978.

Stayer, James M. *Anabaptists and the Sword*, Second Edition, Lawrence Kansas: Coronado Press, 1976.

Stayer, James M. *The German Peasants' War and Anabaptist Community of Goods*, Montreal: McGill-Queen's U. Press, 1991.

Trouvé, Marianne Lorraine, FSP (general editor). *The Sixteen Documents of Vatican II*, Boston: Pauline Books & Media, 1999.

Volf, Miroslav. *After Our Likeness, The Church as the Image of the Trinity*, Grand Rapids: Eerdmans, 1998.

Weaver, J. Denny. *The Nonviolent Atonement*, Grand Rapids: Eerdmans, 2001.

Weaver, J. Denny, *Becoming Anabaptist, The Origin and Significance of Sixteenth-Century Anabaptism*, Second Edition, Scottdale: Herald Press, 2005.

Weaver, J. Denny, "Parsing Anabaptist Theology: A Review Essay of Thomas N. Finger's *A Contemporary Anabaptist Theology*," *Direction*, Volume 32, N° 2, Fall 2005, 241-263.

Wenger, John C. "The Life and Work of Pilgram Marpeck," *Mennonite Quarterly Review*, July 1938, 137-166.

Wenger, John C. "Additional Note on the Life and Work of Pilgram Marpeck," *Mennonite Quarterly Review*, October 1938, 269-270.

Wenger, John C. "The Theology of Pilgram Marpeck," *Mennonite Quarterly Review*, October 1938, 205-256.

Wenger, John C. "Pilgram Marpeck, Tirolese Engineer and Anabaptist Elder," *Church History* 9, 1940, 24-36.

Williams, George H. *The Radical Reformation*, 1st edition, Philadelphia: Westminster Press, 1962; 3rd edition, Kirksville Missouri: Sixteenth Century Journal Publishers, 1992.

Williams, George. "Popularized German Mysticism as a Factor in the Rise of Anabaptist Communism," in: W. Muller & W. Zeller, *Glaube, Geist und Geschichte: Festschrift für Ernst Benz*, Leiden, 1967, 290-312.

Williams, George. "Sanctification in the Testimony of Several So-Called Schwärmer," *Mennonite Quarterly Review*, January 1968, 5-25.

Wiswedel, W. "Pilgram Marbeck und seine Bedeutung für das Schrifttum der Täufer," in *Bilder und Führergestalten der Täufer*. Band 3. Kassel: Oncken, 1952, 69-80.

Wray, Frank. "The *Vermanung* of 1542 and Rothmann's *Bekentnisse*," *Archiv für Reformationsgeschichte* 47, 1956, 243-251.

Yoder, John Howard. *Nevertheless. The Varieties of Religious Pacifism*, Scottdale: Herald Press, 1971.

Yoder, John Howard. *The Priestly Kingdom. Social Ethics as Gospel*, The University of Notre Dame Press, 1984, 46-62.

Yoder, John Howard. *The Politics of Jesus*, Second Edition, Grand Rapids: Eerdmans, 1994.

Yoder, John Howard. *To Hear the Word*, Eugene OR: Wipf and Stock Publishers, 2001.

Yoder, John Howard. *Preface to Theology, Christology and Theological Method*, Grand Rapids: Brazos Press, 2002.

Yoder, John Howard. *Anabaptism and Reformation in Switzerland*, Kitchener: Pandora Press, 2004.

Ziegler, D.J. "Marpeck versus Butzer: A Sixteenth Century Debate over the Uses and Limits of Political Authority," in Smith, C.S., *Sixteenth Century Essays and Studies*, Volume II, Saint Louis: The Foundation for Reformation Research, 1971, 95-107.

About Pandora Press

Pandora Press is a small, independently owned press dedicated to making available modestly priced books that deal with Anabaptist, Mennonite, and Believers Church topics, both historical and theological. We welcome comments from our readers.

Visit our full-service online Bookstore:
www.pandorapress.com

Peter C. Erb , ed., *Martyrdom in an Ecumenical Perspective: A Mennonite-Catholic Conversation* (Kitchener: Pandora Press, 2007). Softcover, 200 pages. ISBN978-1-894710-81-7 ISSN 1711-9480

Neal Blough, *Christ in our Midst: Incarnation, Church and Discipleship in the theology of Pilgram Marpeck* (Kitchener: Pandora Press, 2007). Softcover, 275 pages. ISBN 978-1-894710-77-0

James Urry, *None but Saints* (Kitchener: Pandora Press, 2007). Softcover, 370 pages. ISBN 1-894710-71-8

Werner O. Packull, *Peter Riedemann: Shaper of the Hutterite Tradition* (Kitchener: Pandora Press, 2007). Softcover, 252 pages. ISBN 978-894710-76-3

H.G. Mannhardt, *The Danzig Mennonite Church: Its Origins and History from 1569-1919*, translated by Victor G. Doerksen (Kitchener: Pandora Press, 2007). Softcover, 286 pages. ISBN 978-1-889239-04-0

R. Martens, M. Jantzen and H. Neufeldt, *Windows to a Village: Life Studies of Yarrow Pineers* (Kitchener, Pandora Press, 2007). Softcover, 444 pages. ISBN 978-1894710-79-4

Gerke van Hiele with Marion Bruggen, Ina ter Kuile and Frans Misset, *Encountering the Eternal One: A Guide for Mennonite Churches* (Kitchener: Pandora Press, 2006) Softcover, 120 pages. ISBN 1-894710-75-4

Richard MacMaster, *Mennonite and Brethren in Christ Churches of New York City* (Kitchener: Pandora Press, 2006) Softcover, 366 pages. ISBN 1-894710-70-3

Peter Riedemann, *Love is like Fire: The Confession of an Anabaptist Prisoner* (Kitchener: Pandora Press, 2006) Softcover, 84 pages. ISBN 1-894710-72-X

Andreas Ehrenpreis and Claus Felbinger, *Brotherly Community: The Highest Command of Love* (Kitchener: Pandora Press, 2006) Softcover, 146 pages. ISBN 1-894710-74-6

Jakob Hutter, *Brotherly Faithfulness: Epistles from a Time of Persecution* (Kitchener: Pandora Press, 2006) Softcover, 250 pages. ISBN 1-894710-73-8

Robert John Russell, *Cosmology, Evolution, and Resurrection Hope* (Kitchener: Pandora Press, 2006) Softcover, 118 pages. ISBN 1-894710-67-3

Nathan E. Yoder and Carol A. Scheppard, eds., *Exiles in the Empire: Believers Church Perspectives on Politics* (Kitchener: Pandora Press, 2006) Softcover, 266 pages. Scriptural and topical indexes. ISBN 1-894710-68-1

Helmut Isaak, *Menno Simons and the New Jerusalem* (Kitchener: Pandora Press, 2006) Softcover, 158 pages. Bibliography. ISBN 1-894710-69-X

Leah Dawn Bueckert and Daniel Schipani, eds. *Spiritual Caregiving in the Hospital. Windows to Chaplaincy Ministry* (Kitchener: Pandora Press, 2006) Softcover, 230 pages. ISBN 1-894710-65-7

Lawrence M. Yoder, *The Muria Story. A History of the Chinese Mennonite Churches in Indonesia* (Kitchener: Pandora Press, 2006). Softcover, 386 pages. ISBN 1-894710-60-6

Ralph Lebold, *Strange and Wonderful Paths. The Memoirs of Ralph Lebold.* (Kitchener: Pandora Press, 2006). Softcover, 236 pages. Bibliography, index. ISBN 1-894710-66-5

Karl Koop, ed. *Confessions of Faith in the Anabaptist Tradition, 1527-1660* (Kitchener: Pandora Press, 2006). Softcover, 366 pages. Scripture index. ISBN 1-894710-62-2

Alle Hoekema and Hanspeter Jecker, eds. *Testing Faith and Tradition. A Global Mennonite History: Europe* (Kitchener: Pandora Press, 2006; co-published with Good Books). Softcover, 324 pages. Indexes. ISBN 1-56148-550-0

John A. Lapp and C. Arnold Snyder, gen.eds., *Anabaptist Songs in African Hearts. A Global Mennonite History: Africa* (Kitchener: Pandora Press, 2006; co-published with Good Books) Softcover, 292 pages. Indexes. ISBN 1-56148-549-7

Harry Loewen, *Between Worlds. Reflections of a Soviet-born Canadian Mennonite* (Kitchener: Pandora Press, 2006). Softcover, 358 pages. Bibliography. ISBN 1-894710-63-0

H. H. Drake Williams III, ed., *Caspar Schwenckfeld. Eight Writings on Christian Beliefs* (Kitchener: Pandora Press, 2006). Softcover, 200 pages. Index. ISBN 1-894710-64-9

Maureen Epp and Carol Ann Weaver, eds., *Sound in the Land: Essays on Mennonites and Music* (Kitchener: Pandora Press, 2006). Softcover, 220 pages. Bibliography. ISBN 1-894710-59-2

Geoffrey Dipple, *"Just as in the Time of the Apostles": Uses of History in the Radical Reformation* (Kitchener: Pandora Press, 2005). Softcover, 324 pages. Bibliography and index. ISBN 1-894710-58-4.

Harry Huebner, *Echoes of the Word: Theological Ethics as Rhetorical Practice* Anabaptist and Mennonite Studies Series (Kitchener: Pandora Press, 2005). Softcover, 274 pages. Bibliography and index. ISBN 1-894710-56-8 ISSN 1494-4081

John F. Haught, *Purpose, Evolution and the Mystery of Life,* Proceedings of the Fourth Annual Goshen Conference on Religion and Science, ed. Carl S. Helrich (Kitchener" Pandora Press, 2005). Softcover, 130 pages. Index. ISBN 1-894710-55-X

Gerald W. Schlabach, gen. ed., *Called Together to be Peacemakers: Report of the International Dialogue between the Catholic Church and Mennonite World Conference 1998-2003* (Kitchener: Pandora Press, 2005). Softcover, 77 pages. ISBN 1-894710-57-6 ISSN 1711-9480

Rodney James Sawatsky, *History and Ideology: American Mennonite Identity Definition through History* (Kitchener: Pandora Press, 2005). Softcover, 216 pages. Bibliography and index. ISBN 1-894710-53-3 ISSN 1494-4081

Harvey Neufeldt, Ruth Derksen Siemens and Robert Martens, eds., *First Nations and First Settlers in the Fraser Valley (1890-1960)* (Kitchener: Pandora Press, 2005). Softcover, 287 pages. Bibliography and index. ISBN 1-894710-54-1

David Waltner-Toews, *The Complete Tante Tina: Mennonite Blues and Recipes* (Kitchener: Pandora Press, 2004) Softcover, 129 pages. ISBN 1-894710-52-5

John Howard Yoder, *Anabaptism and Reformation in Switzerland: An Historical and Theological Analysis of the Dialogues Between Anabaptists and Reformers* (Kitchener: Pandora Press, 2004) Softcover, 509 pages. Bibliography and indexes. ISBN 1-894710-44-4 ISSN 1494-4081

Antje Jackelén, *The Dialogue Between Religion and Science: Challenges and Future Directions* (Kitchener: Pandora Press, 2004) Softcover, 143 pages. Index. ISBN 1-894710-45-2

Ivan J. Kauffman, ed., *Just Policing: Mennonite-Catholic Theological Colloquium 2001-2002* (Kitchener: Pandora Press, 2004). Softcover, 127 pages. ISBN 1-894710-48-7.

Gerald W. Schlabach, ed., *On Baptism: Mennonite-Catholic Theological Colloquium 2001-2002* (Kitchener: Pandora Press, 2004). Softcover, 147 pages. ISBN 1-894710-47-9 ISSN 1711-9480.

Harvey L. Dyck, John R. Staples and John B. Toews, comp., trans. and ed. *Nestor Makhno and the Eichenfeld Massacre:* (Kitchener: Pandora Press, 2004). Softcover, 115 pages. ISBN 1-894710-46-0.

Jean Janzen, *Elements of Faithful Writing* (Kitchener, Pandora Press, 2004). Softcover, 49 pages. ISBN 1-889239-03-8

Jeffrey Wayne Taylor, *The Formation of the Primitive Baptist Movement* (Kitchener: Pandora Press, 2004). Softcover, 225 pages. Bibliography and index. ISBN 1-894710-42-8 ISSN 1480-7432.

James C. Juhnke and Carol M. Hunter, *The Missing Peace: The Search for Nonviolent Alternatives in United States History*, 2nd ed. (Kitchener: Pandora Press, 2004) Softcover, 339 pp. Index. ISBN 1-894710-46-3

Louise Hawkley and James C. Juhnke, eds., *Nonviolent America: History through the Eyes of Peace* (North Newton: Bethel College, 2004, co-published with Pandora Press) Softcover, 269 pages. Index. ISBN 1-889239-02-X

Karl Koop, *Anabaptist-Mennonite Confessions of Faith: the Development of a Tradition* (Kitchener: Pandora Press, 2004) Softcover, 178 pages. Index. ISBN 1-894710-32-0

Lucille Marr, *The Transforming Power of a Century: Mennonite Central Committee and its Evolution in Ontario* (Kitchener: Pandora Press, 2003). Softcover, 390 pages. Bibliography and index, ISBN 1-894710-41-x

Erica Janzen, *Six Sugar Beets, Five Bitter Years* (Kitchener: Pandora Press, 2003). Softcover, 186 pages. ISBN 1-894710-37-1

T. D. Regehr, *Faith Life and Witness in the Northwest, 1903–2003: Centenninal History of the Northwest Mennonite Conference* (Kitchener: Pandora Press, 2003). Softcover, 524 pages. Index, ISBN 1-894710-39-8

George F. R. Ellis, *A Universe of Ethics Morality and Hope: Proceedings from the Second Annual Goshen Conference on Religion and Science* (Kitchener: Pandora Press, 2003) Softcover, 148 pages. ISBN 1-894710-36-3

Donald Martin, *Old Order Mennonites of Ontario: Gelassenheit, Discipleship, Brotherhood* (Kitchener: Pandora Press, 2003). Softcover, 381 pages. Index. ISBN 1-894710-33-9

Mary A. Schiedel, *Pioneers in Ministry: Women Pastors in Ontario Mennonite Churches, 1973-2003* (Kitchener: Pandora Press, 2003) Softcover, 204 pages. ISBN 1-894710-35-5

Harry Loewen, ed., *Shepherds, Servants and Prophets* (Kitchener: Pandora Press, 2003) Softcover, 446 pages. ISBN 1-894710-35-5

Robert A. Riall, trans., Galen A. Peters, ed., *The Earliest Hymns of the Ausbund: Some Beautiful Christian Songs Composed and Sung in the Prison at Passau, Published 1564* (Kitchener: Pandora Press, 2003) Softcover, 468 pages. Bibliography and index. ISBN 1-894710-34-7

John A. Harder, *From Kleefeld With Love* (Kitchener: Pandora Press, 2003) Softcover, 198 pages. ISBN 1-894710-28-2

John F. Peters, *The Plain People: A Glimpse at Life Among the Old Order Mennonites of Ontario* (Kitchener: Pandora Press, 2003) Softcover, 54 pages. ISBN 1-894710-26-6

Robert S. Kreider, *My Early Years: An Autobiography* (Kitchener: Pandora Press, 2002) Softcover, 600 pages. Index ISBN 1-894710-23-1

Helen Martens, *Hutterite Songs* (Kitchener: Pandora Press, 2002) Softcover, xxii, 328 pages. ISBN 1-894710-24-X

C. Arnold Snyder and Galen A. Peters, eds., *Reading the Anabaptist Bible: Reflections for Every Day of the Year* (Kitchener: Pandora Press, 2002) Softcover, 415 pages. ISBN 1-894710-25-8

C. Arnold Snyder, ed., *Commoners and Community: Essays in Honour of Werner O. Packull* (Kitchener: Pandora Press, 2002) Softcover, 324 pages. ISBN 1-894710-27-4

James O. Lehman, *Mennonite Tent Revivals: Howard Hammer and Myron Augsburger, 1952-1962* (Kitchener: Pandora Press, 2002) Softcover, xxiv, 318 pages. ISBN 1-894710-22-3

Lawrence Klippenstein and Jacob Dick, *Mennonite Alternative Service in Russia* (Kitchener: Pandora Press, 2002) Softcover, viii, 163 pages. ISBN 1-894710-21-5

Nancey Murphy, *Religion and Science* (Kitchener: Pandora Press, 2002) Softcover, 126 pages. ISBN 1-894710-20-7

Biblical Concordance of the Swiss Brethren, 1540. Trans. Gilbert Fast and Galen Peters; bib. intro. Joe Springer; ed. C. Arnold Snyder (Kitchener: Pandora Press, 2001) Softcover, lv, 227 pages. ISBN 1-894710-16-9

Orland Gingerich, *The Amish of Canada* (Kitchener: Pandora Press, 2001) Softcover, 244 pages. Index. ISBN 1-894710-19-3

M. Darrol Bryant, *Religion in a New Key* (Kitchener: Pandora Press, 2001) Softcover, 136 pages. Bib. refs. ISBN 1-894710- 18-5

Trans. Walter Klaassen, Frank Friesen, Werner O. Packull, ed. C. Arnold Snyder, *Sources of South German/Austrian Anabaptism* (Kitchener: Pandora Press, 2001; co-published with Herald Press.) Softcover, 430 pages. Indexes. ISBN 1-894710-15-0

Pedro A. Sandín Fremaint y Pablo A. Jimémez, *Palabras Duras: Homilías* (Kitchener: Pandora Press, 2001). Softcover, 121 pages. ISBN 1-894710-17-7

Ruth Elizabeth Mooney, *Manual Para Crear Materiales de Educación Cristiana* (Kitchener: Pandora Press, 2001). Softcover, 206 pages. ISBN 1-894710-12-6

Esther and Malcolm Wenger, poetry by Ann Wenger, *Healing the Wounds* (Kitchener: Pandora Press, 2001). Softcover, 210 pages. ISBN 1-894710-09-6.

Otto H. Selles and Geraldine Selles-Ysselstein, *New Songs* (Kitchener: Pandora Press, 2001). Poetry and relief prints, 90 pages. ISBN 1-894719-14-2

Pedro A. Sandín Fremaint, *Cuentos y Encuentros: Hacia una Educación Transformadora* (Kitchener: Pandora Press, 2001). Softcover 163 pages. ISBN 1-894710-08-8.

A. James Reimer, *Mennonites and Classical Theology: Dogmatic Foundations for Christian Ethics* (Kitchener: Pandora Press, 2001) Softcover, 650 pages. ISBN 0-9685543-7-7

Walter Klaassen, *Anabaptism: Neither Catholic nor Protestant*, 3rd ed (Kitchener: Pandora Press, 2001) Softcover, 122 pages. ISBN 1-894710-01-0

Dale Schrag & James Juhnke, eds., *Anabaptist Visions for the new Millennium: A search for identity* (Kitchener: Pandora Press, 2000) Softcover, 242 pages. ISBN 1-894710-00-2

Harry Loewen, ed., *Road to Freedom: Mennonites Escape the Land of Suffering* (Kitchener: Pandora Press, 2000) Hardcover, large format, 302pages. ISBN 0-9685543-5-0

Alan Kreider and Stuart Murray, eds., *Coming Home: Stories of Anabaptists in Britain and Ireland* (Kitchener: Pandora Press, 2000) Softcover, 220pages. ISBN 0-9685543-6-9

Edna Schroeder Thiessen and Angela Showalter, *A Life Displaced: A Mennonite Woman's Flight from War-Torn Poland* (Kitchener: Pandora Press, 2000) Softcover, xii, 218 pages. ISBN 0-9685543-2-6

Stuart Murray, *Biblical Interpretation in the Anabaptist Tradition*, Studies in the Believers Tradition (Kitchener: Pandora Press, 2000) Softcover, 310pages. ISBN 0-9685543-3-4 ISSN 1480-7432.

Loren L. Johns, ed. *Apocalypticism and Millennialism* (Kitchener: Pandora Press, 2000) Softcover, 419 pages. Indexes. ISBN 0-9683462-9-4 ISSN 1480-7432

Later Writings by Pilgram Marpeck and his Circle. Volume 1. Trans. Walter Klaassen, Werner Packull, and John Rempel (Kitchener: Pandora Press, 1999) Softcover, 157 pages. ISBN 0-9683462-6-X

John Driver, *Radical Faith. An Alternative History of the Christian Church*, ed. Carrie Snyder. Kitchener: Pandora Press, 1999) Softcover, 334 pages. ISBN 0-9683462-8-6

C. Arnold Snyder, *From Anabaptist Seed.* (Kitchener: Pandora Press, 1999) Softcover, 53 pages. ISBN 0-9685543-0-X
 Also available in Spanish translation: *De Semilla Anabautista*, from Pandora Press only.

John D. Thiesen, *Mennonite and Nazi? Attitudes Among Mennonite Colonists in Latin America, 1933-1945* (Kitchener: Pandora Press, 1999) Softcover, 330 pages. Bibliography, index. ISBN 0-9683462-5-1

Lifting the Veil, ed. Leonard Friesen; trans. Walter Klaassen (Kitchener: Pandora Press, 1998). Softcover, 128 pages. ISBN 0-9683462-1-9

Leonard Gross, *The Golden Years of the Hutterites,* rev. ed. (Kitchener: Pandora Press, 1998). Softcover, 280 pages. Index. ISBN 0-9683462-3-5

William H. Brackney, ed., *The Believers Church: A Voluntary Church,* (Kitchener: Pandora Press, 1998). Softcover, viii, 237 pages. Index. ISBN 0-9683462-0-0 ISSN 1480-7432

An Annotated Hutterite Bibliography, compiled by Maria H. Krisztinkovich, ed. by Peter C. Erb (Kitchener: Pandora Press, 1998). (Ca. 2,700 entries) 312 pages. Softcover, electronic, or both. ISBN (paper) 0-9698762-8-9/(disk) 0-9698762-9-7

Jacobus ten Doornkaat Koolman, *Dirk Philips. Friend and Colleague of Menno Simons,* trans. W. E. Keeney, ed. C. A. Snyder (Kitchener: Pandora Press, 1998). Softcover, xviii, 236 pages. Index. ISBN: 0-9698762-3-8

Sarah Dyck, ed./tr., *The Silence Echoes: Memoirs of Trauma & Tears* (Kitchener: Pandora Press, 1997). Softcover, xii, 236 pages. ISBN: 0-9698762-7-0

Wes Harrison, *Andreas Ehrenpreis and Hutterite Faith and Practice* (Kitchener: Pandora Press, 1997). Softcover, xxiv, 274 pages. Index. ISBN 0-9698762-6-2

C. Arnold Snyder, *Anabaptist History and Theology: Revised Student Edition* (Kitchener: Pandora Press, 1997). Softcover, xiv, 466 pages. Index, bibliography. ISBN 0-9698762-5-4

Nancey Murphy, *Reconciling Theology and Science: A Radical Reformation Perspective* (Kitchener, Ont.: Pandora Press, 1997). Softcover, x, 103 pages. Index. ISBN 0-9698762-4-6

The Limits of Perfection: A Conversation with J. Lawrence Burkholder 2nd ed., with a new epilogue by J. Lawrence Burkholder, Rodney Sawatsky and Scott Holland, eds. (Kitchener: Pandora Press, 1996). Softcover, x, 154 pages. ISBN 0-9698762-2-X

C. Arnold Snyder, *Anabaptist History and Theology: An Introduction* (Kitchener: Pandora Press, 1995). Softcover, x, 434 pages. Index, bibliography. ISBN 0-9698762-0-3

Pandora Press
33 Kent Avenue Kitchener, ON N2G 3R2
Tel.: (519) 578-2381 / Fax: (519) 578-1826
E-mail: info@pandorapress.com
Web site: www.pandorapress.com